The New US Strategy towards Asia

Barack Obama's 'rebalancing' or 'pivot' strategy, intended to demonstrate continued US commitment to the Asia-Pacific region in a variety of military, economic and diplomatic contexts, was launched with much fanfare in 2011. Implicit in the new strategy is both a focus on China – engagement with and containment of – and a heavy reliance by the United States on its existing friends and allies in the region in order to implement its strategy. This book explores the impact of the new strategy on America's regional friends and allies. It shows how these governments are working with Washington to advance and protect their distinct national interests, while at the same time avoiding any direct confrontation with China. It also addresses the reasons why many of these regional actors harbour concerns about the ability of the United States to sustain the pivot strategy in the long run. Overall, the book illustrates the deep complexities of the United States' exercise of power and influence in the region.

William T. Tow is Professor and Head of the Department of International Relations, College of Asia and Pacific at the Australian National University.

Douglas Stuart is Professor and Chair of International Studies at Dickinson College and also an Adjunct Research Professor at the US Army War College.

T0347253

Routledge Security in Asia Pacific Series

Series Editors
Leszek Buszynski, Strategic and Defence Studies Centre, the Australian
National University, and William Tow, Australian National University.

Security issues have become more prominent in the Asia-Pacific region because of the presence of global players, rising great powers and confident middle powers, which intersect in complicated ways. This series puts forward important new work on key security issues in the region. It embraces the roles of the major actors, their defence policies and postures, and their security interaction over the key issues of the region. It includes coverage of the United States, China, Japan, Russia, the Koreas, as well as the middle powers of ASEAN and South Asia. It also covers issues relating to environmental and economic security as well as transnational actors and regional groupings.

The New US Strategy towards Asia

Adapting to the American pivot

Edited by
William T. Tow and Douglas Stuart

LONDON AND NEW YORK

First published 2015 by Routledge

2 Park Square, Milton Park, Abingdon, Oxfordshire OX14 4RN
711 Third Avenue, New York, NY 10017

Routledge is an imprint of the Taylor & Francis Group, an informa business

First issued in paperback 2017

British Library Cataloguing in Publication Data
A catalogue record for this book is available from the British Library

Library of Congress Cataloging in Publication Data
The new US strategy towards Asia : adapting to the American pivot /
edited by William T. Tow and Douglas Stuart.
    pages cm. – (Routledge security in Asia Pacific series ; 30)
    Includes bibliographical references and index.
    1. United States–Foreign relations–Asia. 2. Asia–Foreign relations–
United States. 3. United States–Foreign relations–2009- I. Tow, William T.,
editor. II. Stuart, Douglas T., editor. III. Stuart, Douglas T. Obama's
"rebalance" in historical context. Container of (work):
    DS33.4.U6N48 2015
    327.7305–dc23
                2014027859

ISBN: 978-1-138-82263-4 (hbk)
ISBN: 978-0-8153-5791-9 (pbk)

Typeset in Times New Roman
by Taylor & Francis Books

Contents

List of contributors

Robert Ayson is Professor of Strategic Studies, School of History, Philosophy, Political Science & International Relations, Victoria University, Wellington.

Ralf Emmers is Associate Professor, S. Rajaratnam School of International Studies (RSIS), Nanyang Technological University (NTU), Singapore.

Ken Jimbo is Associate Professor, Faculty of Policy Management, Keio University, Tokyo.

Changsu Kim is Director of the Center for Security and Strategy, Korea Institute for Defense Analyses, Seoul.

Tongfi Kim is Research Fellow, Peace Research Institute, Frankfurt.

Fu-Kuo Liu is Research Fellow, Institute of International Relations, and Executive Director, Center for Security Studies, National Chengchi University, Taipei.

Jeffrey D. McCausland is Visiting Professor of International Security, Dickinson College, and Distinguished Visiting Professor of Research and Minerva Chairholder at the US Army War College, Carlisle, Pennsylvania.

Charmaine G. Misalucha is a US-ASEAN Fulbright Scholar, School of International Service, American University, Washington, DC, and Assistant Professor, International Studies Department, De La Salle University, Manila.

Kitti Prasirtsuk is Director, Institute of East Asian Studies, Thammasat University, and Coordinator, ASEAN Watch Project, Thailand Research Fund, Bangkok.

Mahesh Shankar is Assistant Professor of International Affairs, Skidmore College, Saratoga Springs, New York.

Douglas Stuart holds the J. William and Helen D. Stuart Chair in International Studies, Dickinson College, Carlisle, Pennsylvania.

Brendan Taylor is Associate Professor and Head of the Strategic and Defence Studies Centre, College of Asia and the Pacific, Australian National University, Canberra.

William T. Tow is Professor and Head of the Department of International Relations, College of Asia and the Pacific, Australian National University, Canberra.

Preface

Since formally announcing its 'rebalancing' or 'pivot' strategy in late 2011, the Barack Obama Administration's efforts to prioritize the United States' influence and presence in the Asia-Pacific region have been assessed extensively. Integral to understanding and evaluating this American posture is China's continuing rise as a probable peer competitor to the United States in the region during a time of epic structural change and the protracted threats represented by Asian flashpoints and territorial disputes. The degree to which traditional and emerging US regional allies and partners are willing and able to contribute toward implementing rebalancing will very likely determine its ultimate credibility. The United States, of course, remains a global strategic actor with unparalleled capabilities to project military power to distant parts of the globe. As was the case after the Vietnam War in the late 1970s, however, Washington is once more confronting the imperatives of overcoming intensifying domestic fiscal constraints and sharpening divisions within the American body politic. To a greater extent than at any time in recent history, the long-standing American network of alliances known as the 'San Francisco System', complemented by evolving US relationships with other selected security partners, will need to adapt to a new set of emerging and complex challenges that are now shaping Asia-Pacific geopolitics.

With these factors in mind, the editors of this volume asked a group of respected regional security analysts to join a project designed to gauge how the rebalancing strategy has been received by their own countries and by the Asia-Pacific region. Project members congregated at a two-day workshop convened in Canberra, Australia, during late June 2013. They interacted intensively with each other, with selected policy officials from Australian government agencies, and with invited guests from various regional states' embassies located in Australia's national capital city. The chapters comprising this book resulted largely from these deliberations and from subsequent research conducted in allied/partner capital cities by the chapter contributors.

As is normally the case with such projects, space precludes us from citing every contributor who has supported this enterprise. Some individuals and organizations, however, were essential to this project culminating in what we hope will be a solid review of the rebalancing issue as it has developed to date. In particular, the editors would like to thank Ms Kana Moy who organized and managed the June workshop proceedings with professionalism and cheeriness, and going far beyond her normal administrative responsibilities. Ms Moira Kelly played a key role in the editorial process at Dickinson. Ms Mary-Louise Hickey is the other key individual who must be recognized here. Her editorial skills have been vital in ensuring that this project culminates in a publication intended to stimulate greater policy debate on the rebalancing issue. One could not work with a more patient and more professional colleague.

We must also thank two sponsors, without which the project would never have seen the light of day. The Australian Research Council's Centre of Excellence in Policing and Security (CEPS), administered by Griffith University, provided critical funding underwriting workshop costs and we are extremely grateful to CEPS Director Professor Simon Bronitt for allocating additional funding to ensure that the June workshop proceeded according to plan. We must also acknowledge the US Army War College and the US Department of Defense's Minerva Program for providing the funds that contributed to the costs of American project participants' journeys to Australia and their participation in the workshop. We are also grateful to Dickinson College for supplying timely staffing support to the completion of editorial tasks leading to the production of this book.

The challenge of managing alliance and partnership politics successfully within the broader context of international security has been a long-standing one for US policymakers and for their counterparts in key collaborative states. It is to their efforts that we dedicate this volume.

William T. Tow
Douglas Stuart
June 2014

List of abbreviations

A2/AD	anti-access/area-denial
ADIZ	air defence identification zone
ADMM+	ASEAN Defence Ministers' Meeting Plus
ANZUS	Australia New Zealand United States
APEC	Asia-Pacific Economic Cooperation
ASB	Air–Sea Battle
ASEAN	Association of Southeast Asian Nations
ASEAN+3	ASEAN plus China, Japan and South Korea
AUSMIN	Australia–United States Ministerial Consultations
BMD	ballistic missile defence
C4ISR	command, control, communications, computers, intelligence, surveillance and reconnaissance
CEPS	Centre of Excellence in Policing and Security
DPRK	Democratic People's Republic of Korea
EAS	East Asia Summit
FDI	foreign direct investment
G20	Group of 20
IISS	International Institute for Strategic Studies
IOR-ARC	Indian Ocean Rim Association for Regional Cooperation
ISR	intelligence, surveillance and reconnaissance
JOAC	Joint Operational Access Concept
km	kilometre(s)
KMT	Kuomintang
LACM	land-attack cruise missile
LDP	Liberal Democratic Party
NASA	National Aeronautics and Space Administration
NATO	North Atlantic Treaty Organization
NDPG	National Defense Program Guideline
NPT	Nuclear Non-Proliferation Treaty
NZDF	New Zealand Defence Force
ODA	official development assistance
PLA	People's Liberation Army
QDR	Quadrennial Defense Review

ROK	Republic of Korea
SDF	Self-Defense Force
SEATO	Southeast Asia Treaty Organization
TLAM/N	Tomahawk Land Attack Missile/Nuclear
TPP	Trans-Pacific Partnership
ZOPFAN	Zone of Peace, Freedom and Neutrality

1 Setting the context

Douglas Stuart and William T. Tow

The Barack Obama Administration's 'pivot to Asia' represents the fourth stage in a process of American strategic adjustment which has been ongoing since the late nineteenth century. The first three stages in this process were guided by the concept of the 'Open Door' (following the Spanish–American War), anti-communist containment (following the establishment of the People's Republic of China), and a policy of 'hegemony light' which was based upon the Nixon Doctrine and the US opening to China (Gray 2009). The ongoing pivot campaign is best understood as an effort to preserve 'hegemony light' in the face of an unprecedented shift in global power from West to East.

One essential precondition for the success of the US pivot to Asia is the acceptance of, and the active support for, the pivot by America's regional friends and allies. This volume is designed to help US policymakers and security experts to appreciate the specific strategies, priorities and concerns of these Asia-Pacific governments, as they relate to the pivot. The first section of this book introduces readers to the pivot strategy, and to the situation that Washington faces in the region. Douglas Stuart places the Obama Administration's pivot in historical and geostrategic context. William Tow surveys the policy challenges that Washington faces as it engages in regional 'order building'. Jeffrey McCausland analyses the pivot from the perspectives of deterrence, extended deterrence and reassurance.

The remaining chapters in this volume present the very diverse (and, in some cases, incompatible) points of view of experts from most of America's Asia-Pacific (and Indo-Pacific) partners. Readers will identify certain recurrent themes in these chapters. The first such theme is a generally positive reaction to America's effort to preserve and enhance its influence in the Asia-Pacific region. American representatives often discover that they are 'pushing on open doors' when they meet with their Asian counterparts to discuss the pivot (see Keatley 2013). Contributors to this volume discuss various forms of security cooperation with Washington, including bilateral, multilateral and 'minilateral' arrangements. Many of the authors also express a willingness on the part of their governments to go further in support of the pivot, if the United States can reassure them that the pivot is politically, economically and strategically sustainable. They also seek reassurance from Washington that the pivot will be managed in such a way that it will not force them to choose between China (which is a major source of prosperity for many of these nations) and the United States (which is a major source of security).

Concerns about the sustainability of the pivot have intensified over the last two years, as the United States has been pulled away from Asia by numerous developments, including the Arab Spring, the Syrian civil war, the Iranian nuclear issue and Russia's campaign of coercive diplomacy toward Ukraine. To reassure its Asian friends and allies, the United States replaced the term pivot with a more strategic-sounding term, 'rebalance'. However, most of America's regional partners will keep their options open until they are convinced that the United States is in it for the long haul.

Several contributors to this volume also argue for a multifaceted form of pivot as the best way to bolster regional security without precipitating a confrontation with China. Some commentators express concern that the United States has relied too much on military forms of cooperation, at the expense of economic and diplomatic initiatives. Washington is certainly committed to this type of multifaceted engagement with its regional partners and with Beijing, but US policymakers are also painfully aware that it is only in the military realm that America has a decisive advantage that can be translated into influence in its dealings with China. Several contributors to this volume discuss US plans for a new Air–Sea Battle strategy as a possible tipping point in America's campaign to influence Beijing without encouraging increased hostility.

One reason why it is so difficult for Washington to manage the pivot to Asia is because it must constantly walk a tightrope between contradictory goals. The goal of both engaging and containing China is the most obvious example. Another important challenge for the United States is the need to reconcile policies designed to reassure its regional friends and allies with policies designed to increase 'partner capacity' in the form of defence budgets, basing agreements and security-related memoranda of understanding. Finally, Washington must tread carefully in pursuit of its goal of moving beyond its traditional 'hub-and-spokes' network of bilateral defence arrangements to a more complex and interdependent 'web' arrangement in the Asia-Pacific. As several of the authors in this volume make clear, such US efforts will inevitably confront deeply held resentments and suspicions, and significant territorial disputes between and among key regional security partners.

Since this volume is meant to be an audit of the opinions and interests of America's friends and allies in the Asia-Pacific, it does not include a chapter by a Chinese expert. Beijing is neither a friend nor an ally of Washington. Forty-two years after the US opening to China, the bilateral relationship is still adversarial, and still burdened with the legacy issues that complicated US-Chinese relations at the time of Richard Nixon's visit to Beijing. The American pivot to Asia represents a new chapter in this story, but it is not viewed by Beijing as a positive development. The editors also chose not to include a chapter that summarizes Chinese views on the pivot since those views are uniformly negative and since Chinese policies and statements are discussed by most of the contributors to this volume.

Goals and concerns of America's regional friends and allies

Our survey of the opinions of Asian and Indian defence experts begins with a chapter on America's most important regional ally: Japan. Ken Jimbo notes that Japan 'welcomes the concept' of rebalance, but 'many questions still need to be answered'. He surveys these military and diplomatic questions and then relates them to recent developments in the US-Japan bilateral security relationship and ongoing debates among Japanese defence planners regarding new strategic concepts such as 'dynamic defence' and 'dynamic deterrence'. Not surprisingly, the author focuses much of his attention on Chinese military modernization and China's intentions in the South China and East China Seas. He concludes with a call for US-Japan 'joint development of tailored regional deterrence architecture'.

Changsu Kim presents a South Korean perspective on the US pivot. He concludes that because of special historical and geopolitical circumstances, Seoul views the pivot differently from other Asian governments. These circumstances include: six decades of existential threat from an unpredictable and heavily armed North Korea; close military cooperation with, and dependence upon, Washington since the Korean War; geographic proximity and economic interdependence with an increasingly powerful China; and unresolved disputes with Japan that can be traced back more than a century. Kim refers to these factors to explain why the pivot has relatively little salience for many South Korean defence experts. He concludes that, while the American pivot 'appears quite reasonable' as a guide to US global strategic adjustment, it needs more time to be better understood and supported by key Asian governments, including South Korea.

No Asian government has a greater stake in the success of the American pivot than Taiwan. Fu-Kuo Liu's chapter helps readers to understand both the risks and opportunities of the pivot for Taiwan. At a time when Taiwan is restructuring its forces and undertaking new forms of defence cooperation with Washington in response to dramatic improvements in Chinese military capability, Taipei is concerned that the United States will mismanage the pivot in some way that precipitates a confrontation with Beijing. The author also reminds readers that Taipei's security calculations extend beyond the Taiwan Strait, to include territorial disputes with other regional actors (Japan, the Philippines and Vietnam) in the East China and South China Seas. Like several other contributors to this volume, Liu concludes that the greatest threat to the future of the pivot is America's financial health.

Charmaine Misalucha has contributed the most theoretically ambitious chapter to this volume. The question that she addresses is how the United States 'sold' the idea of the pivot strategy to Southeast Asia. After a survey of the literature relating to strategic communication she discusses how the

Obama Administration has told the 'China story' to its South-East Asian friends and allies in a way that is designed to solicit their support without forcing them to choose between Washington and Beijing. She concludes that the United States has persuaded Southeast Asian governments in general, and the Philippines in particular, that the pivot serves their interests. However, she also recognizes these Asian governments are still not convinced about the sustainability of the idea.

Thailand poses special problems for the Obama Administration as it attempts to 'sell' its pivot to Asia. Kitti Prasirtsuk and William Tow survey these problems and identify their sources. They note that Thailand is a 'reluctant ally' of the United States, and that many of Thailand's security concerns relate to local issues that are not, and cannot be, within the scope of the US-Thai alliance. They stress the Thai foreign policy priority of preserving 'room to manoeuvre' when confronted with evolving great power rivalries, and remind Washington that Thailand is committed to 'an intensifying and comprehensive relationship with China'. The authors applaud the fact that both Washington and Bangkok are cooperating to enhance their capabilities for non-traditional security cooperation (for example, disaster relief), but they caution the United States not to assume that the interests of the two governments converge on other forms of 'hard power' security cooperation. Prasirtsuk and Tow also comment on the 22 May 2014 military coup in Thailand, which has made it even more difficult for Washington to sustain its defence relationship with its 'reluctant ally'.

Ralf Emmers depicts Singapore as a nation acutely aware of its vulnerabilities and realistic about its options. Washington has been viewed as an indispensable source of security since the founding of the Republic of Singapore in 1965. From time to time, Singapore has taken steps to shore up that relationship and encourage Washington to preserve a substantial military presence in Asia. The author cites the decision by the city-state to allow American littoral combat ships to use its facilities as one recent example of this type of bilateral cooperation. However, Emmers also makes it clear that Singapore is closely monitoring US activities in the region for signs that Washington cannot, or will not, sustain its commitment to the pivot. He also reminds readers that Singapore, like virtually every regional partner of the United States, is concerned that Washington will manage the pivot in such a way that it will force America's friends and allies to choose between the United States and China.

Australia has been one of America's most reliable and effective allies since the Second World War, but Brendan Taylor advises readers that it would be a mistake to assume uncritically that Australian defence experts and policymakers are unanimous in their support for the US pivot strategy. Drawing upon a distinction that was developed by Graham Allison, Albert Carnesale and Joseph Nye Jr (1985), Taylor divides Australian commentators into three schools: hawks, doves and owls. The hawks, whom Taylor believes are 'gaining the ascendancy' within the government of Tony Abbott, support close military collaboration with Washington in order to send a strong deterrent message to Beijing. The doves are opposed to any campaign of anti-Chinese containment. Instead, they favour 'working actively to reduce tensions' between Washington and Beijing, even if this requires Canberra to say no to its American ally from time to time (the phrase is from the most influential spokesperson for the dove position, Hugh White 2012–13). The author counts two former prime ministers among the doves: Malcolm Fraser and Paul Keating. Finally, Taylor summarizes the argument of the owls, who support close security cooperation with the United States but reject the argument that this must be at the expense of an active and ambitious policy of diplomatic and economic engagement with China. The author lists former Prime Minister John Howard among the owls. Taylor concludes his discussion of the evolving security debate in Australia by stating that although the US-Australian relationship is in 'remarkably good shape', neither Washington nor Canberra can afford 'undue complacency'.

Every nation in the Asia-Pacific responds to the US pivot according to its unique geostrategic situation and its foreign policy priorities. Robert Ayson makes this very clear in his analysis of New Zealand's reaction to the American strategy. Some of the concerns that dominate the debate in Wellington are shared by all of America's regional friends and allies. Will Washington be able to extricate itself from the larger Middle East? Will budget pressures in the United States mean that the American decision to increase the proportion of US naval assets in the Pacific translate into 'a larger slice of a smaller pie?' However, most of Ayson's chapter focuses on concerns that are specific to New Zealand, because it is 'a long way from many of the places that matter militarily to the United States and to other regional powers', and because New Zealand's geographical orientation is toward the South Pacific. Ayson also notes that the US-New Zealand security relationship, which had been in limbo since the mid-1980s, was actually improving before the announcement of the pivot. So Wellington must be concerned about the possibility that the pivot strategy will actually disrupt the ongoing process of careful and gradual bilateral defence cooperation.

Mahesh Shankar reminds readers that, while the 'core emphasis' of the US pivot is the Asia-Pacific, the US strategy requires an 'Indo-Pacific' orientation if it is to be successful. He quotes former US Secretary of State Hillary Clinton's assertion that Washington has made a 'strategic bet on India's future', and in his chapter he introduces readers to the issues that are likely to determine the success or failure of that bet. While noting that 'by and large' the US pivot is viewed positively in New Delhi, Shankar also discusses the factors that could make India circumspect in the enthusiasm with which it seeks to tie itself closely to the American agenda in the region. These include American mismanagement of the diplomatic aspects of the pivot which might undermine India's 'strategic autonomy'. New Delhi might also become cool to the US pivot if it concludes that America is not able to sustain its commitments to the Indo-Pacific region. Political and economic developments within India could also result in a turning away from foreign affairs, with problematic implications for US-Indian security cooperation.

All of the chapters in this volume make it clear that the American pivot to Asia is still a work in progress, and that its future is by no means certain. At the core of the US strategy is the recognition that Washington cannot 'rebalance' its presence and its influence in the Asia-Pacific without the active support of its regional friends and allies. However, every one of those regional actors is still closely monitoring the pivot in order to assess risks and opportunities. In particular, no regional actor wants to be forced to make a choice between Beijing and Washington. The good news for America and for the pivot is that the United States is fully committed to a policy of productive cooperation with China. The bad news is that American efforts to 'make room for China' could still be overwhelmed by the pressures associated with the evolving power transition situation. As the history of international relations makes clear, power transitions are among the most reliable predictors of war. If America's friends and allies conclude that America's management of the pivot strategy is increasing the risk of either entanglement in a United States–China confrontation or abandonment by Washington in the face of growing Chinese assertiveness, they will rely upon the kinds of insights presented in this volume in order to assess their options and perhaps renegotiate their relations with the United States.

References

Allison, Graham T., Carnesale, Albert and Nye, Jr, Joseph S. (eds) (1985) *Hawks, Doves, and Owls: An Agenda for Avoiding Nuclear War*, New York: W.W. Norton.

Gray, Colin (2009) *After Iraq: The Search for a Sustainable National Security Strategy*, Carlisle, PA: Strategic Studies Institute, US Army War College, January.

Keatley, Robert (2013) 'How China Helps the Pivot', *National Interest*, 21 March, nationalinterest.org/commentary/how-china-helps-the-pivot-8249?page=2 (accessed 11 March 2014).

White, Hugh (2012–13) 'White-Papering the Cracks: A Blueprint for the Asian Century?' *The Monthly*, 85 (December–January).

Part I
Asia's place in America's global strategy

2 Obama's 'rebalance' in historical context

Douglas Stuart

When Barack Obama's Administration first announced plans to accord top priority to the Asia-Pacific in its global foreign policy planning, it referred to the campaign as a 'pivot' to Asia.[1] It soon became clear, however, that the term created problems for Washington, since key friends and allies interpreted a pivot as a brief, tactical manoeuvre.[2] As a result, the United States has settled upon the term 'rebalance' to describe the priority that it accords to the Asia-Pacific. This term makes much more sense, not just from the point of view of marketing, but also from the point of view of historical accuracy, since the Obama Administration's engagement with Asia is the next stage in an American grand strategy of balance of power that has been evolving since the late nineteenth century. The core of this grand strategy has been an American commitment to block any government from achieving hegemonic dominance in the Asia-Pacific. US policies designed to serve this strategy have met with varying degrees of success, but the commitment has endured for over a century. This chapter begins by surveying the history of America's grand strategy in the Asia-Pacific. I then discuss the challenges that the Obama Administration has faced, and will face, in its effort to rebalance US grand strategy in this rapidly changing region.

Phase I: 1784–1907

The history of America's progressive involvement in the Asia-Pacific during the nineteenth century is illustrative of the concept of 'acquisitive individualism', which Robert Kagan (2006: 11) has described as the 'powerful engine' of America's westward expansion. Beginning in 1784, when the *Empress of China* arrived at the port of Whampoa, American merchants were attracted to the Pacific for lucrative trade opportunities: fur pelts (from the United States), silk and tea (from China), and the profits associated with the whaling industry. They were also attracted to the idea of trade routes that were not vulnerable to British naval domination, as was the case in the Atlantic. Lawrence Battistini (1955: 10) notes that by 1832, American traders 'had called at most of the islands in the vast Pacific'. The American flag soon followed the dollar into Asia, and in 1844 Washington signed the Treaty of

Wanghia with Peking. During the rest of the nineteenth century, the United States signed four more treaties with China and eight with Japan (Morse and MacNair 1931: 841). Some of these agreements, such as the treaty between Washington and Tokyo that followed the arrival of Admiral Matthew Perry's 'black ships' in 1853, were the product of coercive diplomacy.[3]

Americans also viewed Asia as a venue for the export of their Christian and enlightenment values. American missionaries were at the forefront of this campaign, and Holly Carter (1989: 4) contends that they were also 'perhaps the most aggressive and outspoken public voices influencing the evolution of US foreign policy in East Asia'.

The success of American merchants and missionaries in Asia created institutionalized interest groups with sufficient political clout to influence key foreign policy decisions relating to the Pacific region.[4] By the end of the nineteenth century, the United States was ready to tie these distinct American policies and interests into a comprehensive doctrine known as the Open Door. President William McKinley summarized the doctrine in his instructions to the US delegation to the Paris peace talks at the end of the Spanish–American War: '[i]t is just to use every legitimate means for the enlargement of American trade; but we seek no advantages in the Orient which are not common to all. Asking only the "open door" for ourselves, we are ready to accord the "open door" to others' (Morse and MacNair 1931: 436). While the principle of equal economic opportunity was at the core of the Open Door, US policymakers also understood the hard power aspects of this doctrine. As Alfred Mahan (1900: 172) noted, 'we cannot be sure of the commercial advantages known as the "open door", unless we are prepared to do our share in holding it open'. Even before it was officially announced in 1899, the logic of the Open Door encouraged the United States to assure itself of permanent access to, and influence in, the Pacific region by the annexation of the Hawaiian Islands.

Concern about the Open Door also contributed to the decision in favour of some form of American dominion over the Philippine Islands in the wake of the US victory in the Spanish–American War. At the end of the war, US policymakers had no clear idea of what they should do with the Philippines, but the logic of the Open Door encouraged Washington not to miss the opportunity to establish a secure foothold on the rim land of Asia. What followed was a brutal counterinsurgency war that lasted from 1899 to 1902. In what one can only hope was a tongue-in-cheek comment, Lieutenant Colonel Mike Fowler (2011) noted that '[t]actics, such as torture, scorched earth, and internment brought short term benefits', but 'current counterinsurgencies should not be too quick to emulate this strategy'. The war fuelled an intense national debate regarding the ethics and the wisdom of an American campaign to take and hold territory in Asia, and ended in what Niall Ferguson (2005: 48) has described as '[d]omestic disillusionment in the face of protracted and nasty conflict'.

Although the outcome of the Philippines war was inconclusive, it established the United States as a permanently influential actor in the Asia-Pacific.

Three other policies during the period from 1897 to 1907 also helped to guarantee America's place in the region: the annexation of Hawaii in 1898, the US deployment of troops to mainland China to help suppress the Boxer Rebellion in 1900, and President Theodore Roosevelt's deployment of the Great White Fleet (which included 16 US battleships) to the Asia-Pacific in 1907. All four policies were understood as serving the concept of the Open Door, which was usually depicted as a benign and principled effort to ensure that America had a 'square deal' in the competition for Asian markets and resources. However, the Open Door was also understood by US policymakers as a way of preserving a multipolar balance of power in Asia so that no European or Asian government could establish regional, and perhaps global, hegemony. This is what Mahan (1910: 144) had in mind when he asserted that '[t]he Open Door is but another way of expressing Balance of Power'.

Washington's actions in Asia during this ten-year period sent the message that the United States was a great power with global interests. It also encouraged key Asian governments to begin to reassess their generally benign views of the United States, setting the stage for the next phase in America's history as a Pacific actor.

Phase II: 1907–73

America's new role as a regional balancer had clear implications for the other rising power in Asia in the early twentieth century. The leaders of the Japanese Navy were serious students of Mahan's writings at the time, and they appreciated how and why both the Open Door doctrine and a growing US naval presence in the Pacific threatened their long-term ambitions (see Dingman 1991). These ambitions had already been made clear by the Japanese – with the domination of Korea in 1876, the occupation of Okinawa in 1879, and victories in the Sino–Japanese War (1894–95) and the Russo–Japanese War (1904–05).

On the other side of the Pacific, the United States was monitoring these developments. As early as 1910, Mahan (1910: 199–200) had, in fact, speculated on the long-term problem that Japan posed for the United States:

> Her nearness to China, Manchuria, Korea, gives the natural commercial advantages that short and rapid transportation always confers ... but the very fact of these near natural markets, and her interest in them, cannot but breed that sense of proprietorship which ... easily glides into the attempt at political control that ultimately means control by force.

Although some experts shared Mahan's concern, most Americans initially favoured Japan in the Russo–Japanese War, because it was assumed that Moscow posed the most immediate threat to the Open Door. Indeed, President Roosevelt responded to news of the Japanese surprise attack on Port Arthur by stating that 'Japan is playing our game' (quoted in Taliaferro 2013:

508). However, one year after Japan's victory, US defence planners began to develop what would become Plan Orange for future war against Tokyo, while Japanese defence planners began to focus more and more of their attention on the American threat.

Michael Hunt and Steven Levine note that both the United States and Japan were trapped in a 'strategic quandary' during the early twentieth century, and that the Philippines was at the heart of this quandary: '[a]ny US fleet strong enough to defend the Philippines was also strong enough to threaten Japan. And any Japanese fleet strong enough to counter the US threat could also command the entire Pacific.' They note that 'US naval strategists ... recognized the strategic vulnerability of the distant colony as early as 1907 ... Abandoning the Philippines and pulling back to a mid-Pacific defensive line anchored by Hawaii might make strategic sense' for US defence planners, 'but such a retreat from dreams of Pacific destiny was politically unpalatable' (Hunt and Levine 2012: 67).

The strategic quandary was exacerbated by economic disputes between the two nations. During the 1920s, US restrictions on immigration and tariff increases angered the Japanese, while Americans complained about Japanese challenges to the Open Door. However, these issues were irritants, compared to a more serious problem of which Tokyo had been aware since the Meiji restoration. Dale Copeland has described this problem as the 'trade–security dilemma': 'Once Japan began modernizing after 1867, it had one major limitation: critical vital goods needed to build an industrial great power lay outside of national boundaries', and 'if they [Japan] expanded into the East Asian theater to compensate for anticipated declines in trade with other great powers, they would likely create mistrust of Japanese intentions, leading to further trade restrictions. Yet they also felt that they had little choice but to expand' (Copeland 2012: 137, 136, 144). With the onset of the depression, and the increase in American and British protectionism, Japan's trade-security dilemma took on the character of a crisis. By 1940, the United States was recognized by Tokyo as the preeminent threat to its survival. In September, the Japanese leadership opted for a Tripartite Treaty with Germany and Italy to balance against the growing threat posed by the United States (see Kawasaki 2012: 224–25).[5] Over the next year, continued American pressure for Japanese retreat from its 'co-prosperity sphere' gradually convinced the Japanese leadership that war with America 'had become the lesser of two evils' (Copeland 2012: 144).

In his provocative book *Cultures of War*, John Dower (2010: 98) explains how '[i]deology, emotion, and wishful thinking at the highest level' led Japanese policymakers to attempt an extraordinary gamble at Pearl Harbor. For the purposes of this chapter, the important lesson is that the Japanese government engaged in extensive strategic debate over several years and still chose a policy that Samuel Eliot Morison (1953: 132) famously (and accurately) described as a 'strategic imbecility'.[6] America's management of the Japan problem during the interwar period provides important lessons for US policymakers who are currently attempting to manage a mixed-adversary relationship with China. Twenty-twenty hindsight supports Michael Full-ilove's (2013: 338) conclusion that 'Roosevelt's belief that he could restrain Tokyo without provoking it proved wrong'. If Washington had been guided by a clearer appreciation of Japan's point of view with regard to the afore-mentioned trade-security dilemma, it might have managed its quarantine strategy differently, or at least been better prepared for a Japanese act of desperation. America's policies during this period also provide additional confirmation for Gordon Craig and Alexander George's (1983: 190, 192) assertion that coercive diplomacy is 'often a beguiling strategy' that 'is in fact more difficult and problematic than is often thought to be the case'. US-Chinese relations are certainly not at a stage where Washington is considering various forms of coercive diplomacy in order to 'shape' Beijing's actions in the Asia-Pacific, but the same could have been said about US-Japanese rela-tions as late as 1936 – five years before Tokyo decided that '[a]n American-imposed peace' was 'less desirable and honourable than a Japanese-initiated war' (Akira Iriye, cited in Fullilove 2013: 339).

Japan's Pearl Harbor gamble transformed the way US policymakers, and the American people, thought about America's role in the world. *Prepared-ness* was the standard against which all future foreign policies would be judged (for an analysis of the 'Pearl Harbor System', see Stuart 2008). In the Asia-Pacific theatre, preparedness demanded that the United States preserve a substantial 'blue zone' basing network after the Second World War ended. As one member of the US Joint Chiefs of Staff explained at the time, 'our aims are to exclude from the former Japanese islands in the Pacific any potential enemy and, secondly, to assume United States control over those portions of the area which are vital to our own security and necessary to our strategic base system'.[7] Preparedness demanded more than an Open Door in the Asia-Pacific. Only US regional hegemony, and the ability to close the door to challengers in the Asia-Pacific, could guarantee American safety.

On the other hand, America was in the process of rapid and dramatic military demobilization after the Second World War, and the Harry S. Truman Administration was committed to keeping tight control of post-war defence budgets. US policymakers also recognized that Asia was only one of the regions that would require American military protection after the war. Influential Americans like Douglas MacArthur and Henry Luce attempted to convince Washington and the American people to accord top priority to Asia, but once US policymakers became convinced that the Soviet Union posed the greatest threat to national security, Russia's geopolitical orientation toward central Europe led US defence planners to focus on Western Europe. A Europe-first strategy was also more attractive than an Asia-first approach, because Western Europe was culturally and politically familiar to US defence planners and manageable by means of a single, geopolitically cohesive, mul-tilateral alliance. By contrast, the vast Asian region was much more culturally and politically complex, much less familiar to Americans, and much harder to envision as a cohesive multilateral alliance system. The result was an historically unprecedented multilateral alliance in Europe, in the form of the North Atlantic Treaty Organization (NATO), and a much looser 'hub-and-spokes' network of bilateral and trilateral alliances in the Asia-Pacific, in the form of the San Francisco System.[8]

By contrast with the NATO story, which begins with a 'big bang' in 1949 and then evolves in a fairly linear fashion over the next four decades (and indeed, up to the present day), the story of the San Francisco System is characterized by fits and starts, diplomatic breakthroughs and setbacks, a war that ended in defeat, and a war that did not end at all. At first, the United States attempted to accord priority to Japan, the Philippines and China. Not surprisingly, ensuring that Japan would never again seek military dominance of the region was America's top priority. It is a striking comment on the continuity of US foreign policy that General MacArthur, the man selected to manage the transformation of Japan, was the son of General Arthur MacArthur, who had served as military governor of the Philippines at the turn of the century. In contrast to the situation in Europe, where the occupation of Germany was managed by four powers, the United States was virtually autonomous in its handling of the Japanese occupation. MacArthur pursued the goals that had been articulated during the Potsdam conference in June 1945: disarmament, punishment of war criminals, reparations and the encouragement of 'democratic tendencies'. Within a year, land reforms had begun, elections had been held, and a new constitution had been put in place (see Dingman 2012: 52–54). The United States also succeeded in its efforts to have Yoshida Shigeru elected prime minister in January 1949. He became associated with the Yoshida Doctrine, which accepted both Japan's pacifist status and a security treaty with the United States in exchange for American protection and Washington's support of Japanese economic revitalization. Over time, the Yoshida Doctrine provided the context for the dramatic rise of the Japanese economy, but it remained to be seen how Japan and the United States would cope with the inherent contradictions of a doctrine that celebrated both Japanese pacifism and Japan's importance as an American ally.

History, geopolitics and the influence of 'sentimental imperialists' (see Thompson *et al.* 1981) all converged to convince Washington that it also needed to continue to accord priority to China after the Second World War. The situation was both complex and fluid, however. President Truman was initially optimistic about the prospects that China could avoid civil war and that the United States could preserve influence in that nation. In a cabinet meeting on 2 August 1946, he noted that 'for the first time we now have a voice in China and for the first time we will be in a position to carry out the policy of 1898' (Cabinet Meeting 1946). Many US defence planners were also hopeful that a pro-American China could function as a restraining influence on an increasingly troublesome Russia.

The Chinese communist victory in 1949 had enormous geopolitical implications for US thinking about the implementation of anti-communist containment. It also had a great psychological impact on Washington and on the American people. When, less than one year later, North Korea invaded South Korea, the United States began to pursue a more 'symmetrical' Asian containment strategy (see Gaddis 1982: 352–57, for his distinction between symmetrical and asymmetrical forms of containment). By the time Truman left office in 1953, however, the problems of overstretch and entrapment associated with symmetrical containment were obvious. As the United States accorded more strategic importance to Asia, key regional governments found that they had greater leverage with Washington. American efforts to control the actions of Syngman Rhee in Korea, Chiang Kai-shek in Taiwan, and (later) Ngo Dinh Diem in South Vietnam, illustrated the problem that John Gaddis (2005: 119–56) has called 'the emergence of autonomy' in the Asia-Pacific. The establishment of the Association of Southeast Asian Nations (ASEAN) in 1967 and its designation of Southeast Asia as a Zone of Peace, Freedom and Neutrality (ZOPFAN) in 1971 added another complication for US planners. Washington nonetheless continued to pursue a symmetrical, anti-communist containment strategy until the catastrophic war in Vietnam, which set the stage for a new American approach to Asia-Pacific security, based on the Nixon Doctrine and the opening to China.

The Nixon Doctrine, which put Asian friends and allies on notice that in the future they would have to take primary responsibility for dealing with internal subversion and, perhaps, external aggression by a non-nuclear enemy, was an attempt by President Richard Nixon to return to the logic of asymmetrical containment in the Asia-Pacific (Gaddis 1982: 304–5). As such, it had the merit of being realistic about what the American people and Congress would support in a post-Vietnam period characterized by knee-jerk neo-isolationism. In conjunction with the opening to China, the Nixon Doctrine helped to make it possible for the Nixon-Henry Kissinger team to scale back American strategic ambitions and obligations across the region. Nixon would later argue that the doctrine was not 'a formula for getting America *out* of Asia, but one that provided the only sound basis for America's staying *in* and continuing to play a responsible role' (quoted in Tow 1991: 294).

Phase two in America's grand strategy in Asia began as a struggle between two rising empires over competing visions of an Open Door in the Asia-Pacific. It evolved after the Second World War – as a result of the decisive victory of one of those empires and the total defeat of the other – into a situation of US hegemonic dominance. From that point, until the latter stages of the Vietnam War, the United States attempted to sustain a preeminent position in the region – and to close the door against regional communist challengers including China, North Korea, North Vietnam and Russia. The setbacks that it experienced set the stage for a process of strategic adjustment that resulted in a more selective and conditional approach to Asia-Pacific containment and the start of a transformed relationship between Washington and Beijing.

Phase III: 1973 to the present

Hunt and Levine (2012: 250) have described the post-Vietnam era as the end of the 'US imperial project in eastern Asia'. They note that the Nixon Doctrine's assertion that Asian governments would have to take greater responsibility for their own security set the stage for 'an ongoing transformation of client states into allies … sensitive issues once largely a matter for Americans to decide became the subject of negotiations and compromise. The day of the diktat was over' (Hunt and Levine 2012: 262).

The end of America's imperial project posed special problems for Japanese policymakers, who found it increasingly difficult to finesse the aforementioned contradictions between the nation's pacifist identity and its treaty obligations to the United States. Japanese leaders tacked between attempts to reassure Washington of the nation's continued value as a security partner (particularly during the Yasuhiro Nakasone era and the 1991 Gulf War), and attempts to keep their focus on economics (which led some Americans to question the reliability of its Asian ally).[9] The US military presence in Okinawa became a special source of neuralgia for both Tokyo and Washington, and remains so to this day.

Washington also faced new geostrategic problems in other parts of Asia after 1973. The opening to China injected a degree of confusion and contradiction into the US-Taiwanese security relationship which is still unresolved. The closure of US military bases in the Philippines and South Vietnam transformed the San Francisco System into a top-heavy arrangement characterized by a substantial US military presence in South Korea and Japan, and a minimal land-based presence in the rest of the western Pacific and Oceania. Yet in spite of these and other setbacks, America's hub-and-spokes alliance network survived to the end of the Cold War and was arguably in a better position than NATO to adapt to post-Cold War challenges. This was at least partly due to the San Francisco System's inherent flexibility and adaptability, and perhaps also a credit to low expectations. In any event, Hunt and Levine (2012: 262) are correct in their assertion that although US diplomacy became much more difficult after 1973, 'these changes … transformed and may actually have strengthened the long-term position of the United States in eastern Asia as a post-imperial power'.

America's post-imperial situation in Asia was made much more manageable by the changes that were taking place in China. The domestic and international problems created by Mao Zedong's Cultural Revolution set the stage for a fundamental overhaul of China's leadership and the nation's grand strategy. Under Deng Xiaoping, Beijing sought to achieve its 'Four Modernizations' by a significant reduction in defence spending and by positive engagement with the US-led global economic order (see Overholt 2008: 107–12). When Beijing chose to act aggressively in 1979 in order to 'teach Vietnam a lesson', it tended to confirm for Chinese policymakers the wisdom of a foreign policy built around economic cooperation and the normalization of relations with the United States.

The gradual normalization of US-Chinese relations was still ongoing when the Berlin Wall came down. It fell to President George H.W. Bush to manage the peaceful conclusion of the Cold War, not just in the European theatre but in the Asia-Pacific as well. The president considered US-Chinese cooperation to be an indispensable precondition for a peaceful and prosperous post-Cold War order. Unfortunately, in a dramatic illustration of Robert Jervis's (1976: 66) claim that 'the central theme of international relations is not evil but tragedy', Bush's plans for an ambitious campaign of engagement with China were derailed by Beijing's brutal crackdown in Tiananmen Square in June 1989. It is hard to say how much progress could have been made in US-Chinese relations if this event had not occurred. What is clear, however, is that in the absence of diplomatic progress, the legacy issues that had complicated US-Chinese relations during the Cold War remained unresolved.

Four legacy issues deserve special note:

- the status of Taiwan;
- Chinese territorial claims in the East China and South China Seas;
- American and Chinese entanglement in the continuing military standoff on the Korean peninsula; and
- fundamental disagreements between Washington and Beijing over values relating to politics, economics and human rights.

(Stuart 2012a: 145–47)

China's dynamic economic growth during this period enhanced the significance of these legacy issues for the United States and its regional friends and allies. It also encouraged many American scholars and policymakers to view Beijing as the next global peer competitor, in accordance with the logic of preparedness. John Mearsheimer (2001: 400) spoke for the influential realist community when he warned that 'if China's economy continues growing at a robust pace … China, like all previous potential hegemons, would be strongly inclined to become a real hegemon'.

President Bill Clinton's efforts to address these problems by tying Beijing into a US-dominated global economy contributed to China's economic rise, but did not bolster bilateral trust or resolve major disputes. The Clinton Administration was also criticized by Asian governments for its handling of the 1997 Asian financial crisis. America's influence and reputation were further undermined during George W. Bush's presidency. Following the 11 September 2001 terrorist attacks on the United States, Bush's 'global war on terror' pulled America's focus away from Asia at a time when Beijing was pursuing an ambitious and productive 'friends with everybody' campaign across the region. By Bush's second term, Kishore Mahbubani (2008) was justified in stating that 'American diplomacy is being trumped by Chinese diplomacy' throughout the Asia-Pacific.

These were the circumstances that confronted Obama at the start of his presidency in 2009. As Jeffrey Bader (2012: 2), Obama's senior director of

East Asian affairs in the National Security Council, has recently observed: 'whatever successes the Bush administration had achieved in the region, they were contaminated by the fallout from problems elsewhere … the general perception in Asia in 2009 was that the United States was distracted by the war in Iraq and global war on terrorism and was economically weakened.' Of course, America's economic weakness was more than a perception by the time Obama entered the White House. The 2007–08 financial crisis had dealt a body blow to the US economy and convinced most governments and experts that 'the unprecedented shift in relative wealth and economic power roughly from West to East now under way will continue' (National Intelligence Council 2008: iv).[10]

Obama's 'rebalancing' strategy

The Obama Administration responded to these challenges in two ways. First, it accorded top priority to domestic economic and infrastructure problems. In his first National Security Strategy, the president called for a campaign of 'renewal' based on the assumption that 'our strength and influence abroad begins with the steps we take at home' (White House 2010).[11] The Obama team's second response was to declare publicly its intention to place Asia at the top of its list of regional priorities. Both policies faced serious risks, and if not managed well the two policies had the potential to be mutually exclusive. A policy of domestic renewal required deep cuts in defence spending and an increased reliance on civilian instruments of power so that diplomacy, aid and economic engagement could substitute for more expensive and less appropriate military actions. However, such a strategy ran counter to the military-dominated system of policy formulation and implementation that had been in place in Washington for over five decades. Obama also had to convince the American people that it was both safe and necessary for his Administration to focus more of its attention at home, without sending a message of indiscriminate retrenchment.[12] Obama's plan to accord top priority to Asia was also fraught with potential problems, the most obvious being the need for the United States to extricate itself from the Middle East and resist the temptation to become involved in future international conflicts outside the Asia-Pacific region. Perhaps the biggest risk that both the policy of domestic renewal and the reorientation toward Asia faced was the possibility that key friends and allies would not be willing or able to take greater responsibility for their security, and that they would not allow the United States to 'lead from behind' in the shaping of a new security order (see Stuart 2012a). In this regard, the Obama team's two-pronged strategy faced many of the same problems that the Nixon Doctrine had confronted in the 1970s.[13]

All things considered, the Obama Administration has navigated these shoals very effectively.[14] To set the foundation for his policy of domestic 'renewal', the president began the process of removing US forces from Iraq (completed in 2011) and announced plans to remove most American troops from Afghanistan by the end of 2014. The president has also tried to address the pervasive national fear that is at the core of America's global war on terror. In an important speech on 23 May 2013, Obama reminded the American people that the nation had been at war for over a decade, at a cost of over US$1 trillion, and that these efforts had been 'helping to explode our deficits and constraining our ability to nation-build here at home'. While recognizing that '[n]either I, nor any President, can promise the total defeat of terror', he assured his listeners that '[t]argeted action against terrorists, effective partnerships, diplomatic engagement and assistance [foreign aid] … can significantly reduce the chances of large-scale attacks on the homeland and mitigate threats to Americans overseas' (Obama 2013).

Critics on the right were quick to attack the president for wishful thinking. John Bolton (2013) called the speech '[c]onfused, contradictory and often detached from reality'. The president was also criticized from the left. Although she applauded Obama for 'acknowledging that the United States must shift away from a perpetual state of war against terror', Danya Greenfield (2013) complained that 'Obama did not go far enough in addressing the most worrisome aspects of the current drone campaign, nor did he assure observers that greater transparency and accountability would indeed be forthcoming'. The president could take some reassurance from the fact that the speech was attacked from both extremes of the political spectrum, but the speech represented only the first step in an extremely difficult process of weaning the American people and Congress away from the politics of fear and the overreliance on hard power instruments to address complex foreign policy situations.[15]

Obama also deserves to be commended for his management of the 'rebalancing' campaign in the Asia-Pacific. As previously noted, when Obama came into office, he was burdened with some serious handicaps in his effort to bolster US influence in the Asia-Pacific. As the president was reminded during the 2010 G20 (Group of 20) summit in Seoul, he could not take for granted that Asian governments would be willing to defer to Washington in the management of global economic issues (see Chan *et al.* 2010). He also had to adapt his regional policies to the fact that while the United States is still viewed by many Asian governments as their primary source of security, they now see China as their principal source of prosperity. Managing this balancing act has been especially difficult for South Korea, which serves as one of the two anchors of the US-led alliance system in the region, but which views China as its most important trading partner.[16] Edward Luttwak has been unfairly critical of Seoul for what he sees as its failure to stand up to China. South Korea has, in fact, pursued an ambitious and assertive foreign policy which has preserved the US-South Korean security relationship while enhancing its influence and options in the Asian region (see Luttwak 2012: 169–79).

The diplomatic and economic problems that the United States has faced in the Asia-Pacific have been offset to some extent by the leverage that Washington has been able to extract from the fact that many Asia-Pacific governments are reassessing the value of America's role as a regional balancer. Confronted with growing Chinese power and influence, key Asian governments are undergoing a process that Robert Cooper (2003: 41) has described (in the case of Western Europe) as a transition from postmodernism to a posture of 'defensive modernism'. The characteristic behaviours of postmodern states are the rejection of war as an instrument for resolving international disputes and the reliance on negotiation and economic inducements to resolve conflicts and facilitate cooperation. By contrast, a state undergoing the transition to a posture of defensive modernism will accept, grudgingly to be sure, the need to bolster its security either by developing the military capabilities to defend its national interests or by relying on others for protection. Writing in 2003, Cooper noted that Japan had evolved into a model postmodern state in the Asian region:

> It has self-imposed limits on defence spending and capabilities. It is no longer interested in acquiring territory nor in using force ... [however] postmodernism in one country is possible only up to a point and only because its security treaty with the US enables it to live as though its neighbourhood were less threatening. If China develops in an unpromising fashion ... Japan could be forced to revert to defensive modernism.
>
> (Cooper 2003: 41)

Until recently, America's regional hegemony made it possible for most of the governments of Southeast Asia to replicate Japan's postmodern behaviour, according top priority to economic development and domestic political concerns (see Tellis 2012: 5–8). Some of these governments have also exploited American protection by engaging in distinctly postmodern forms of multilateral cooperation. ASEAN's reliance upon the aforementioned ZOPFAN concept is a case in point. With the rise of China, however, many Asia-Pacific governments have increased their defence budgets and adapted their military strategies to the demands of regional power balancing. This has opened up a rich realm of opportunity for Washington, as it seeks to bolster its presence and influence in the Asia-Pacific theatre. As Robert Keatley (2013) has observed, 'Washington officials often find themselves pushing on open doors' when they meet with their Asian counterparts to discuss issues relating to security. The Obama team is well aware, however, that it cannot push too hard or too fast. In particular, Washington cannot ask, or be perceived to be asking, Asia-Pacific governments to support a strategy of anti-Chinese military containment. They also recognize that while Washington needs to focus on relations with China, it will only succeed if these efforts are 'embedded in a multifaceted campaign that resonates with the specific strategic interests and concerns of its regional friends and allies' (Kurt Campbell, in National Security in the 21st Century 2012).

The San Francisco network of US-led alliances will continue to be the most reliable foundation for America's campaign of reassurance and recruitment in the Asia-Pacific (see Stuart 2012b). As previously mentioned, one of the great strengths of the San Francisco System is its flexibility, which is an especially valuable quality in a period of fundamental strategic adjustment. The American-led hub-and-spokes alliance network has served as a reassuring point of reference for Asian governments as they make decisions that have long-term strategic implications. It has also served as a shield, behind which various Asia-Pacific actors have been able to investigate and develop new forms of 'minilateral' security cooperation with regional neighbours (see Stuart 2012a: 148–50).

As Washington moves forward with its campaign to reassure and recruit Asia-Pacific governments, it will have to continue to weigh its actions against the ultimate goal of 'making room for China', both regionally and globally.[17] Neither history nor international relations theory encourage optimism in this regard. Indeed, power transition situations are among the most reliable pre-dictors of war in the international relations literature. On the other hand, there are characteristics of the US-Chinese situation – most notably the nuclear standoff between the two nations – which encourage both sides to avoid conflict and favour bilateral cooperation. There are also some encouraging signs that the two governments accept, in principle, David Lampton's (2013: 57) assertion that '[c]ooperation is especially important given that global economic, environmental, and health challenges are likely to raise security concerns that rival or supplant in importance the traditional security preoccupations of the twentieth century'.

It is safe to say that the US-Chinese relationship is still at a stage that Steven Lobell, Jeffrey Taliaferro and Norrin Ripsman (2012: 23) have descri-bed as a 'permissive international environment', in which both sides have at their disposal numerous options which could lead to the kind of cooperative relationship for which both President Obama and Chinese President Xi Jinp-ing called during their 2013 meeting in California.[18] However, there are also reasons to be very concerned about both nations' ability to pursue these options.

In the case of China, the most serious problem is that as the nation becomes more economically and militarily powerful, it will redefine its national interests in ways that precipitate conflicts with other nations. Wang Jisi (2011: 77) has described China's 'core interests' as 'sovereignty, security, and development'. This is a deceptively straightforward statement. In fact, all three core interests are undergoing constant reassessment by Chinese policy-makers as China takes on more and more global and regional responsibilities. The situation is made more dangerous by the fact that as China modernizes, it is experiencing bureaucratic growing pains. Battles over turf between major government agencies have created policy confusion and encouraged risk taking (see Shambaugh 2011). Finally, as China becomes militarily stronger it will be increasingly tempted to try to 'solve' some of its major security pro-blems. Andrew Nathan and Andrew Scobell (2012: 5, 6, 3–7) have described these security problems in terms of four concentric circles: within China, on

China's borders, within the 'six nearby multistate regional systems' that surround China, and throughout 'the rest of the world'. Like Kagan's (2003: 31) well-known analogy of the man who must deal with a bear in the woods, China will become increasingly willing to do something about some of these threats as it becomes increasingly confident that it has the capability to succeed.

Whether or not China concludes that threats to its security are intolerable will depend to a great extent on US policies over the next decade. This is why the evolving debate over Air–Sea Battle (ASB) is of more than operational and budgetary significance. ASB has been presented as a logical and necessary response to a growing Chinese capability to threaten America's ability to move with impunity and maintain bases throughout the western Pacific. It calls for the development and deployment of long-range precision strike systems capable of 'networked, integrated, attack-in-depth to disrupt, destroy and defeat' Chinese weapons in the first stage of a conflict (Air–Sea Battle Office 2011). The title harks back to Air–Land Battle, America's Cold War doctrine which relied upon deep-strike systems to compensate for Russia's conventional force advantages along NATO's central front, but the comparison is dangerously misleading for two reasons. First, America and China are not locked in a Cold War struggle, and Beijing does not pose the kind of military threat that Moscow posed during the Cold War. Indeed, according to the IISS (2012b: 233):

> With a fleet of more modern submarines and naval escorts, more capable fighter aircraft and advanced armoured vehicles, it [the People's Liberation Army, or PLA] is now superior to the armed forces of less developed countries in Southeast Asia; the PLA also now matches the capabilities of Taiwan. However, a lack of war-fighting experience … questions over training and morale, and key capability gaps … mean that it remains inferior to more technologically proficient militaries in the region, such as South Korea and Japan, and far behind that of the US.

The second reason why the United States would be unwise to develop a precision deep-strike system modelled on Air–Land Battle is because it would significantly increase the already strong sense of vulnerability and insecurity among Chinese policymakers. In order to be successful, an ASB doctrine will need to be capable of taking out ballistic missiles and C4ISR (command, control, communications, computers, intelligence, surveillance and reconnaissance) systems on the Chinese mainland in the first stage of a US–Chinese confrontation. Chinese defence planners would inevitably interpret such a capability as a direct threat to their nuclear deterrent, and they would have to make their plans accordingly. Some aspects of ASB, such as proposals for the hardening and dispersal of US military assets in the western Pacific, can and should be pursued, but nothing that the Chinese have done to date justifies ratcheting up the bilateral tension by making China's land-based systems more vulnerable to a pre-emptive strike.

There is also a real risk that if the United States presses its regional friends and allies for support of ASB, some of these governments may pursue leash-slipping strategies or even decide to scrap their security ties with Washington (see Layne 2006: 30–36, regarding leash slipping). As noted in this chapter, most Asia-Pacific states are currently appreciative of America's rebalancing and are willing to provide conditional support for an enhanced American presence. Key Asian governments are also improving their own military capabilities and investigating new arrangements for what Luttwak (2012: 41–45) calls 'geo-economic' balancing against Beijing.[19] However, these policies could be reversed if Asian governments come to agree with Benjamin Schreer (2013: 31) that ASB 'risks making the Chinese military an enemy at a time when … allied grand strategy is still aimed at integrating Beijing in a cooperative Asian security order'. The net effect of this sequence of events would be an Asian region that is less conducive to American interests and ultimately less secure.

ASB may also precipitate open-ended disputes between Washington and key Asian friends and allies by forcing these Asian governments to confront publicly the most likely scenario for the US recourse to ASB: a conflict with China over Taiwan. The status of Taiwan within the San Francisco System is an issue that all parties have been able to finesse since at least 1979, but if planning for ASB places key Asian governments in the position where they have to commit to the defence of Taiwan, then Washington may not like the decisions that these governments make.

It would be naive to discount the impressive pace of Chinese military modernization, and it would be irresponsible for US policymakers not to make plans for the time when China might surpass the United States in defence spending. The Stockholm International Peace Research Institute has speculated that this might occur by 2035 (quoted in *Economist* 2012), but a great deal can happen in two decades, and the danger that China will ultimately surpass the United States as a global or regional hegemon pales by comparison with the shorter-term danger that US actions will back the Chinese into a corner in ways that will fuel dangerous risk-taking behaviour by Beijing. Furthermore, as illustrated by Chinese debates over the nation's vulnerability to economic and resource strangulation, China is already acutely aware of America's current threat potential. Washington can do little to reassure China about this, but there is no reason to tighten the screws any further.[20]

Conclusion

This chapter began with a survey of America's history as an Asia-Pacific actor. My purpose was to make the point that there is nothing tentative or anecdotal about the current US campaign to rebalance to Asia. The Obama Administration is building upon a long tradition of direct American involvement in the Asia-Pacific. The process has not been linear. At various points (1902, 1947, 1973) American policymakers have had to scale back their ambitions regarding the US role and presence in the Asian theatre, but since at least 1899, with the declaration of the Open Door policy, Washington has recognized significant national interests in the Asia-Pacific. The overriding national interest during this entire period has been the preservation of a regional balance of power. Obama's rebalancing campaign is a continuation of, rather than a departure from, this grand strategy.

My brief historical survey also provides two cautionary lessons for contemporary US policymakers. The first lesson has to do with the ease and speed with which economic issues (broadly defined to include questions of access to resources) can come to be seen as matters of national survival. US-Japanese relations during the interwar period are an obvious illustration. As Japan's economy grew, economic and resource issues increasingly came to be defined in terms of national security. When the United States sought to use economic instruments to pressure Tokyo into abandoning its expansionist policies, it exacerbated the trade-security dilemma for Japanese policymakers and set the stage for Japan's act of 'strategic imbecility' in Pearl Harbor.

In the conclusion to his study of US-Japanese relations during the interwar period, Copeland (2012: 146) asserts that '[t]he closest parallel in today's environment is clearly China'. The Clinton Administration's campaign of economic engagement with China was guided by a liberal faith in the benign effects of financial and trade relations. During this period, US-Chinese economic ties were often cited as a counter-argument to conservatives who interpreted Chinese military modernization as an indicator that Beijing would be America's next global peer competitor. Over time, however, much of the debate within the Washington policy community has shifted, so that both specific Chinese economic policies and Chinese defence spending are being placed on the negative side of the US conflict–cooperation ledger. The influential annual *Report to Congress of the US-China Economic and Security Review Commission* is a good example of this trend (see US-China Economic and Security Review Commission 2012). If the United States is serious about 'making room for China' as a global and regional actor, it will have to make a concerted effort to assist Beijing in its efforts to manage its economic challenges, while continuing to defend US economic interests and the liberal economic order.[21]

The second cautionary lesson is that the United States should not place too much faith in military solutions to problems in Asia. Former US Secretary of Defense Gates is certainly correct that 'any future defense secretary who advises the president to again send a big American land army into Asia … should "have his head examined"' (Shanker 2011). However, an equally important insight is that Washington can be seduced by technology into overestimating the ease and under-estimating the risks associated with the use of long-range precision strike instruments to 'shape' Chinese behaviour. This lesson speaks directly to the ongoing debate about ASB.

My recommendations that the United States should pursue closer economic ties with China and steer clear of the most threatening aspects of ASB may be interpreted by some as an argument for appeasement. However, I share with Avery Goldstein (2013: 49–50) a conviction that, '[f]or at least the next decade, while China remains relatively weak, the gravest danger in Sino–American relations is the possibility the two countries will find themselves in a crisis that could escalate to open military conflict'. I am also convinced that the United States will lose the support of many of its regional friends and allies if it fails to be guided by this concern.

Notes

1 Kurt Campbell, former US Assistant Secretary of State for East Asian and Pacific Affairs, jokingly made a case for an alternative term: 'pirouette'. See his statement during a public event at Georgetown University involving four former assistant secretaries of state for East Asian and Pacific Affairs (National Security in the 21st Century 2012).

2 In his contribution to this volume, Ralf Emmers (Chapter 10) notes that Singapore 'initially dislike[d] the term "pivot" as it suggested that the United States might in the future pivot away ... it therefore preferred the later rebranding of the US policy move as a "rebalancing" of forces'.

3 Perry's fleet was deployed after a previous mission under Commander James Biddle had been rebuffed by the Japanese in 1846.

4 An interesting theoretical argument regarding the impact of economic activity and regime type on foreign policy decisions is provided by Papayoanou (1996).

5 Tsuyoshi Kawasaki's balance-of-threat argument perhaps goes too far, however, in downplaying the bandwagoning considerations that contributed to the Japanese decision. See Schweller (1994).

6 See the discussion of Morison's claim in Dower (2010: 115).

7 Minutes of the Meetings of the Joint Staff Planners, 1946–47, #243, quoted in Tow (1991: 343).

8 The post-war debates that culminated in a Europe-first strategy are discussed in Stuart and Tow (1990: 24–46).

9 Anti-Japanese sentiment in the United States probably peaked in 1991 with the publication of *The Coming War with Japan*. See Friedman and LeBard (1991).

10 The National Intelligence Council presented this prediction as a 'relative certainty'.

11 Supporting arguments are provided by Haass (2013) and Brzezinski (2012).

12 Not surprisingly, Obama's statements and policies encouraged a lively debate among experts regarding the pros and cons of US global retrenchment. See, for example, Parent and MacDonald (2011), and Brooks et al. (2012).

13 The similarity may be most striking in the European theatre. Just as the Nixon and Gerald Ford Administrations faced special problems in Europe, Obama has had to manage a difficult process of pressing NATO allies to take greater responsibility for defence burden sharing without creating an irreparable rupture in the alliance. This has been especially difficult because US policymakers are deeply frustrated with the fact that Washington contributes 75 percent of the NATO defence budget at a time when key alliance members are pursuing even deeper cuts in defence spending. See former Secretary of Defense Robert Gates's remarks in Jaffe and Birnbaum (2011).

14 The International Institute for Strategic Studies (IISS), which is not known for its effusiveness, supports this conclusion, noting in 2012 that '[i]n the realm of foreign policy ... the United States continued to move on to more sensible, firmer ground'. Obama was commended for his management of Iraq, Afghanistan, Libya, Syria and, in particular, the 'global war on terror', which has been 'replaced by a more pragmatic approach, one that more accurately reflected America's true interests

and played to its strengths'. The IISS also approved of Obama's 'deliberate shift of strategic attention to the Pacific Ocean'. See IISS (2012a: 23).
15 Micah Zenko and Michael Cohen (2012) develop arguments that support efforts to reduce America's focus on security.
16 China accounts for 25 percent of South Korea's total exports, and 16 percent of its total imports. See Trading Economics (2013).
17 The phrase was made popular by White (2010).
18 See, for example, President Xi's reference to a 'new historic starting point' for bilateral relations, in Calmes and Myers (2013).
19 For some anecdotal information relating to Japan's use of economic instruments, see *Economist* (2013: 44).
20 For an assessment of America's ability to threaten Chinese shipping as a form of 'offshore control', see Hammes (2012).
21 See, for example, Lampton's (2013: 52) practical recommendations, which include greater opportunities for local-level economic cooperation, policies designed to '[e]ncourage greater employment-generating FDI [foreign direct investment]', and a commitment on the part of both governments to favour inclusive multilateral economic and diplomatic arrangements.

References

Air–Sea Battle Office (2011) 'The Air-Sea Battle Concept Summary', Story Number: NNS111109-17, 9 November, www.navy.mil/submit/display.asp?story_id=63730 (accessed 15 August 2013).
Bader, Jeffrey (2012) *Obama and China's Rise: An Insider's Account of America's Asia Strategy*, Washington, DC: Brookings Institution.
Battistini, Lawrence (1955) *The United States and Asia*, New York: Praeger.
Bolton, John (2013) 'John Bolton: Barack Obama Declares Defeat in Global War on Terror', *The Daily Beast*, 28 May, www.thedailybeast.com/articles/2013/05/28/john-bolton-barack-obama-declares-defeat-in-global-war-on-terror.html (accessed 15 August 2013).
Brooks, Stephen G., Ikenberry, G. John and Wohlforth, William C. (2012) 'Don't Come Home, America: The Case Against Retrenchment', *International Security*, 37 (3): 7–51.
Brzezinski, Zbigniew (2012) *Strategic Vision: America and the Crisis of Global Power*, New York: Basic Books.
Cabinet Meeting (1946) Friday, 2 August, Harry S. Truman Presidential Library, www.trumanlibrary.org/calendar/cabinet_minutes/index.php?date=1946-08-02 (accessed 14 August 2013).
Calmes, Jackie and Myers, Steven Lee (2013) 'Obama and Xi Tackle Cybersecurity as Talks Begin in California', *New York Times*, 8 June.
Carter, K. Holly Maze (1989) *The Asian Dilemma in US Foreign Policy: National Interest Versus Strategic Planning*, Armonk, NY: M.E. Sharpe.
Chan, Sewell, Stolberg, Sheryl Gay and Sanger, David E. (2010) 'Obama's Trade Strategy Runs into Stiff Resistance', *New York Times*, 11 November.
Cooper, Robert (2003) *The Breaking of Nations: Order and Chaos in the Twenty-First Century*, New York: Atlantic Monthly Press.
Copeland, Dale (2012) 'Economic Interdependence and the Grand Strategies of Germany and Japan, 1925–41', in Jeffrey W. Taliaferro, Norrin M. Ripsman and Steven E. Lobell (eds) *The Challenge of Grand Strategy: The Great Powers and the Broken*

Balance Between the World Wars, Cambridge: Cambridge University Press, pp. 120–46.

Craig, Gordon A. and George, Alexander (1983) *Force and Statecraft: Diplomatic Problems of our Time*, New York: Oxford University Press.

Dingman, Roger (1991) 'Japan and Mahan', in John Hattendorf (ed.) *The Influence of History on Mahan: The Proceedings of a Conference Marking the Centenary of Alfred Thayer Mahan's The Influence of Sea Power Upon History, 1660–1783*, Newport, RI: Naval War College Press, pp. 49–66.

——(2012) 'Truman's Gift: The Japanese Peace Settlement', in James Matray (ed.) *Northeast Asia and the Legacy of Harry S. Truman: Japan, China, and the Two Koreas*, Kirksville, MO: Truman State University Press, pp. 46–72.

Dower, John (2010) *Cultures of War: Pearl Harbor, Hiroshima, 9-11, Iraq*, New York: W.W. Norton.

Economist (2012) 'China's Military Rise: The Dragon's New Teeth', 7 April.

——(2013) 'Hand in Hand', 1 June.

Ferguson, Niall (2005) *Colossus: The Rise and Fall of the American Empire*, New York: Penguin.

Fowler, Mike (2011) 'Philippine Counterinsurgency Strategy: Then and Now', *Small Wars Journal*, 18 January, smallwarsjournal.com/blog/journal/docs-temp/651-fowler. pdf (accessed 14 August 2013).

Friedman, George and LeBard, Meredith (1991) *The Coming War with Japan*, New York: St Martin's Press.

Fullilove, Michael (2013) *Rendezvous with Destiny: How Franklin D. Roosevelt and Five Extraordinary Men Took America into War and into the World*, New York: Penguin.

Gaddis, John (1982) *Strategies of Containment: A Critical Appraisal of Postwar American National Security Policy*, New York: Oxford University Press.

——(2005) *The Cold War: A New History*, New York: Penguin Press.

Goldstein, Avery (2013) 'First Things First: The Pressing Danger of Crisis Instability in US–China Relations', *International Security*, 37(4): 49–89.

Greenfield, Danya (2013) 'Obama's Drone Speech Misses the Mark', *Foreign Policy*, 4 June, mideast.foreignpolicy.com/posts/2013/06/04/obama_s_drone_speech_misses_the_mark (accessed 15 August 2013).

Haass, Richard (2013) *Foreign Policy Begins at Home: The Case for Putting America's House in Order*, New York: Basic Books.

Hammes, T.X. (2012) 'Offshore Control: A Proposed Strategy', *Infinity Journal*, 2(2), www.infinityjournal.com/article/53/Offshore_Control_A_Proposed_Strategy/ (accessed 15 August 2013).

Hunt, Michael and Levine, Steven (2012) *Arc of Empire: America's Wars in Asia from the Philippines to Vietnam*, Chapel Hill, NC: University of North Carolina Press.

IISS (International Institute for Strategic Studies) (2012a) *Strategic Survey 2012: The Annual Review of World Affairs*, London: IISS.

——(2012b) *The Military Balance, 2012*, London: IISS.

Jaffe, Greg and Birnbaum, Michael (2011) 'Gates Rebukes European Allies in Farewell Speech', *Washington Post*, 10 June.

Jervis, Robert (1976) *Perception and Misperception in International Politics*, Princeton, NJ: Princeton University Press.

Kagan, Robert (2003) *Of Paradise and Power: America and Europe in the New World Order*, New York: Knopf.

——(2006) *Dangerous Nation: America's Place in the World from its Earliest Days to the Dawn of the Twentieth Century*, New York: Random House.

Kawasaki, Tsuyoshi (2012) 'The Rising Sun Was No Jackal: Japanese Grand Strategy, the Tripartite Pact, and Alliance Formation Theory', in Jeffrey W. Taliaferro, Norrin M. Ripsman and Steven E. Lobell (eds) *The Challenge of Grand Strategy: The Great Powers and the Broken Balance Between the World Wars*, Cambridge: Cambridge University Press, pp. 224–45.

Keatley, Robert (2013) 'How China Helps the Pivot', *The National Interest*, 21 March, nationalinterest.org/commentary/how-china-helps-the-pivot-8249 (accessed 15 August 2013).

Lampton, David (2013) 'A New Type of Major-Power Relationship: Seeking a Durable Foundation for US–China Ties', *Asia Policy*, 16(July): 51–68.

Layne, Christopher (2006) 'The Unipolar Illusion Revisited: The Coming End of the United States' Unipolar Moment', *International Security*, 31(2): 7–41.

Lobell, Steven E., Taliaferro, Jeffrey W. and Ripsman, Norrin M. (2012) 'Introduction: Grand Strategy between the World Wars', in Jeffrey W. Taliaferro, Norrin M. Ripsman and Steven E. Lobell (eds) *The Challenge of Grand Strategy: The Great Powers and the Broken Balance Between the World Wars*, Cambridge: Cambridge University Press, pp. 1–36.

Luttwak, Edward N. (2012) *The Rise of China vs. the Logic of Strategy*, Cambridge, MA: Belknap Press of Harvard University Press.

Mahan, Alfred Thayer (1900) *The Problem of Asia and its Effect Upon International Policies*, London: Sampson, Low, Marston and Company.

——(1910) *The Interest of America in International Conditions*, Boston, MA: Little, Brown and Co.

Mahbubani, Kishore (2008) 'Smart Power, Chinese Style', *The American Interest*, 3(4), www.the-american-interest.com/article-bd.cfm?piece=406 (accessed 13 August 2013).

Mearsheimer, John (2001) *The Tragedy of Great Power Politics*, New York: Norton.

Morison, Samuel Eliot (1953) *History of United States Naval Operations in World War II, volume 3, The Rising Sun in the Pacific*, New York: Little, Brown.

Morse, Hosea and MacNair, Harley (1931) *Far Eastern International Relations*, Boston, MA: Houghton Mifflin.

Nathan, Andrew and Scobell, Andrew (2012) *China's Search for Security*, New York: Columbia University Press.

National Intelligence Council (2008) *Global Trends 2025: A Transformed World*, Washington, DC: US Government Printing Office.

National Security in the 21st Century (2012) 'Webcast: Forging Consensus: US-Asia Policy in the Next Administration', Georgetown University, Washington, DC, 1 November, www.georgetown.edu/webcast/usasia-policy.html (accessed 14 August 2013).

Obama, Barack (2013) 'Obama's Speech on Drone Policy', *New York Times*, 23 May.

Overholt, William (2008) *Asia, America, and the Transformation of Geopolitics*, Cambridge: Cambridge University Press.

Papayoanou, Paul (1996) 'Interdependence, Institutions, and the Balance of Power: Britain, Germany, and World War I', *International Security*, 20(4): 42–76.

Parent, Joseph and MacDonald, Paul (2011) 'The Wisdom of Retrenchment: America Must Cut Back to Move Forward', *Foreign Affairs*, 90(6): 32–47.

Schreer, Benjamin (2013) 'Planning the Unthinkable War: "AirSea Battle" and its Implications for Australia', Barton, ACT: Australian Strategic Policy Institute, April.

Schweller, Randall (1994) 'Bandwagoning for Profit: Bringing the Revisionist State Back In', *International Security*, 19(1): 72–107.

Shambaugh, David (2011) 'Coping with a Conflicted China', *Washington Quarterly*, 34(1): 7–27.

Shanker, Thom (2011) 'Warning Against Wars Like Iraq and Afghanistan', *New York Times*, 25 February.

Stuart, Douglas (2008) *Creating the National Security State: A History of the Law That Transformed America*, Princeton, NJ: Princeton University Press.

——(2012a) '"Leading from Behind": Toward a New US Strategy for the Asia-Pacific', *Korean Journal of Defense Analysis*, 24(2): 141–55.

——(2012b) 'San Francisco 2.0: Military Aspects of the US Pivot Toward Asia', *Asian Affairs: An American Review*, 39(4): 202–18.

Stuart, Douglas and Tow, William T. (1990) *The Limits of Alliance: NATO Out-of-Area Problems Since 1949*, Baltimore, MD: Johns Hopkins University Press.

Taliaferro, John (2013) *All the Great Prizes: The Life of John Hay, from Lincoln to Roosevelt*, New York: Simon and Schuster.

Tellis, Ashley (2012) 'Uphill Challenges: China's Military Modernization and Asian Security', in Ashley Tellis and Travis Tanner (eds) *Strategic Asia 2012–13: China's Military Challenge*, Washington, DC: National Bureau of Asian Research, pp. 1–24.

Thompson, James, Stanley, Peter and Perry, John (1981) *Sentimental Imperialists: The American Experience in East Asia*, New York: Harper & Row.

Tow, William T. (1991) *Encountering the Dominant Player: US Extended Deterrence Strategy in the Asia-Pacific*, New York: Columbia University Press.

Trading Economics (2013) 'South Korea Balance of Trade', July, www.tradingeconomics.com/south-korea/balance-of-trade (accessed 15 August 2013).

US-China Economic and Security Review Commission (2012) *2012 Report to Congress of the US-China Economic and Security Review Commission*, Washington, DC: US Government Printing Office, November.

Wang Jisi (2011) 'China's Search for a Grand Strategy: A Rising Great Power Finds its Way', *Foreign Affairs*, 90(2): 68–79.

White, Hugh (2010) 'Power Shift: Australia's Future between Washington and Beijing', *Quarterly Essay*, 39 (September).

White House (2010) *National Security Strategy*, Washington, DC: White House, May.

Zenko, Micah and Cohen, Michael (2012) 'Clear and Present Safety: The United States is More Secure than Washington Thinks', *Foreign Affairs*, 91(2): 79–93.

3 Rebalancing and order building

Strategy or illusion?

William T. Tow

Recent developments in the Middle East and the Barack Obama Administration's response to them might have created the misperception that the United States' role as the custodian of the post-war liberal internationalist order may be dissipating. US military interventionism to underwrite or restore the norms and rules of that order appears to be giving way to American preoccupations with domestic economic strains, political paralysis and long-term geopolitical fatigue. As Timothy Garton Ash recently observed, 'the American people are "sick and tired" of [the United States engaging in wars that have] cost trillions of dollars, while they've been losing their jobs and homes, struggling to get by'. While isolationism has intermittently shaped US foreign policy following long periods of conflict, Ash notes that 'this time feels different', because it is no longer a rising power but one 'fearfully conscious of relative decline' and wary of traditional American predominance being superseded by relentless Chinese growth (Ash 2013).

If this proposition is accurate, it represents an historic sea change in US foreign policy and in how Washington will relate to its long-standing global alliances in Europe (through the North Atlantic Treaty Organization, or NATO) and in the Asia-Pacific (via its network of bilateral alliance systems with selected regional states, collectively known as the San Francisco System). It would also have significant implications for the credibility of the so-called 'rebalancing' or 'pivot' strategy initially announced by President Obama in November 2011 – an initiative designed to *enhance* US geopolitical influence in Asia and its contiguities (such as the Indian Ocean) over the ensuing decade. As two critics of rebalancing have recently insisted, '[b]y over-dramatizing and overselling an evolutionary development of US foreign policy, the Obama Administration risks providing false reassurances to allies of Washington's ability to deliver on its promises' (Klingner and Cheng 2012).

Recent American behaviour in Northeast Asia, however, has challenged the proposition that the United States is undergoing inevitable strategic decline. Robust demonstrations of US air and naval power during a standoff with North Korea in March 2013 and similar signals directed toward China after that country declared an air defence identification zone (ADIZ) in the East China Sea have signalled the Obama Administration's determination to implement a credible 'rebalancing' strategy in the Asia-Pacific. It is argued in this chapter that the United States will proceed to cultivate and broaden this initiative. It will do so, however, incrementally and selectively rather than comprehensively. The United States will pursue limited forms of rebalancing because it has a continuing need to apply symbolic measures to underscore American power as a factor in Asia-Pacific security.

Initially, the San Francisco System served as a 'hub-and-spokes' mechanism of bilateral alliance politics through which Washington could extend security guarantees and manage resource allocations separately with each 'junior ally' (Cha 2009/10). Evolving structural change in regional and global politics is likely to compel American and allied policymakers to move away from this asymmetrical approach. Due to increasingly strained finances, the American public's growing war-weariness, and continued pressures for the United States to remain strategically involved in other theatres (especially the Middle East), Washington will lobby its Asia-Pacific allies to play more significant roles in pursuing mutual regional security interests. The extent to which they can and will meet this expectation will determine the rebalancing strategy's future viability. To what extent US regional allies will meet American expectations is uncertain. The most favourable outcome would be the San Francisco System's transformation from a Cold War 'threat-centric' alliance framework into a mechanism that is more oriented toward regional 'order building'. This outcome would be consistent with the restructuring envisioned by US officials who shaped that strategy. For example, Kurt Campbell, Obama's US assistant secretary of state for East Asian affairs during his first term in office, has insisted that rather than focusing on preventing China from achieving 'hegemonic transition' at the United States' expense, rebalancing was introduced as a means to 'embed the [Sino–American] relationship in a larger multilateral context … which seek to prevent misunderstandings from getting out of hand' (quoted in Potter 2012). In a definitive address delivered to the Center for Strategic and International Studies in November 2012, National Security Advisor Tom Donilon (2012) explained that US policy was focusing on 'a sustained and multi-dimensional strategy' of rebalancing rather than 'simply … a shifting of military resources'. Both Campbell and Donilon, however, have acknowledged that regional allies and partners, along with China, have focused more on the specific military dimensions of rebalancing than Washington intended. Current trends in Asia-Pacific security politics point to military and geopolitical factors continuing to dominate US relations with allies and strategic partners.

This chapter is divided into three parts. Initially, the evolving relevance of US bilateral alliance relationships in an Asia-Pacific region that has undergone extensive structural change for more than two decades is discussed. These relationships' continued importance will hinge upon such issues as forging updated and common perceptions about the San Francisco System's overarching purpose and the perceived ability of the United States to exercise continued leadership over that alliance framework. A brief assessment is then offered of the extent to which US bilateral alliances can transition from a threat-centric to a more order-centric alliance framework. In theory, such a transition would facilitate the implementation of a broader rebalancing initiative such as that envisioned by the Obama Administration. In practice, however, still outstanding and emerging regional security dilemmas have impeded any such transition from taking place. So too have regional uncertainties about the future of Sino–American relations.

A third section of the chapter focuses on the rebalancing strategies' advertised goal of strengthening 'partner capacity': the willingness and capability of America's regional allies to assume greater responsibility in their intra-alliance relations with Washington. US officials have emphasized that shifting from 'traditional' alliance management, where asymmetry between the United States and its regional allies was a fundamental principle, to a more nuanced and equal set of security relationships with allies and partners, will be a long-term process, taking years and perhaps decades to achieve. It remains unclear whether such change will result in America's friends accepting more direct responsibility for regional order building, or supporting a reinvigorated San Francisco System as a threat-centric instrument for the containment of China.

The policy challenges are formidable. Will current and emerging regional threats become so intense as to render order-building efforts irrelevant? Can American and allied policymakers be successful in redefining or regenerating alliance purpose in an era of rapid and dynamic regional change? Or will American policymakers and their regional counterparts be compelled by other factors (excessive budgetary strains, polarization in domestic politics, or ideological shifts that generate intensified nationalism) to embrace strategic postures similar to those pursued during the Cold War? As these challenges unfold, the San Francisco System's value as a source of Asia-Pacific security environment will be increasingly tested.

Responding to structural change

The San Francisco System's purpose was straightforward when the bilateral alliances constituting that alliance network were originally conceived in the early 1950s. Growing Soviet military power in Eurasia fuelled an American desire for containment based on security alliances with selected European and Asia-Pacific states. The question for Washington was how to implement its containment strategy. American policymakers believed that the United States shared a 'collective identity' with its future NATO allies because of similar cultures, shared histories and common values. No corresponding identity appeared to be operative in Asia. Instead, the relatively weak, divided and ideologically diverse states located in that region precluded any viable multilateral security grouping similar to NATO (Hemmer and Katzenstein 2002). In Northeast Asia, as a defeated wartime adversary, Japan's nascent democracy could barely rebuild the country's shattered economy. Conflict exploded on the Korean peninsula in mid-1950 soon after Chiang Kai-shek's pro-Western regime was defeated by communist opponents, relegating it to governing only a small offshore island, Taiwan. Japan, South Korea and Taiwan were all deemed by early Cold War US policymakers as potential recalcitrants inclined to destabilize Northeast Asia without firm American control. As Victor Cha has since argued, Washington opted to restrain these three states from 'aggressive behavior' that could entrap the United States in future Northeast Asian conflicts. It thus imposed bilateral 'pacts of restraint' that would not interfere with its efforts to contain Soviet and (after late 1949) communist Chinese power (see Cha 2009/10: 158, 163).

In Southeast Asia, after a brief and ill-fated effort to establish the Southeast Asia Treaty Organization (SEATO) via signing the Manila Pact in late 1954, the United States reinforced its support for bilateralism in that sub-region as well. SEATO never represented the type of substantive US defence commitment that was offered to the NATO allies – a promise of an immediate response if a European member state were attacked (Hemmer and Katzenstein 2002: 579). There was no commensurate joint command structure in SEATO compared to the Supreme Allied Command in NATO. Even the nature of SEATO's membership was fluid, with the status of three Indochinese 'protocol member states' never really clarified: Vietnam and Laos accepted SEATO's provisions but Cambodia rejected them, eventually opting for neutrality between East and West. US military inaction during the Laotian neutrality crisis in 1961–62 was soon followed by a Soviet–American deal to observe the Indochinese states' de facto non-aligned status. This chain of events signalled SEATO's practical death knell years before its formal demise in June 1977 (Buszynski 1983: 81–83). British and French resistance to activating SEATO for defending Laos against further communist inroads led President John F. Kennedy – himself unenthusiastic about committing US forces in the defence of that landlocked Southeast Asian country – to finesse a reinforcement of the United States' separate bilateral defence commitment to Thailand. The March 1962 Rusk–Thanat agreement quickly superseded the Manila Pact as the operative document for US-Thai bilateral security relations. From the Philippines' perspective, meanwhile, its SEATO membership had never really matched the importance that country had assigned to the bilateral 1951 Mutual Defense Treaty between the United States and the Philippines.

Christopher Hemmer and Peter Katzenstein (2002: 597) have noted that the whole SEATO episode reflected a 'strong note of condescension in many of the US discussions of SEATO … Many American policymakers did not see [recently decolonized] Asians as ready or sufficiently sophisticated to enjoy the trust and the same degree of power that the United States had offered to European states'. Joseph Siracusa (2012: 456) has further observed that '[t]he United States [only] sustained the principle of collective security in Southeast Asia to provide the necessary sanction for its largely unilateral or bilateral strategies'.

Even as the Cold War was drawing to a close, US policymakers elected to preserve the San Francisco System's asymmetrical character and had little time for what multilateral security initiatives were being proposed by their regional counterparts. Soviet leader Mikhail Gorbachev's 1986 Pacific Ocean conference proposal, designed largely to replicate in Asia the confidence-building measures in the 1975 Helsinki Accords that solidified *détente* in Europe, was rejected by the United States because it included a cap on naval forces operating in the western Pacific. American officials also reacted adversely to Australian Foreign Minister Gareth Evans's July 1990 proposal for a Conference on Security Cooperation in Asia. Evans later insisted they did so because the United States tended to take the view that 'any approach to regional security in the Asia Pacific that does not focus wholly on the maintenance of traditional Western alliance discipline ... is destined to slip quickly down the slope and over the precipice of unacceptable policy concessions' (Evans and Grant 1992: 111). While acknowledging that rapid structural change in the Asia-Pacific would necessitate greater adaptability in US alliance politics, US Secretary of State James Baker nevertheless maintained that Washington's 'loose network' of bilateral alliances, coupled with its growing economic ties in the region, would continue to be the foundation for US strategy in the Asia-Pacific (Baker 1991: 5, 7).

Washington could still prioritize bilateralism at a time when regional allies and partners feared that the end of the Cold War would lead to US strategic retrenchment from the region. The Nixon Doctrine, announced in August 1969, had already foreshadowed the United States' intention to reduce its force presence in Asia as the Vietnam War was winding down. Less than ten years later, the Jimmy Carter Administration announced it would withdraw all US ground forces from South Korea – a decision only suspended after intelligence information revealed that North Korean military strength was much greater than originally estimated. Ronald Reagan's Administration, however, reversed its predecessor's inclination for downsizing the United States' regional force presence, opting to build up US military capabilities and strengthen America's security alliances and coalitions in response to what it viewed to be a growing and more active Soviet threat in the region (Godwin 1988: 48–49).

Although that threat was specifically designated as his Administration's key strategic concern, Reagan's policies should not be equated to the Obama Administration's rebalancing strategy, which was designed to reassure US Asia-Pacific allies and partners that the United States would become more strategically involved in their region. Indeed, much of the Reagan Administration's early strategic outlook was shaped by the Weinberger Doctrine (enunciated by US Secretary of Defense Caspar Weinberger). It served notice that apart from the unlikely event of a direct superpower confrontation, the United States would not initiate the use of military force abroad unless it had strong public support and could be assured of victory (Wortzel 1996). This strategic outlook was clearly a manifestation of the residual impact of the Vietnam War, and of President Reagan's determination to focus on the 'big picture' of Soviet–American strategic relations (see, for example, Dibb 2013).[1] Like

Carter before him, however, Reagan anticipated 'swinging' US forces stationed in Asia to the Persian Gulf in response to any conflict that might erupt in the latter theatre. Asian allies were urged to develop more formidable self-defence capabilities to pick up the slack (Dibb 2013: 49–50).

Reagan's successor, George H.W. Bush, oversaw a successful US-led military intervention against Iraq, and anticipated that a post-Cold War 'peace dividend' could provide new opportunities for further US force reductions in Asia. In April 1990, and again in April 1992, the Bush Administration released two East Asia Strategy Initiative reports to Congress. These reports outlined a 'strategic framework' that anticipated the reduction of US force levels in Asia from 135,000 to 100,000 and which assigned greater defence burden-sharing responsibilities to America's regional allies (for background, see Stuart and Tow 1995: 6–20; Winnefeld *et al.* 1992: 33–34; Goh 2004: 51–53; Cossa *et al.* 2009: 12). To counterbalance growing allied uncertainties over the US regional defence role in response to such cutbacks, Secretary of Defense Dick Cheney proffered assurances to Asia-Pacific security allies and partners that its bilateral security guarantees would remain strong. He insisted that sufficient force levels and basing support would be maintained for US operations in the area to meet future threats if the allies worked with Washington to complement defence cooperation by assuming greater responsibility for their own security (Wortzel 1996: 6).

As US force reductions were implemented in the region, intensified multilateral security dialogues became viewed by the Bill Clinton Administration as a complement to, but not a replacement for, the San Francisco System. As the first post-war president not to be confronted with a Soviet global threat, Clinton and his advisers believed that bilateral and multilateral security approaches could be credibly managed even while Congress was questioning the continued rationale for substantial US force deployments in Asia. During his confirmation hearing before the Senate Committee on Foreign Relations in March 1993, Assistant Secretary of State for East Asian and Pacific Affairs-designate Winston Lord (1993) explicitly stated that effective co-responsibility was a key US policy goal (see also Goh 2004: 53). Simultaneously, the Association of Southeast Asian Nations (ASEAN) member states expressed a desire for the United States to remain involved in their region while they looked for ways to encourage China's participation in multilateral security.

Two additional East Asia Strategy reports were released in 1995 and 1998. Both reaffirmed the United States' determination to remain a critical strategic player in the Asia-Pacific. On the premise that Northeast Asia had been assigned the bulk of attention by US policymakers, the 1998 report specifically emphasized the need for the United States to upgrade its military relations and training with Southeast Asian allies and partners. The major thrust of that document, however, was to reaffirm that US bilateral alliances in the region were 'the cornerstone of regional security'. In contrast to being directed toward containing a specific threat, the San Francisco System was now being described as increasingly 'interest centric', supporting the common objective of 'regional security and stability', and contributing to 'the concurrent and complementary development of constructive ties with non-allied states' (United States Department of Defense 1998; see also USIA Foreign Press Center 1998).

Clinton underscored his support for this objective by visiting all five formal US bilateral allies during two Asia-Pacific trips in April and November 1996. In Japan and the Philippines he emphasized the need to enhance logistical components of military cooperation (including updating the US-Japanese defence guidelines and renewing a Visiting Forces Agreement with the Philippines). In South Korea, he advanced a joint US-South Korean peace proposal for a four-party dialogue with China and North Korea while pledging Washington's continued support for its alliance with Seoul (Clinton 1996b). In Thailand he emphasized the importance of alliance politics in the pursuit of non-traditional security objectives (Clinton 1996a).

President George W. Bush assumed office determined to repair traditional strategic relations with the Asia-Pacific's bilateral security allies that he believed had been neglected by the Clinton Administration in favour of forging closer ties with China – a country Bush labelled during his presidential campaign as a 'strategic competitor'. While acknowledging the impact of the 11 September 2001 terrorist strikes in New York and Washington as catalysts for major change on how international security should be perceived and managed, the 2001 Quadrennial Defense Review noted that 'Asia is gradually emerging as a region susceptible to large-scale military competition'; the United States could not shirk from the responsibility of assuring its allies and friends that it would continue to be a reliable security partner. In that context, it stated: 'US alliances, as well as its wide range of bilateral security relationships, are a centerpiece of American security' (United States Department of Defense 2001: 4, 5).

Allied and partner responses to the Bush Administration's security postures were mixed. Bush was successful in strengthening US-Japanese security ties, in no small part due to his close personal relationship with Koizumi Junichiro, who was Japan's prime minister in the period 2001–06. The same conclusion can be drawn about American relations with Australia and its prime minister, John Howard. US-Indian relations also clearly strengthened during Bush's term in office. Bush's relations with South Korean President Kim Dae Jung and his successor, Roh Moo-hyun, became strained, however, over what the White House considered to be excessive South Korean appeasement of North Korean President Kim Jong-il, whom Bush detested. The Philippines and Thailand joined ASEAN and other Asian states in projecting at least some discomfort over what one respected US Republican congressman, writing in early 2005, described as 'the manner in which the administration ... exercised America's extraordinary primacy in world affairs, so much so that one can imagine a range of scenarios in which even our friends in Asia resist future Washington initiatives' (Leach 2005: 213).

To sum up, the Nixon Doctrine reconstituted US global strategy nearly half a century ago by reconciling the United States' security interests in the Asia-Pacific with the imperative to prioritize its commitments and ration resources directed toward that region. As China's wealth and power grew, and Asia acquired greater prosperity and geopolitical importance, US policymakers struggled to define how American power could best be applied to an Asia-Pacific undergoing rapid structural change without diminishing their country's influence in other parts of the world. Part of this calibration process involved retaining sufficient credibility with US allies and partners so that they would be willing and capable of working with the United States and with each other to sustain a balance of power and ultimately to build a peaceful regional order. The key variable for success in this context was China's gradual enmeshment into a US-dominated international order. Rebalancing is the latest US version of this strategy.

Prospects for Sino–American cooperation

When President Obama assumed office in 2009, the momentum for regional order-building in the Asia-Pacific appeared to be intensifying. The Declaration of ASEAN Concord II (better known as Bali Concord II) had set out ambitious plans for the formation of an ASEAN Community with politico-security, economic and socio-cultural components. This initiative has since been endorsed to various degrees by China within the auspices of ASEAN+3 (China, Japan and South Korea) meetings and by the United States within the East Asia Summit (EAS). The American decision to join the EAS was a landmark development in its own right, given Washington's traditional preference for coordinating regional security issues within its alliance network.

In December 2008, a China–Japan–South Korea trilateral summit involving the leaderships of all three countries convened in Fukuoka, Japan. South Korean President Lee Myung-bak spearheaded the formation of a permanent secretariat for this grouping in Seoul. He proposed a formal roadmap (Trilateral Cooperation Vision 2020) to spur intensified trading ties, environmental cooperation and human security collaboration between the three powers. South Korea and China negotiated a separate strategic cooperative partnership in 2008 to foster greater trade and confidence building in Northeast Asia.

There were some setbacks, however. Beijing and Washington privileged ASEAN+3 and the EAS as the best means to underwrite ASEAN's vision of community building. This underscored their wariness of each other's preferences as to how order building might flow from Southeast Asia to encompass the Asia-Pacific region-at-large. By late 2013, moreover, the trilateral summit appeared to have dissolved as Chinese and Korean animosities intensified over what China and South Korea viewed to be the excessive nationalist tendencies of a conservative Japanese government led by Shinzō Abe. There seemed to be little hope that any progress on trade relations could 'spill over' to facilitate serious discussion on historical grievances, territorial issues, or security on the Korean peninsula (*Asahai Shimbun* 2013). Indeed, until late November 2013, the only common security policy that Japan and South Korea seemed to share was their mutual affiliation with the San Francisco System.

This situation changed dramatically with China's announcement of its ADIZ on 23 November 2013. The geographic space covered by this zone includes the tiny Diaoyu/Senkaku Islands contested by China and Japan. Speculation has been rife for years that these islets sit atop rich oil and natural gas reserves. The ADIZ also overlaps the submerged Socotra Rock where South Korea has established a science observation facility and which it claims as part of its exclusive economic zone, calling it 'Idedo' (China refers to it as the Suyan Rock). While the Abe government and its South Korean counterpart led by Park Geun-hye still have little regard for each other, the shared concern about Beijing's threatening behaviour has encouraged Tokyo and Seoul to move closer to Washington. Emulating the American response of dispatching unannounced military aircraft (including B-52 bombers) into the zone, South Korean and Japanese military aircraft have flown through the ADIZ without previously reporting flight plans to China as the latter country demanded. South Korean and Japanese policymakers view the Chinese move as an effort by President Xi Jinping and his counterparts in Beijing to establish Chinese dominance away from its own shores and well out into Pacific waters at a time when they perceive the United States' influence weakening in the Middle East and elsewhere, and American power waning as a result of political discord at home. As one observer noted:

> Beijing has now turned control of the air space around the Senkaku into a litmus test of the US security commitment to east Asia. For Washington to accept the Chinese restrictions would be to send a signal to every other nation in the region that the US cannot be relied on to defend the status quo against Chinese expansionism ... Mr Obama, accused of presiding over a collapse of US power in the Middle East, cannot afford to back down over the Senkaku.
>
> (Stephens 2013)

What does the recent spiralling of regional flashpoints in the East China and South China Seas and the Korean peninsula imply for future Sino–American cooperation and Asia-Pacific order building? Driven by its domestic population's intensified nationalism, can China's leaders be 'conditioned' over time to accept the type of rebalancing originally envisioned and promoted by key US policy officials during the Obama Administration's first term of office? To a great extent, the answer to these questions rests upon the degree to which China and the United States can collaborate with each other and with other Asia-Pacific states to define what Campbell has labelled 'rules of the road' based on mutual respect and strengthened by institutional approaches to regional confidence building and conflict avoidance.

In this context, US rebalancing must be more effective at providing China with incentives. They must strike a judicious balance between resistance to 'face diplomacy' (where Beijing's leadership relentlessly privileges and pursues its national interests), and the encouragement of 'smile diplomacy' (where China engages in regional security dialogues and institutional forums as a means of building up diplomatic influence) (on 'face diplomacy', see Gries 2004; Shambaugh 2013: 57; on 'smile diplomacy', see Holmes 2013). China's hard-line approach to territorial disputes in the region's maritime environs reflects the first tendency. Its exploitation of President Obama's absence from the 2013 Asia-Pacific Economic Cooperation (APEC) and EAS, where President Xi and Chinese Premier Li Keqiang played down those disputes and empha-sized the growth of Chinese-ASEAN economic interaction, exemplifies the second pattern. If rebalancing is to unfold as the comprehensive American approach to regional involvement originally envisioned by that policy's architects, the United States will need to do better at reassuring its allies and partners' confidence that it will be consistently and reliably involved in *all* aspects of regional development.

Obama's absence from the critical institutional summits in late 2013 left the 'much-promoted but already anemic American "pivot" to Asia ... further undercut' (Perlez 2013). Subsequent efforts by US Vice President Joseph Biden, during a swing through Northeast Asia in early December 2013, to preserve the rebalancing strategy's credibility and durability had to be made in the context of reaffirming the value of enduring Sino–American ties. One respected Australian analyst aptly summarized the complexity of Biden's diplomatic challenge: 'Washington must walk a fine line, reassuring allies without emboldening them and projecting strength to China without belli-gerence. Yet at the moment, friends and adversaries alike are increasingly concluding that America's heart is not in the rebalance' (Fullilove 2013). More alarmingly, China's initial response to Obama's rebalancing initiative reflected its fears that rebalancing was nothing more than a containment policy directed against it (Liao 2013).[2]

In the absence of a clearer US policy direction for rebalancing, the pro-spects for regional order building will decline commensurately. Both the United States and China will be more likely to edge toward reinforcing their bilateral security ties in the region, engaging with multilateral security insti-tutions only if by doing so they can realize zero-sum outcomes for their own national interests. President Xi's October 2013 visits to Indonesia and Malaysia prior to APEC and the EAS reflected Chinese efforts to strengthen bilateral ties with the two key states in the Malay world. This process was defended by the participants as the next steps in China's economic and dip-lomatic relations with ASEAN, which would be strengthened as a result of Xi's visits.

US policy planners have also played the bilateral–multilateral game in order to bolster regional security. The United States criticized China on mul-tilateral grounds for not observing what Washington views as 'international norms' when it established its ADIZ in the East China Sea (Cha 2013). The Obama Administration's immediate policy response, however, was firmly bilateral in nature: embracing the San Francisco System's traditional deterrence strategy. It warned China that it would defend Japan against any external attack directed toward the Diaoyu/Senkaku Islands, given that Japan had long exercised 'administrative control' of the islands. It is unlikely that the United States, China or Japan will favour a multilateral approach to territorial negotiations or conflict avoidance in the East China Sea. Beijing and Washington still view multilateral forums predominantly as instruments to check one another's power.

It also seems improbable that Washington or Beijing will favour 'power-sharing' arrangements with the other. The divergent Chinese and American visions of regional order will not be modified sufficiently any time soon for both to support a liberal-internationalist regional security model underpinned by 'trust building' or comprehensive security initiatives.[3] Neither will bilateralism's continued primacy be compatible with a more nationalistic – and arguably more expansionist – China settling for a 'hierarchical and multi-tiered' Asia-Pacific order led by the United States (as argued by Goh 2013).

China is clearly an emerging regional power, but to what extent could it ever really be considered a US 'partner'? A survey conducted in mid-2012 of both American and Chinese elites and publics, co-sponsored by the Carnegie Endowment for International Peace and the China Strategic Culture Promotion Association, found that while there was a 'low level of strategic trust' in each country toward the other, only small minorities in each country perceived the other country as an outright enemy (Carnegie Endowment for International Peace 2013: 1). The pursuit of bilateral economic cooperation, the sharing of global leadership and the dampening of military tensions ranked high in both countries' survey groups. Realizing these objectives, the Carnegie report concluded, could provide the basis for a more positive long-term Sino–American relationship. The annual United States–China Strategic and Economic Dialogue, implemented in 2009, has made notable progress in cooperation on such key issues as climate change, cyber security and bilateral investment practices. Although criticized by hard-liners in both countries as constituting nothing more than 'talk shops', the Dialogue has enhanced information sharing between the Chinese and US governments in ways that 'create a certain baseline of predictability and structure to the tricky US-Chinese relationship. The relative permanence and regularity of these channels offer a degree of assurance that diplomatic relations may not be allowed to regress beyond a certain point' (Boon 2013).

Institutionalization of dialogues, however, is not sufficient to achieve a fully fledged great power partnership. Partnership only becomes manifest when two or more parties are prepared to collaborate on difficult political issues. In this regard, several important tests now confront Sino–American relations. The most immediate and compelling will be to what extent Chinese and US leaders will coordinate their policies towards an increasingly weakened, but nonetheless erratic and dangerous nuclear North Korea. The stabilization of the East China and South China Seas disputes through confidence-building security measures looms almost as large. So too does the need to shape more cooperative approaches to the politics of nuclear deterrence and missile defence. Until Beijing and Washington prove able to negotiate effectively on such issues, the prospects of their development of a meaningful great power partnership remain improbable.

US efforts to encourage enhanced partner capacity

Speaking at the Shangri-La Dialogue in June 2012, US Secretary of Defense Leon Panetta linked the US rebalancing strategy to partner capacity-building. He insisted that the United States would 'play an essential role in promoting strong partnerships that strengthen the capabilities of the Pacific nations to defend and secure themselves'. The United States would do so, he declared, by working to 'modernize and strengthen our alliances and partnerships in [the Asia-Pacific] region' and by implementing updated initiatives related to forward basing, joint patrols and training, intelligence sharing, and other concrete forms of politico-security cooperation, including initiatives undertaken with China (Panetta 2012). Other US policymakers have underscored the need for America's five formal treaty allies in the Asia-Pacific to become more 'nimble and adaptive' in their own right so as better to meet emerging regional security challenges independently and in tandem with their senior US ally and to deter more effectively 'provocation from the full spectrum of state and non-state actors' (Clinton 2011b; see also Odom 2012: 9). The United States is also committed to economic, diplomatic and military cooperation with 'emerging powers' in the Asia-Pacific, and to preserving regional stability, promoting a 'rules-based' regional security order, and encouraging democracy and human rights (Clinton 2011a; see also Odom 2012: 9–10). This approach is more wide ranging than the version of partner capacity-building normally applied by the US Department of Defense, which favours '*[t]argeted efforts to improve the collective capabilities and performance of the* [US] *Department of Defense and its partners*' (United States Department of Defense 2006: 3, emphasis in original; see also Paul *et al.* 2013: 8).

US policymakers have also been able to reach at least partial bilateral consensus with other regional states on such issues as maritime security, counterterrorism and regional order-building to a degree where the application of a 'partnership' concept is more than an exercise in hyperbole. The precondition for further progress is the United States identifying common security interests with the countries in question and shared thinking on how to realize those interests. Partnership is further enhanced by similar values in approaching interest fulfilment. This precept was explicated by the US Department of Defense in its 2012 document on sustaining US global leadership: 'we will seek to be the security partner of choice, pursuing new partnerships with a growing number of nations ... whose interests and viewpoints are merging into a common vision of freedom, stability, and prosperity' (United States Department of Defense 2012: 3).

Partnerships can often supplement existing alliances and relationships rather than supplant them. 'Side talks' convened at multilateral regional summits, independent 'minilateral' interactions, and joint bilateral security declarations exemplify the processes that the United States has undertaken with select Asia-Pacific countries. Practical forms of cooperation with specific partners have been recently developed through counterterrorism and anti-piracy measures with Indonesia, defence technology collaboration, joint military exercises, defence equipment sales to India, nuclear non-proliferation measures with Malaysia, maritime security and military logistical coordination with Singapore, nascent joint naval collaboration with Vietnam, and intelligence-sharing and peace-building coordination with New Zealand (Odom 2012: 12; White House 2013).

How can partner capacity-building success be measured? A recent RAND Corporation report has advanced several conditions that, when met, appear to confirm partner capacity-building effectiveness. Among the most significant of these are: 1) when US objectives align with partner nation security objectives, baseline capabilities and absorptive capacity; 2) when the partner nation invests its own funds to support or sustain capacity; and 3) when partner capacity-building is substantial and consistent over time (Paul *et al.* 2013: 87–93). It is not yet evident that the overall US rebalancing strategy in Asia is meeting all of these conditions.[4]

Progress in implementing the US force posture initiatives envisioned under rebalancing has perhaps been most evident in Washington's strategic relations with its two key maritime allies in the Asia-Pacific: Japan, the traditional 'linchpin' of the US bilateral regional alliance network, and Australia, the San Francisco System's 'southern anchor'. Japan and Australia are playing a central role in the increase of US Marines' deployment to the Asia-Pacific, with an estimated growth to around 22,000 by the time realignment is completed in 2020 (National Institute for Defense Studies 2013: 313). By the end of 2013, Japanese Prime Minister Abe appeared to be close to resolving long-standing basing issues in Okinawa that would reaffirm a US Marine and naval military presence there, although up to 5,000 Marines would be shifted from Okinawa to Guam (Hayashi 2013). The rotational presence of the small but highly symbolic Marine Air–Ground Task Force in Darwin will facilitate American and Australian capabilities to interact with Southeast Asian militaries. Australia recently committed further expenditure to support the pre-positioning of US military equipment in Darwin and the modernization of airbases in northern Australia which could be accessed by US Air Force components (Schreer 2013). The central Japanese government is financially committed to building substantially more military and civilian infrastructure in Okinawa as part of its evolving 'dynamic defence' posture (underwritten by increased defence spending from 2014 onward). Australia cannot currently afford a commensurate defence increase (American officials have complained that Australia should be spending more than 1.67 percent of its gross national product on its military) but its targeted support for the Marine Air–Ground Task Force initiative goes some way in conforming to the partner capacity-building criterion for partner nation financial support. Japan and Australia, moreover, support the rebalancing policy's objective of deployment of 60 percent of US naval power in the Pacific (including six aircraft carriers) as consistent with their own national security objectives.

However, the broader contours of the rebalancing strategy pose serious long-term challenges for these two stalwart US allies. Japan's increasingly tenuous relations with China threaten to entrap the United States into a military confrontation with Beijing. Meanwhile, Japan's territorial disputes and historical tensions with South Korea, another vital American ally in Northeast Asia, are hardly compatible with the rebalancing strategy's vision of a more stable and economically driven region. As for Australia, at the time of writing, having opted to prioritize its military alliance with the United States over its increasingly important Chinese economic partner, the conservative Australian government led by Tony Abbott now confronts a China angry over Canberra's criticism of its implementation of the new East China Sea ADIZ (the Chinese ambassador in Canberra was summoned by Australia's foreign ministry to 'please explain'). It has further alienated Beijing by Abbott's and Australian Foreign Minister Julie Bishop's observation that Japan is Australia's 'best friend in Asia' (Keck 2013). Australia is also dealing with strained relations with its northern Indonesian neighbour over disclosures of Australian intelligence monitoring of Jakarta's policy elites and its management of forced people's movements from Indonesian to Australian shores. None of these episodes conforms to the original 'sustained and multidimensional strategy' of rebalancing originally envisioned by the Obama Administration.

US capacity building with South Korea focuses on issues related to South Korea's pursuit of an independent foreign policy diplomacy towards North Korea and China. Even before assuming her office in early 2013, South Korean President Park launched a form of trust building to overcome what she termed the 'Asia paradox' – an imbalance between growing Asia-Pacific wealth and scant security cooperation (Park 2012; see also Cheon 2013). Later refined to become the 'Northeast Asian Peace and Cooperation Initiative', Park's *trustpolitik* has been designed to strengthen Chinese–South Korean relations as a means of leveraging greater stability on the Korean peninsula while hedging this approach with a credible alliance deterrent against North Korea.

The major South Korean diplomatic objective is to 'peacefully manage the evolution of the regional balance of power, establish a cooperative mechanism for working with China, and address regional security issues, such as North Korea, territorial disputes, and human security concerns' (Chun 2013: 16). This objective can only be met, however, if it remains underwritten by an adaptive but still credible US-South Korean bilateral alliance. Achieving this condition will entail overcoming several challenges in alliance management. These include eventually realizing a smooth transition of wartime operational control to the South Korean joint chiefs of staff (at time of writing scheduled for 2015), greater coordination to develop a comprehensive counter-missile strategy directed toward North Korean weapons of mass destruction and missile delivery systems, and employing 'a full range of military capabilities' needed to maintain a successful extended deterrence strategy (see United States Forces Korea 2013: 3). It is encouraging that recent tensions between the United States and South Korea over how best to apply deterrence strategy on the Korean peninsula and over the maximum range and payload of South Korean ballistic missiles have been largely moderated. In October 2012, the United States and South Korea agreed that South Korean ballistic missile ranges would be increased from 300 km to 800 km (Agence France-Presse 2013; Nuclear Threat Initiative 2013). In late 2013, the two allies announced a 'tailored deterrence' strategy for responding to different threat scenarios of a North Korean nuclear strike against South Korea.

Rebalancing was initially viewed by many within and outside the Obama Administration as correcting the United States' long-term strategic neglect of Southeast Asia (IISS 2012). As other regionally-based analysts have observed, however, many of the new US posture's intended Southeast Asian beneficiaries initially feared that it would 'overmilitarize' their neighbourhood by worsening what they viewed as an already too intense strategic competition between the United States and China (Emmerson 2012; Graham 2013: 306–7).

Limited but relatively low-key initiatives have been undertaken by Washington with Southeast Asian allies and partners, including the rotational deployment of US littoral combat ships in Singapore, increased US military assistance and basing access to the Philippines, and accelerated maritime security, disaster relief and naval ship servicing initiatives with Vietnam. These measures are consistent with the general idea of capacity building, but fall short of being robust examples of how the three key partner capacity-building criteria cited above can be fulfilled. The positions of Indonesia and Malaysia on rebalancing have remained ambiguous, with political legacies of non-alignment trumping various factions in both countries that have demonstrated a greater interest in exploiting American desires to interact more comprehensively with them. Thailand (as discussed in Kitti Prasirtsuk's and William Tow's chapter) has visibly turned toward China in a post-Cold War security environment. It has turned down several recent US requests to access its U-Tapao airbase for alleged space tracking of climate change and for disaster relief missions, fearing that it could become entrapped as an unwitting collaborator in US intelligence surveillance and naval balancing vis-à-vis China (see Prasirtsuk 2013: 35).

President Obama's absence from the key Asian summits hosted by Brunei and Indonesia in late 2013 has rekindled the very type of apprehension by ASEAN members that rebalancing was designed to avoid: a perception that US domestic turmoil over budget politics and partisan advantage has combined with its still enduring preoccupations with the Middle East and Northeast Asia to relegate their own sub-region's status and its partnership capacity-building potential to the backwaters of US policy formulation. This process is more complex than a first impression that the United States is 'either in or out' of Southeast Asia might lead one to believe.

Two 'outlier' polities – India and Taiwan – must be factored into US thinking about rebalancing and capacity building. Indian policymakers operate in a country that constitutes the South Asian component of the US 'Indo-Pacific' rebalancing strategy. They perceive their support of that strategy as a way to circumvent what they deem to be a growing power gap between China and India (China's gross domestic product is four times larger than India's, and Beijing's defence spending is creating a similar capability gap; Mohan 2013: 23). In October 2013, President Obama and Indian Prime Minister Manmohan Singh met in New York to issue a Joint Declaration on Defense Cooperation foreshadowing their determination to accelerate the two countries' defence technology collaboration. US Deputy Secretary of Defense Ashton Carter announced that India was now included within a 'Group of Eight' that have access to high-end US defence technologies with a minimum of export controls (*Times of India* 2013b). True to its long-term preference for adhering to a broad-based, non-aligned posture, however, Indian diplomats were quick to point out that this new agreement would not supplant long-standing and extensive Indo-Russian commercial defence ties, and within three weeks Singh had signed a new confidence-building agreement with China to maintain 'peace and tranquillity' on the Sino–Indian border (*Times of India* 2013a; Chandran 2013). During the second half of 2013, the Indian government modified its 26 percent cap on foreign direct investment in the country's defence sector, in effect since 2001 (each application to exceed this level will now be reviewed on a case-by-case basis), but until greater policy clarity on this issue is reached, the US and other foreign defence suppliers will still remain 'reluctant to provide advanced technology and expertise' (IISS 2013: 264).[5] This will qualify other progress on partner capacity-building between the United States and India.

The official US position on Taiwan's role in rebalancing and, more directly, on how Taiwan fits into American partner capacity-building policy, was recently set out by a US State Department official's Congressional testimony: 'The United States has also played an important role in ensuring continued cross-Strait stability, consistent with the Taiwan Relations Act and our one-China policy. The United States makes available to Taiwan defense articles and services necessary to enable Taiwan to maintain a sufficient self-defense capability' (Yun 2013). Independent analysis is less sanguine. While Taiwan has publicly welcomed rebalancing, its territorial claims mirror those of the Chinese mainland and are therefore often at odds with Japan in the East China Sea and with ASEAN claimants in the South China Sea. A recent study has noted that Taiwan is therefore 'not strongly associated' with the thrust of US rebalancing strategy and that its views on territorial issues tend to 'exacerbate tensions and work against US efforts to calm regional tensions' (Sutter *et al.* 2013: 21; see also Huang 2013).

From a partner capacity-building standpoint, Taiwan's *National Defence Report 2013* projected that China would be capable of successfully invading Taiwan by 2020, with China's 2nd Artillery Corps recently deploying anti-ship ballistic missiles opposite the Taiwan Strait to supplement its already formidable short-range ballistic missile defence force deployed in Fujian against key Taiwanese targets (Neill 2013; Ministry of National Defense, Taiwan 2013). Washington has been careful in recent years to ensure that the Taiwan security issue has not assumed centre stage in Sino–American relations. It still reserves the prerogative to initiate military sales to the Taiwanese when required in an effort to retain a credible 'cross-strait military balance' relative to an increasingly powerful China. The United States is Taiwan's sole military collaborator, but one which is significantly constrained by its need to balance its lingering security commitment to that island with Sino–American conflict avoidance. Given this context, Taiwan is perhaps the most difficult challenge confronting Washington's rebalancing politics as they apply to its network of alliances and partners in the Asia-Pacific region.

Conclusion

Contemporary historians could not be faulted for thinking about US 'rebalancing' in the Asia-Pacific as just 'more of the same'. The rise of China has been a key factor in that region's post-war environment since 1949. The San Francisco System has always been at least partially geared toward neutralizing Beijing's ambitions. The Soviet Union's demise has merely accentuated this reality. Nor has the Asian security environment changed so much as to alter radically other enduring challenges for US security policy there:

- how to sustain and promote US strategic interests in the region on a cost-effective basis;
- how to encourage regional allies and partners to bolster their defence capacities in ways that will allow them to share the burden of underwriting the United States' vision of regional stability and prosperity; and
- how to shape the behaviour of potential rivals to US influence in the region in ways most conducive to support of a regional order predicated on free markets, democratization, and enduring human rights and security.

Greater US sensitivity to the possible advantages of participating in and developing viable multilateral institutions is a recent development. However, Washington has yet to strike a successful balance between assuring China, as its major regional rival, that it will not use multilateral forums or mechanisms to marginalize or isolate it in the Asia-Pacific community, while still extending sufficiently credible security guarantees to its allies and other regional partners to deflect aggressive Chinese (or North Korean) behaviour.

Complicating this task is the American need to exercise sensitivity towards those allies and partners who desire some form of strategic affiliation with the United States, but who prefer not to appear as if they are coalescing against China. This is a particularly challenging concern for successive US Administrations which have viewed with favour 'greater ongoing coordination multilaterally across allied relationships' by forging informal groupings such as the Australia–Japan–US Trilateral Strategic Dialogue and the more recent US–Japan–India Trilateral Meeting (Gill 2013: 8; Baker and Glosserman 2013: 89).[6]

The ultimate determinant of the success of the US rebalancing strategy will be the extent to which China accepts that this initiative contributes to long-term regional stability as defined by Beijing. President Obama and other US officials have argued strongly that rebalancing is not synonymous with the 'balance of power' strategy directed against China but is, as one respected China watcher has observed, a 'win–win' or absolute gains strategy where American power and presence benefits not just US interests but facilitates an overall atmosphere of regional cooperation with China and other rising powers (Saunders 2013: 2–3). To date, Beijing does not accept this premise. It still believes that the original Clinton–Campbell–Donilon game plan for developing a comprehensive version of rebalancing has been supplanted by a zero-sum logic associated with US military planners (Liao 2013: 109).

At the same time as ensuring the security of its allies, the United States has little choice but to look for ways to reassure the Chinese about American bilateral security politics, encourage greater Chinese cooperation in regional institution building, and work with Beijing to derive common approaches for stabilizing ongoing regional crises and avoiding crisis escalation. If rebalancing can facilitate this process, its label will become appropriately less important than its substance.

Notes

1 Paul Dibb argues that the worst-case perceptions held by the United States and the Soviet Union regarding one another's nuclear intentions nearly precipitated a nuclear war during Reagan's first term of office.
2 Kai Liao (2013), a research fellow for the Knowfar Institute for Strategic and Defense Studies in Beijing, asserts that a review of work on China by the Pentagon's Office of Net Assessment suggests that US policy has been directed toward sustaining US strategic primacy in the region at China's expense.
3 Hugh White (2010, 2012) has advanced the Sino–American power-sharing vision most vigorously. A powerful critique of this argument is offered by Denny Roy (2013). The liberal-internationalist vision has been developed by G. John Ikenberry and Jitsuo Tsuchiyama (2002).
4 The RAND Corporation document argues that partner capacity-building is an 'evolving concept' that entails the training and equipping of partner military and non-military components, but does not include the broadly based objectives envisioned by Hillary Clinton and other US officials.
5 For recent developments on this issue from an Indian perspective, see Indicia Research & Advisory (2013).

6 On the Trilateral Strategic Dialogue, see Tow *et al.* (2008); on the US–Japan–India Trilateral Meeting, consult Reuters (2011).

References

Agence France-Presse (2013) 'S Korea–US Sign Plan to Deter N Korea Nuclear Strike', 2 October, www.globalpost.com/dispatch/news/afp/131002/s-korea-us-sign-plan-deter-n-korea-nuclear-strike-1 (accessed 23 January 2014).

Asahai Shimbun (2013) 'Senior Diplomats from Japan, S Korea, China Fail to Break the Ice', English-language edition, 8 November.

Ash, Timothy Garton (2013) 'This Crisis Resolves Little in Syria but Says a Lot About the United States', *Guardian*, 12 September.

Baker, Carl and Glosserman, Brad (eds) (2013) 'Doing More and Expecting Less: The Future of US Alliances in the Asia Pacific', *Issues & Insights*, 13(1), Honolulu: Pacific Forum CSIS, January.

Baker, III, James A. (1991) 'America in Asia: Emerging Architecture for a Pacific Community', *Foreign Affairs*, 70(5): 1–18.

Boon, Hoo Tiang (2013) 'The Growing Institutionalisation of US–China Relations', *East Asia Forum*, 3 August, www.eastasiaforum.org/2013/08/03/the-growing-institutionalisation-of-us-china-relations/ (accessed 25 December 2013).

Buszynski, Leszek (1983) *SEATO: The Failure of an Alliance Strategy*, Singapore: Singapore University Press.

Carnegie Endowment for International Peace (2013) *US–China Security Perceptions Survey: Findings and Implications*, Washington, DC: Carnegie Endowment for International Peace and China Strategic Culture Promotion Association.

Cha, Victor (2009/10) 'Powerplay: Origins of the US Alliance System in Asia', *International Security*, 34(3): 158–96.

——(2013) 'The Opportunity for the US in China's Overreach', *Washington Post*, 7 December.

Chandran, D. Suba (2013) 'Border Defence Agreement', Institute of Peace and Conflict Studies, 27 October, www.ipcs.org/article/china/india-china-an-assessment-of-october-2013-agreements-border-defence-4151.html (accessed 29 December 2013).

Cheon, Seongwhun (2013) 'Trust – The Underlying Philosophy of the Park Gyun-Hye Administration', *Korea Chair Platform*, Washington, DC: Office of the Korea Chair, Center for Strategic and International Studies, 6 May, csis.org/files/publication/130506_Trust_President_Park.pdf (accessed 28 December 2013).

Chun, Chaesung (2013) 'US Strategic Rebalancing to Asia: South Korea's Perspective', *Asia Policy*, 15(January): 13–17.

Clinton, Hillary (2011a) 'America's Pacific Century', *Foreign Policy*, 18(November): 56–63.

——(2011b) 'On America's Pacific Century', Speech at East–West Center, Honolulu, 10 November, fpc.state.gov/176998.htm (accessed 22 January 2014).

Clinton, William J. (1996a) 'Text: President Clinton 11/26 Speech at Chulalongkorn University', 26 November, www.usembassy-israel.org.il/publish/press/whouse/archive/november/wh11127.htm (accessed 28 November 2013).

——(1996b) 'The President's News Conference with President Kim Young-sam of South Korea in Cheju', 16 April, The American Presidency Project, www.presidency.ucsb.edu/ws/?pid=52677 (accessed 28 November 2013).

Cossa, Ralph, Glosserman, Brad, McDevitt, Michael A., Patel, Nirav, Przystup, James and Roberts, Brad (2009) *The United States and the Asia-Pacific Region: Security Strategy for the Obama Administration*, Washington, DC: Center for a New American Security, February.

Dibb, Paul (2013) 'The Nuclear War Scare of 1983: How Serious was It?' Special Report, Canberra: ASPI, October, www.aspi.org.au/publications/publication_details. aspx?ContentID=385 (accessed 22 January 2014).

Donilon, Tom (2012) 'President Obama's Asia Policy & Upcoming Trip to Asia', Remarks by National Security Advisor Tom Donilon – As Prepared for Delivery, Office of the Press Secretary, The White House, 15 November, www.whitehouse.gov/the-press-office/2012/11/15/remarks-national-security-advisor-tom-donilon-prepared-delivery (accessed 17 September 2013).

Emmerson, Donald (2012) 'Challenging ASEAN: The US Pivot through Southeast Asia's Eyes', *Global Asia*, 7(4): 22–26.

Evans, Gareth and Grant, Bruce (1992) *Australia's Foreign Relations: In the World of the 1990s*, Carlton, Victoria: Melbourne University Press.

Fullilove, Michael (2013) 'The "Pivot" has Run Out of Puff', *US News and World Report*, 4 December, www.usnews.com/opinion/articles/2013/12/04/bidens-trip-is-not-enough-to-save-obamas-pivot-to-asia (accessed 7 December 2013).

Gill, Bates (2013) 'Alliances Under Austerity: What Does America Want?' Centre of Gravity Paper #10, Canberra: Strategic and Defence Studies Centre, Australian National University, September.

Godwin, Paul H.B. (1988) 'The United States and Asia: The Success of Continuity?' in William P. Snyder and James Brown (eds) *Defense Policy in the Reagan Administration*, Washington, DC: National Defense University Press, pp. 45–82.

Goh, Evelyn (2004) 'The ASEAN Regional Forum in United States East Asian Strategy', *Pacific Review*, 17(1): 47–69.

——(2013) *The Struggle for Order: Hegemony, Hierarchy, and Transition in Post-Cold War East Asia*, Oxford: Oxford University Press.

Graham, Euan (2013) 'Southeast Asia in the US Rebalance: Perceptions from a Divided Region', *Contemporary Southeast Asia*, 35(3): 305–32.

Gries, Peter Hayes (2004) *China's New Nationalism: Pride, Politics, and Diplomacy*, Berkeley, CA: University of California Press.

Hayashi, Yuka (2013) 'US, Japan Move to Shore Up Military Base in Okinawa', *Wall Street Journal*, 25 December.

Hemmer, Christopher and Katzenstein, Peter J. (2002) 'Why is there No NATO in Asia? Collective Identity, Regionalism, and the Origins of Multilateralism', *International Organization*, 56(3): 575–607.

Holmes, James R. (2013) 'Chinese Soft Power: Another Typhoon Haiyan Victim', *The Diplomat*, 14 November, thediplomat.com/tag/smile-diplomacy/ (accessed 7 December 2013).

Huang, Alexander Chieh-cheng (2013) 'Taiwan in an Asian "Game of Thrones"', *Asia Policy*, 15(January): 18–20.

IISS (International Institute for Strategic Studies) (2012) 'US Rebalance: Potential and Limits in Southeast Asia', *Strategic Comments*, 49(19 December), www.iiss.org/en/publications/strategic%20comments/sections/2012-bb59/us-rebalance-potential-and-limits-in-southeast-asia-c5a7 (accessed 28 December 2012).

——(2013) *The Military Balance 2013*, London: Routledge for the IISS.

Ikenberry, G. John and Tsuchiyama, Jitsuo (2002) 'Between Balance of Power and Community: The Future of Multilateral Security Co-operation in the Asia-Pacific', *International Relations of the Asia-Pacific*, 2(1): 69–94.

Indicia Research & Advisory (2013) *Indicia Weekly Brief*, 7–13 October, indicia.in/weeklybrief/7-13October2013 (accessed 29 December 2013).

Keck, Zachary (2013) 'Australia's Delicate China–Japan Balancing Act', *The Diplomat*, 17 October, thediplomat.com/2013/10/australias-delicate-china-japan-balancing-act/ (accessed 28 December 2013).

Klingner, Bruce and Cheng, Dean (2012) 'US Asian Policy: America's Security Commitment to Asia Needs More Focus', *Backgrounder*, #2175, Washington, DC: The Heritage Foundation, 7 August, www.heritage.org/research/reports/2012/08/americas-security-commitment-to-asia-needs-more-forces (accessed 18 September 2013).

Leach, James A. (2005) 'A Congressional Perspective on Asia and the Pacific', in Robert M. Hathaway and Wilson Lee (eds) *George W. Bush and East Asia: A First Term Assessment*, Washington, DC: Woodrow Wilson International Center for Scholars, pp. 195–214.

Liao, Kai (2013) 'The Pentagon and the Pivot', *Survival*, 55(3): 95–114.

Lord, Winston (1993) 'A New Pacific Community: Ten Goals for American Foreign Policy', *Foreign Policy Bulletin*, 3(6): 49–53.

Ministry of National Defense, Taiwan (2013) *National Defense Report 2013*, Taipei: Ministry of National Defense.

Mohan, C. Raja (2013) 'India: Between "Strategic Autonomy" and "Geopolitical Opportunity"', *Asia Policy*, 15(January): 21–25.

National Institute for Defense Studies (2013) *East Asian Strategic Review 2013*, Tokyo: Japan Times.

Neill, Alexander (2013) 'Taiwan: The Missing Piece in the Rebalance Puzzle', *The Strategist*, October, www.aspistrategist.org.au/taiwan-the-missing-piece-in-the-rebalance-puzzle/ (accessed 29 December 2013).

Nuclear Threat Initiative (2013) 'South Korea', *NTI*, July, www.nti.org/country-profiles/south-korea/delivery-systems/ (accessed 28 December 2013).

Odom, Jonathan G. (2012) 'What Does a "Pivot" or "Rebalance" Look Like? Elements of the US Strategic Turn Towards Security in the Asia-Pacific Region and its Waters', *Asia-Pacific Law and Policy Journal*, 14(1): 1–32.

Panetta, Leon (2012) 'Shangri-La Security Dialogue: As Delivered by Secretary of Defense Leon E. Panetta', Singapore, 2 June, www.defense.gov/speeches/speech.aspx?speechid=1681 (accessed 25 December 2013).

Park Geun-hye (2012) 'Speech', Presidential Candidate of the Saenuri Party, Korea in a Transforming World: A New Frontier for Peace and Cooperation, Seoul Foreign Correspondents' Club, Seoul, 8 November.

Paul, Christopher, Clarke, Colin P., Grill, Beth, Young, Stephanie, Moroney, Jennifer D.P., Hogler, Joe and Leah, Christine (2013) *What Works Best When Building Partner Capacity and Under What Circumstances?* Santa Monica, CA: RAND Corporation, www.rand.org/content/dam/rand/pubs/monographs/MG1200/MG1253z1/RAND_MG1253z1.pdf (accessed 25 December 2013).

Perlez, Jane (2013) 'Cancellation of Trip by Obama Plays to Doubts of Asia Allies', *New York Times*, 4 October.

Potter, Ben (2012) 'US Says its Asia "Pivot" Went Too Far', *Australian Financial Review*, 23 August.

Prasirtsuk, Kitti (2013) 'The Implications of US Strategic Rebalancing: A Perspective from Thailand', *Asia Policy*, 15(January): 31–37.

Reuters (2011) 'US, India, Japan to Meet After Obama's "Asia Pivot"', 5 December, www.reuters.com/article/2011/12/05/us-usa-asia-talks-idUSTRE7B42EQ20111205 (accessed 29 December 2013).

Roy, Denny (2013) 'The Problem with Premature Appeasement', *Survival*, 55(3): 183–202.

Saunders, Phillip C. (2013) 'The Rebalance to Asia: US–China Relations and Regional Security', *INSS Strategic Forum*, Washington, DC: National Defense University, August.

Schreer, Ben (2013) 'Strategic Posture Review: Australia', *World Politics Review*, 26 November, www.worldpoliticsreview.com/articles/13405/strategic-posture-review-australia (accessed 26 December 2013).

Shambaugh, David (2013) *China Goes Global: The Partial Power*, Oxford: Oxford University Press.

Siracusa, Joseph M. (2012) *Encyclopedia of the Kennedys: The People and Events that Shaped America, Volume 2: I–R*, Santa Barbara, CA: ABC-CLIO.

Stephens, Philip (2013) 'China has Thrown Down a Gauntlet to America', *Financial Times*, 28 November.

Stuart, Douglas T. and Tow, William T. (1995) *A US Strategy for the Asia-Pacific*, Adelphi Paper 299, London: Routledge for the International Institute for Strategic Studies, December.

Sutter, Robert G., Brown, Michael E. and Adamson, Timothy J.A., with Mochizuki, Mike M. and Ollapally, Deepa (2013) 'Balancing Acts: The US Rebalance and Asia-Pacific Stability', Washington, DC: Sigur Center for Asian Studies, George Washington University, August.

Times of India (2013a) 'Defence Ties with US not at Russia's Expense, India says', 1 October.

——(2013b) 'US Submits List of 10 Defence Technologies for Transfer to India', 2 October.

Tow, William, Auslin, Michael, Medcalf, Rory, Tanaka, Akihiko, Feng, Zhu and Simon, Sheldon W. (2008) *Assessing the Trilateral Strategic Dialogue*, NBR Special Report #16, Seattle and Washington, DC: National Bureau of Asian Research, December.

United States Department of Defense (1998) 'The United States Security Strategy for the East Asia-Pacific Region 1998', Washington, DC: United States Department of Defense, 25 November, www.fas.org/man/docs/easr98.html (accessed 3 November 2013).

——(2001) *Quadrennial Defense Review Report*, Washington, DC: United States Department of Defense, September.

——(2006) 'Building Partnership Capacity: QDR Execution Roadmap', Washington, DC: United States Department of Defense, May.

——(2012) 'Sustaining US Global Leadership: Priorities for 21st Century Defense', Washington, DC: United States Department of Defense, January.

United States Forces Korea (2013) 'Joint Communiqué: The 45th ROK–US Security Consultative Meeting', 2 October, Seoul, www.defense.gov/pubs/Joint%20Communique,%2045th%20ROK-U.S.%20Security%20Consultative%20Meeting.pdf (accessed 28 December 2013).

USIA Foreign Press Center (1998) 'Unofficial Transcript: Campbell on East Asia Strategy Report', Briefing, Washington, DC, 24 November, www.fas.org/man/docs/98112410.htm (accessed 3 November 2013).

White, Hugh (2010) 'Power Shift: Australia's Future Between Washington and Beijing', *Quarterly Essay*, 39 (September).

——(2012) *The China Choice: Why America Should Share Power*, Collingwood, Victoria: Black Inc.

White House (2013) 'US–India Joint Security Declaration on Defense Cooperation', 27 September, www.whitehouse.gov/the-press-office/2013/09/27/us-india-joint-declaration-defense-cooperation (accessed 25 December 2013).

Winnefeld, James A., Pollack, Jonathan D., Lewis, Kevin N., Pullen, L.D., Schrader, John Y. and Swaine, Michael D. (1992) *A New Strategy and Fewer Forces: The Pacific Dimension*, Santa Monica, CA: RAND.

Wortzel, Larry M. (1996) 'The ASEAN Regional Forum: Asian Security Without an American Umbrella', Carlisle, PA: Strategic Studies Institute, US Army War College, December, www.hsdl.org/?view&did=487437 (accessed 23 January 2014).

Yun, Joseph (2013) 'Rebalance to Asia II: Security and Defense: Cooperation and Challenges', Statement before the Senate Committee on Foreign Affairs Subcommittee on East Asian and Pacific Affairs, Washington, DC, 25 April, www.state.gov/p/eap/rls/rm/2013/04/207981.htm (accessed 29 December 2013).

4   Deterrence, the twenty-first century, and the 'pivot'

Jeffrey D. McCausland

Introduction

Thucydides observed in his history of the Peloponnesian Wars that one of the primary motivators of Athenian foreign policy was 'interests' (Robinson 1957: 71). This remains as true in the twenty-first century as in ancient Greece. As a result, modern policymakers would all agree that the national strategy of any country must focus on national interests and be built on three variables. First, what are the 'ends' of strategy or the goals that the nation is trying to accomplish alone or in concert with friends and allies that further their interests? Second, what are the 'ways' or policies that are formulated in order to move the nation in the direction of a better future? Finally, what are the 'means' or resources available to the government of any nation that can be devoted to securing these objectives, and how can they be husbanded in a fashion to maximize their potential?

US President Barack Obama underscored the criticality of American interests in the Pacific as the United States ended its long involvement in the Iraq War and began a drawdown of its forces in Afghanistan. He observed in January 2012 that US interests were 'inextricably linked to developments in the arc extending from the Western Pacific and East Asia into the Indian Ocean region and South Asia'. This fact, he argued, created a 'mix of evolving challenges and opportunities' that the United States must address. Consequently, he directed that while the American military 'will continue to contribute to security globally, *we will of necessity rebalance toward the Asia-Pacific region*' (United States Department of Defense 2012: 2, emphasis in original). This was in many ways not surprising. US Secretary of State Hillary Clinton had provided the rationale and strategic logic for this shift in American strategy in a *Foreign Policy* article in November 2011, where she had described the Asia-Pacific region's importance as 'a key driver of global politics' (Clinton 2011: 57). This is clearly true. One need only consider that the Asia-Pacific region is 'home to two-thirds of the world's population' and its fastest growing economies. 'The annual flow of US investment into East Asia has increased from $22.5 billion in 2009 to $41.4 billion in 2011'. American exports to the region totalled over US$320 billion in 2012, which is a growth rate of 8 percent since 2008 (Yun 2013).

Renewed emphasis on American interests in the Pacific was further reflected in remarks by US Secretary of Defense Chuck Hagel at the June 2013 Shangri-La Dialogue in Singapore. Hagel (2013: 2) noted that, '[t]he first decade of this new century has reaffirmed that this region is becoming the center of gravity for the world's population, global commerce, and security'. He further observed that a range of emerging threats existed that included North Korea's nuclear/missile programmes, ongoing land and maritime disputes, proliferation of weapons of mass destruction, and threats from cyberspace.

The success or failure of America's 'pivot' to Asia will be determined in large part by Washington's ability to develop and sustain a viable and appropriate deterrence posture in the Asia-Pacific. The concept of deterrence is not new in strategy formulation. Raoul Naroll, Vern Bullough and Frada Naroll (1974) have observed that deterrence was part of Chinese strategy in 116 BC. In the modern age, many Western strategists would agree that deterrence is a natural outgrowth of the theory of balance of power, which has been the basis for Western diplomacy since the Congress of Vienna in 1815. It is also not a new concept when considering American national security strategy in the Pacific. In the spring of 1940, President Franklin Roosevelt directed that the American Pacific Fleet be repositioned from the West Coast to Pearl Harbor in Hawaii. Roosevelt made this decision in an effort to deter continued Japanese expansion in the Pacific. He overrode the objections of many senior naval officers who believed that the fleet's redeployment was a very risky strategy.

Today, American leaders must fully consider all of the implications of the pivot or the rebalancing of American power to the Pacific. They must also consider the lessons from American deterrence policies during the Cold War that can be applied to relations with allies and partners in Asia as well as to China and North Korea.

Some general comments about the pivot are necessary at the outset. First, while the term 'pivot' will be used in this analysis, almost no one in official Washington likes the term. It may have been useful for the Obama Administration politically, as it described a turning away from eight years of the policies of Republican President George W. Bush and underscored one of President Obama's primary objectives: ending the wars in Iraq and Afghanistan. Strategically, however, the term raised concerns among some of the United States' traditional allies in Europe, and raised questions about America's commitment to remain a global power. Second, while this analysis will focus on the military and security components of the pivot, the pivot must encompass all of the elements of power – diplomatic, economic, political and informational, if it is to be a successful regional strategy. Third, this shift in policy focus is largely and in many ways surprisingly bipartisan. Both Republican and Democrat policymakers seem to agree that the ongoing dramatic changes in the world economy demand a greater American emphasis on the Pacific region. Still, it is very likely that the two parties will differ over the 'means' to be applied to affect this new strategy. Fourth, US presidents have frequently been surprised by events in foreign affairs that they never anticipated when they entered the Oval Office. Ronald Reagan could not have anticipated Grenada. President George H.W. Bush could not have predicted a major war in the Persian Gulf, and his successor, Bill Clinton, was surprised by a war in Kosovo. President George W. Bush was poised to place greater emphasis on the US role in the Pacific in the initial months of his Administration prior to the events of 11 September 2001.

Finally, the Asia-Pacific region is *not* Europe. While this may strike many as trite or superficial, it is an important observation. There is much the United States can learn from its Cold War experience, which had a large European focus, but American policy during that era was largely threat-centric and concerned with an opponent that freely espoused expansionist views motivated by both ideological and historical reasons. By contrast, current US efforts in the Pacific are largely 'order' centric. The United States wishes to maintain the essential Asian security order while improving opportunities for economic and social development in the face of new emerging problems.

American deterrence thinking

An understanding of deterrence would seem appropriate in light of President Obama's comments and the overall understanding of the concept in relation to US policy in the Asia-Pacific region. For this analysis, 'deterrence is simply the persuasion of one's opponent that the costs and/or risks of a given course of action he might take outweigh its benefits' (George and Smoke 1974: 11). It can perhaps be better understood as an equation: deterrence = credibility x capability (Rosecrance 1975: 3). This is expressed as a product instead of a sum since if either component is zero there is no overall deterrent effect. However, it is also important to remember that a nation's deterrent doctrine is not by itself a national security strategy, but rather a crucial component.

'Capability' includes nuclear forces, but it further encompasses conventional military forces, command and control, intelligence gathering, trained personnel and so on. In this regard, President Obama's 2012 defence strategic guidance provides direction to the Pentagon as the American military reorients its capabilities and capacities to prepare for challenges in the Pacific region (see United States Department of Defense 2012). As a result, all of the American military services are making adjustments. The First and Third Marine Expeditionary Forces and the Army's 25th Infantry Division are all returning to their home stations in the region. The Army has also designated its First Corps as 'regionally aligned' to the Pacific. The Navy will forward base 60 percent of its naval assets to the Pacific by 2020, and the Air Force will also allocate 60 percent of its overseas-based forces to the region. There will also be diversions of space and cyber capabilities to the region in order to augment the speed, range and flexibility of US Air Force assets (Hagel 2013: 5).

American defence spending for the foreseeable future would also seem to stress capabilities that are consistent with a greater focus on the Pacific

(Sherbo 2012). The Air Force and Navy plan to retain 11 aircraft carriers and ten air wings, as well as a big-deck amphibious fleet and the current strategic bomber force. Planned future investments include funding for a new long-range bomber, the new Afloat Forward Staging Base, increased emphasis on cruise missiles launched by submarines, and upgrades to both tactical sensors and electronic warfare capabilities.

Finally, there is an ongoing effort to renew and expand bilateral defence relationships across Asia. These include new Guidelines for Japan–US Defense Cooperation and implementation of the Strategic Alliance 2015 with South Korea. Expanded relations between Australia and the United States began in November 2011 following an agreement signed by Prime Minister Julia Gillard and President Obama. Australia agreed to allow several thousand American Marines to deploy on six-monthly rotations to bases in northern Australia. Subsequently, the two countries have expanded cooperation relating to cyber security and cyberspace. The United States is also expanding its bilateral defence relationships with a number of countries in the region including Malaysia, Myanmar, New Zealand, the Philippines, Singapore, Thailand and Vietnam. It is important to note, however, that unlike Europe during the Cold War, any effort to create a multilateral military alliance is considered both inappropriate and counterproductive.

'Credibility' in the Asia-Pacific is provided by announced doctrines, national military strategies, exercises and so on. Many Asian security analysts have argued that the new military doctrine of Air–Sea Battle is focused primarily on the Pacific region in an effort to enhance the overall credibility of the pivot as a regional strategy. The Air–Sea Battle doctrine and associated technologies will have a direct bearing on possible challenges to freedom of navigation or possible future military operations in the Taiwan Strait, South China Sea, or off the coast of the Korean peninsula. However, it also has clear relevance in other regions such as the Persian Gulf, the Arabian Sea, or even the Mediterranean, where issues of sea denial or anti-access might occur in the future.

The United States will continue its reliance on carrier-battle groups as perhaps the clearest manifestation of power projection. The rapid growth in the number and accuracy of missiles that can be launched from the littoral landmass and strike targets at sea is a threat that the US military believes it must meet. Many strategic analysts believe that both China and Iran are committed to the development of 'no-go zones' in the maritime areas off their respective coasts. As a result, the United States is confronted with a strategic choice – risk the loss of military access to areas considered vital to American security, or explore options for preserving access (Krepinevich *et al.* 2003).

In April 2010, the United States released an updated *Nuclear Posture Review Report*, which is also an essential part of the 'credibility' component (see United States Department of Defense 2010). The report announced significant changes as well as points of continuity in American declaratory policy that have direct application in the Asia-Pacific region. The United

States pledged not to use or threaten the use of nuclear weapons against any non-nuclear state that was in compliance with the Nuclear Non-Proliferation Treaty (NPT) and its obligations. This would appear to be a direct message to North Korea and Iran. The report also asserted that if any state eligible for such assurances were to use chemical or biological weapons against the United States or its allies, the United States would respond with a massive conventional strike. Furthermore, Washington declared that it reserved the right to reconsider this policy further based on the continued evolution or proliferation of biological weapons. Still, there were also obvious points of continuity with earlier statements. The United States would hold accountable any state, terrorist group or non-state actor that assisted a terrorist effort to acquire or use weapons of mass destruction. Finally, the United States reaffirmed its adherence to a nuclear triad 'capability', although at reduced levels.

In June 2013, the Department of Defense released a report on the nuclear employment strategy of the United States (see United States Department of Defense 2013b). The Obama Administration had directed the Department and other appropriate agencies of the American government to conduct this additional analysis in the aftermath of the *Nuclear Posture Review Report*. The purpose of this effort was to examine US deterrence requirements in order better to align US nuclear planning with the current and emerging security environment. It further considered what options should be provided to any president in the event that deterrence failed, and assessed the following additional sixth objective to those outlined in the *Nuclear Posture Review Report*: '[a]chieve US and Allied objectives if deterrence fails' (United States Department of Defense 2013b: 2).

American strategic thinking during the Cold War and in its aftermath has included planning for deterrence through denial and punishment. Both concepts still have application today. The objective of deterrence during the Cold War was the leadership of the Soviet Union (and perhaps China). Deterrence sought to prevent or deter aggression while (according to George Kennan's 'long telegram') waiting for the Soviet Union to collapse due to its 'internal contradictions'. Today, deterrence seeks to affect the calculation of various state actors (for example, China, Iran, North Korea and the Russian Federation) as well as non-state actors.

Deterrence is also about perceptions and actions in one region that may resonate elsewhere around the globe. During the Cold War, the United States entered into a number of strategic alliances in the Pacific with the Philippines, South Korea, South Vietnam and Taiwan. Many of these alliances were based on more than the specific geopolitical value of the ally to Washington. In the case of South Korea, for example, the US response to the North Korean invasion in 1950 was intended to send a clear message to both the Kremlin and the Chinese that reaffirmed America's determination to contain Soviet-sponsored communist military expansionism. Washington fought the Korean War in large measure to defend US credibility, not to defend strategic territory that was deemed vital to American interests (Ross 2013: 29–30; see also

Stueck 1981). The same is true today. As many experts have argued, US policy towards Iran and its desire to acquire nuclear weapons will have an impact on the attitudes of Pacific actors such as North Korea.

In March 2012, General C. Robert Kehler, Commander, US Strategic Command, described contemporary deterrence as:

> [F]undamentally about influencing an actor's decisions. The deterrence decision calculus still revolves around familiar concepts like imposing costs and denying benefits; however, in today's world we also strive to highlight the consequences of restraint (benefits of the status quo) ... Its practice encompasses both the nuclear and a strong conventional offensive force, missile defenses where appropriate, unfettered access and use of space and cyberspace, and, in all warfare areas, modern capabilities that are resilient and sustained.
>
> (Kehler 2012: 8–9)

Consequently, many American security experts now argue that the United States must adopt a complementary effort of 'dissuasion' which could play an important role in strategy for the Asia-Pacific region. Dissuasion seeks to discourage others from developing capabilities or adopting courses of action contrary to American interests. It is also designed to induce restraint in potential adversaries, channel their strategies and resources in less threatening directions, and complicate their respective military planning. Dissuasion also involves the careful synchronization of all the elements of hard and soft American power to reduce the robustness of an adversary's capabilities and to potentially 'buy time' (Lowery 2012).

Variations and aspects of deterrence

There are several variations on the central concept of deterrence that have been important in the past. These will undoubtedly also be critical in the development of American deterrence thinking with respect to major state actors in Asia. These include minimum deterrence, extended deterrence and reassurance.

Minimum deterrence

While we often view efforts to acquire nuclear weapons as offensive, it is also necessary to consider that states seek to acquire such weapons as part of a minimal strategy to enhance their overall security. Minimum deterrence may be considered a cost-effective approach for the leaders of small states. Consequently, North Korea's intent to create and expand its nuclear stockpile is based on a desire to gain prestige and leverage, as well as to deter perceived threats posed by Washington. As the American strategist Stephen Walt once observed, 'American policy-makers clearly understand the logic of minimum deterrence or they would not be so worried when a state like North Korea or

Iran makes a move to join the nuclear club' (quoted in Forsyth *et al.* 2010: 3; Lowery 2012).

The goals of the North Korean leadership have been fairly consistent since its inception in 1948. They include reunification of the peninsula under Pyongyang's control (which is only attainable by expelling the United States), and a firm commitment to the perpetuation of the Kim family regime (Office of the Secretary of Defense 2012: 1; see also Flynn 2013: 14–15). Nuclear weapons have played an increasing role in overall North Korean strategy for the past decade. In April 2010, the Korean Central News Agency discussed a North Korean Foreign Ministry memorandum on nuclear weapons. In this document, the North Korean leadership stated 'the mission of the nuclear armed forces of the DPRK [Democratic People's Republic of Korea] is to deter and repulse aggression and attack on the country and the nation till the nuclear weapons are eliminated from the peninsula and the rest of the world. The DPRK has invariably maintained the policy not to use nuclear weapons against non-nuclear states or threaten them with nukes as long as they do not join nuclear weapons states in invading or attacking it' (quoted in McDevitt 2011).

Pyongyang conducted its initial nuclear test in 2006, followed by a more unambiguously successful test in 2009, and another in February 2013. This latter test was coupled with the successful launch of the Unha-3 rocket in December 2012, which was also able to place a small satellite into temporary orbit. This suggested that Pyongyang was developing the capability to launch missiles that could not only hold targets in Northeast Asia at risk but also potentially strike US territory. These improvements in North Korean 'capabilities' also enhanced the 'credibility' of their overall minimum deterrence posture. In the aftermath of United Nations Security Council sanctions imposed following its missile launch and the 2013 nuclear test, Pyongyang attempted to expand the 'credibility' of its minimum deterrent posture. This included threats to launch a pre-emptive nuclear strike against the United States and South Korea which included a propaganda video of an imagined missile strike on Washington, DC and the White House.

At this juncture, it is still unclear what nuclear capabilities North Korea possesses. It is important to realize that the Unha-3, while associated with ballistic missile technology, was not a ballistic missile. North Korea has, however, unveiled an 18-metre-long, three-stage, liquid-fuelled missile that has been named the KN-08 by American experts. Many believe this weapon will give North Korea an intercontinental capability. At the time of writing there had not been any flight tests of the KN-08, but six mock-ups appeared in a parade in Pyongyang to celebrate the 100th anniversary of Kim Il-sung's birth. Pyongyang has also continued to expand its short- and medium-range ballistic missiles which could threaten targets up to 1,600 km and potentially carry a nuclear weapon. Furthermore, the untested Musudan missile, which was first displayed in October 2010, is believed to have a maximum range of 2,400 km (IISS 2013: 269–70; see also Elleman 2013).

It is further believed that the first two nuclear tests conducted by North Korea used plutonium. Experts estimate that this would leave Pyongyang sufficient stockpiles of active material for building four to eight nuclear weapons, depending on the design and desired yield. North Korea's ability to accelerate its production of fissile material is scenario dependent. A study in 2012 examined six different scenarios over the next five years. The range of total weapons production varied from 14 to 48 nuclear warheads (Thielmann 2013).

There is also disagreement among some intelligence experts over whether or not North Korea has achieved the technological ability to miniaturize the components necessary to create a nuclear warhead that could subsequently be mounted on any of these missile systems. The US Defense Intelligence Agency released an unclassified report indicating that it had 'moderate confidence' that North Korea had nuclear weapons that could fit on a ballistic missile; however, this was subsequently disputed by a United States Department of Defense (2013c) press statement.

American experts now appear convinced that the North Korean leadership may see the benefits of negotiating with the United States, but is 'no longer willing to negotiate over eliminating its nuclear and ballistic missile programs' (Flynn 2013: 14; United States Department of Defense 2013c). The regime in Pyongyang now seems convinced that it must maintain, if not increase, its nuclear stockpile as a guarantor of its security. Consequently, while the North Korean leadership may be willing to negotiate on security guarantees, a final peace treaty will have to eventuate with the elimination of international economic sanctions and clear international recognition that North Korea is a nuclear power and has the sovereign right to maintain its arsenal.

This is contrary to one of the guiding assumptions of the 1994 Agreed Framework between the US and the DPRK whereby North Korea was willing eventually to negotiate its nuclear programme away in return for a package of economic and diplomatic benefits. Indeed, in the aftermath of the fall of Libyan dictator Muammar Gaddafi, North Korean official statements noted that Gaddafi's decision to give up his nuclear programme had been a grave mistake, and this also showed Pyongyang's ideology of a powerful military 'was the only way to keep the peace' (Rapp-Hooper and Waltz 2011).

This presents a dilemma for America's deterrent posture in the region as well as its overall strategy. American military forces (conventional and nuclear) will attempt to deter future North Korean aggression through a threat to punish Pyongyang by retaliation (Colby 2013), but there is no possibility that any American Administration could accept North Korea as a nuclear power. Furthermore, even if the North Korean leadership were willing to negotiate the elimination of its nuclear stockpile, the level of transparency required would hardly be acceptable to the world's most hermetically sealed regime. Indeed, such a verification regime would threaten the very viability of the regime. Some commentators reacted to the arrival of the young Kim Jong-un as the new North Korean leader (following his father's death) by stating that this might well mean that an opportunity was emerging for improved relations. It now appears, however, that there is no chance that the younger Kim will change the regime's long-standing priorities, and the possibility of improved relations may actually be even more remote (Hoare 2013).

This suggests that American strategy towards North Korea must not solely focus on deterrence. The threat of massive retaliation may continue to contain and deter any future North Korean aggression, but it will only serve to maintain the status quo. North Korea is a failed state, but it is a failed state with nuclear weapons. The crisis on the Korean peninsula in the spring of 2013 would seem to suggest that there are two likely outcomes over the long term: war, which would likely include the use of nuclear weapons, or North Korea's internal dissolution. The former would be disastrous for the peninsula and region despite the fact that it would likely result in the destruction of the regime. The latter would result in millions of refugees fleeing south, massive regional economic dislocation, and a possible loss of control over North Korean nuclear weapons. Consequently, the United States must maintain a deterrent posture that contains North Korea, but Washington must also, in concert with its South Korean and Japanese allies, seek alternative policies that avoid either calamity.

Extended deterrence

Throughout the Cold War, the United States, through its declaratory posture and force structure, extended its 'nuclear umbrella' over its North Atlantic Treaty Organization (NATO) and Asian allies which included Australia, Japan and South Korea. So-called extended deterrence attempted 'to prevent a military attack against an ally by threatening [some form of] retaliation' (Tow 1991: 32). During the Cold War, the United States and the Soviet Union provided such extended guarantees to allies. Experts have argued that this was motivated by a belief that neither superpower could tolerate the loss of prestige and credibility that would follow an unavenged attack on one of its allies.

Some have suggested that extended deterrence reflected a shared concern by the United States and the Soviet Union that the spread of nuclear weapons would complicate their relationship and make it more dangerous (Moran and Russell 2009). Therefore, it is argued, extended deterrence has contributed somewhat to a slowing down in the spread of nuclear weapons. There can be little doubt that Japan and South Korea could produce nuclear weapons if they desired. As American allies, both nations have chosen not to do so, which demonstrates their belief that the US nuclear security guarantee remains intact (Barnett 2004: 174).

This having been said, scholars would agree that American extended deterrence in Asia has been at best ambiguous in terms of conditions and type of response to any attack on an ally. While this may have had the advantage of reinforcing US conventional deterrence strategy, it has made the overall effort difficult to manage (Tow 1991: 33–35). The United States has attempted to make its deterrent in Asia more credible through direct reference to the requirement for regional deterrence in the *Nuclear Posture Review Report*, and in the subsequent 'Report on Nuclear Employment Strategy of the United States' released in 2013 (United States Department of Defense 2010: 31–37, 2013b).

There are two primary focal points of American extended deterrence strategy in Asia. First are concerns about the possibility of an attack by North Korea against South Korea and possibly Japan as well. Second is a growing belief that the United States must seek to discourage growing assertiveness and territorial and maritime claims by China in the South China Sea and East China Sea.

The Korean peninsula

Since its inception, South Korea has sought to underscore its close ties with the United States in order to bolster extended deterrence in dealing with the threat posed by North Korea. The strategy inherent in the US-South Korean alliance has combined deterrence through denial and deterrence through punishment. The two countries have developed a strong conventional defence that could deny Pyongyang the ability to be successful in reunifying the peninsula under its control by force of arms. They have buttressed this effort with a clear promise and with the associated forces that threaten overwhelming retaliation in the event that aggression should occur.

History, however, has shown that in responding to North Korean provocations, short of an actual invasion, the deterrent equation may in fact be reversed (McDevitt 2011: 2). The American–South Korean alliance is prepared to respond at every level of war, and their allies enjoy clear military advantages over North Korea including nuclear weapons. Many would argue that these capabilities do not provide a distinct advantage when dealing with lower-level challenges from Pyongyang, such as the sinking of the South Korean naval vessel *Cheonan*, or the artillery attack against Yeonpyeong Island in 2010. North Korea has so far been able to deter any military response to such provocations by its ability to inflict unacceptable consequences on South Korea. North Korea has not only maintained a large military force, but has positioned massive amounts of conventional artillery and rockets along the demilitarized zone between the two countries. Thus, North Korea could launch a massive barrage against Seoul at any moment, which would turn the city into a 'sea of fire', as North Korean propaganda frequently describes it.

The attacks by North Korea in 2010 sent shockwaves through the South Korean population and political leadership. The deaths of over 40 South Korean sailors aboard the *Cheonan* stunned the nation, but the subsequent killing of civilians on Yeonpyeong Island was even more disturbing. These were the first civilian deaths caused by a direct military attack since the end of the Korean War in 1953. As a result, the South Korean political and military leadership developed a new strategy that included policy and operational changes. This new strategy, dubbed 'proactive deterrence', was announced in March 2011 by President Lee Myung-bak as part of an approved and updated Defense Reform Plan 307 (Denmark 2011).

With this shift, the South Korean leadership has reoriented from deterrence by denial to deterrence by punishment, based on the belief that its responses to the two North Korean provocations had been passive and only served to restore the *status quo ante*. Many commentators also complained that Seoul's reaction to the two attacks had further constrained its military's ability to shape a more favourable end-state in a crisis and ceded the initiative to North Korea. Defense Reform Plan 307 called on the South Korean military to be prepared to move beyond solely self-defence and take prompt, focused, but potentially disproportionate retaliation (and in some cases possibly even pre-emptive action) in order to raise the costs to Pyongyang of low-level attacks (Rhee 2011; see also Kim 2012). There have been suggestions that the South Korean leadership has informed Washington that a future attack similar to the artillery barrage against Yeonpyeong Island would result in a full-scale response by South Korea. Seoul was no longer going to 'turn the other cheek'. This new policy has serious implications for escalation control on the peninsula, and for extended deterrence.

A crisis did arise on the Korean peninsula in spring 2013 in the aftermath of the North Korean nuclear test of 12 February. On 7 March, the United Nations Security Council, with the cooperation of China, adopted Resolution 2094 that further condemned Pyongyang for this action and imposed new sanctions. In response, North Korea announced that it was withdrawing from the 1953 Korean Armistice Agreement, severed all contacts with South Korea including the joint industrial zone at Kaesong, and announced that it was stepping up preparation for war. In the weeks that followed, North Korea threatened 'pre-emptive nuclear strikes' not only against targets in the region but also against US territory, although most experts doubted that the North Koreans had a capability to do so. Pyongyang also asserted that Key Resolve and Foal Eagle, the annual joint American and South Korean military exercises that were conducted between 13 March and 30 April, were escalatory and provocative. As tensions on the peninsula rose, a number of nations announced that they were considering the evacuation of their personnel from Pyongyang. Furthermore, in the midst of the crisis, Kim Jong-un announced at a meeting of the Supreme People's Assembly that a further expansion of North Korea's nuclear arsenal and a stronger economy were his top priorities (Klug and Kim 2013). North Korea also moved its medium-range Musudan missiles closer to their launch sites in what was believed to be preparation for a test launch (Kim and Kim 2013). Although such a test was not conducted, North Korea launched a number of short-range missiles and rockets in late May at about the time that tensions receded.

In response, the United States took a number of actions to underscore both American and South Korean military capabilities as well as the credibility of the extended deterrent posture. Despite North Korean rhetoric, Washington and Seoul continued with the planned military exercises. This included repositioning US Navy warships and sea-based radars closer to the peninsula. The United States also flew B2 and B52 bombers, as well as stealth F22 fighters, over South Korea during these exercises in what were called 'deterrence' missions (Kim 2013). In addition, US Secretary of State John Kerry, former National Security Advisor Thomas E. Donilon and Deputy Secretary of Defense Ashton Carter issued public statements that reiterated American support for Seoul. These were clearly synchronized with South Korean official statements expressing confidence in American security guarantees. The United States and South Korea also announced a new agreement on detailed contingency planning to counter limited attacks by North Korea. Many experts had argued that the lack of such detailed planning had made it difficult for Seoul to assess its options in the aftermath of the 2010 attacks.

It is unclear if these actions will deter North Korean attacks in future, but Washington can consider other options. President George H.W. Bush directed the removal of all American tactical nuclear weapons from South Korea in the early 1990s. The *Nuclear Posture Review Report* nonetheless made it clear that the United States retained 'the capacity to re-deploy non-strategic nuclear systems in East Asia, if needed, in times of crisis' (United States Department of Defense 2010: 32). The B61 bomb is the last truly 'tactical' nuclear weapon in the US inventory, and the United States has committed to its continued development (United States Department of Defense 2010: 39). The American fiscal year 2014 budget request included US$537 million for the B61 life extension programme (Taylor and Collina 2013: 27). In the *Nuclear Posture Review Report*, Washington wished to make this part of its extended deterrence posture unambiguous. It intended to maintain the capacity and policy to reintroduce such weapons into the Korean peninsula if the situation dictated in future.

The United States also appears prepared to examine carefully the command relationships between American and South Korean forces in times of conflict. In 1994, South Korea assumed peacetime control of its armed forces from the United States, but the American four-star general in charge of South Korea/US Combined Forces Command remained responsible for all forces in time of conflict. In 2006, the two nations announced that South Korea would assume wartime control of its forces in April 2012. However, shortly after the sinking of the *Cheonan*, the two sides agreed to delay this handover until December 2015. It now appears likely that American and South Korean leaders will announce a further delay in order to underscore the continued commitment of the United States to the defence of its ally (Burns 2013).

Adjusting to the rise of China

As previously suggested, the American pivot strategy is designed in part to counter increasing Chinese assertiveness. Territorial and maritime disputes with the nations that border the South China Sea, and Beijing's ongoing disagreement with Japan over the islands in the East China Sea, continue to be significant concerns. In the South China Sea, Beijing disputes the maritime boundary in the Gulf of Tonkin as well as off the coasts of Brunei, Malaysia, the Philippines and Vietnam. The interests of the nations involved include fishing, the potential exploitation of suspected oil and natural gas deposits on the ocean floor, and strategic control of important international shipping lanes.

In the East China Sea, Japan and China are involved in a dispute over small islands (known as the Senkaku in Japan and Diaoyu in China) that has raised concerns in Tokyo about China's growing military power. Japanese alarm was further heightened by numerous popular demonstrations in China over this issue. It increased even further following an unofficial meeting of Chinese officials, scholars and military leaders at Renmin University. This was part of what appeared to be a semi-official campaign by the Chinese government which has argued that Beijing should also assert its historical claims to the island of Okinawa, home to 1.3 million Japanese citizens and 27,000 American troops (Perlez 2013).

As a matter of national priority, China is also pursuing a long-term, comprehensive military modernization programme, 'designed to improve the capacity of its armed forces to fight and win short-duration, high-intensity regional military conflict' (United States Department of Defense 2013a: i). Many experts believe these expanded capabilities are intended to provide Beijing with the ability to advance territorial claims and build influence abroad while expanding its ability to deter any potential adversary. These improvements include advanced short- and medium-range missiles, land attack/anti-ship cruise missiles, long-range conventional strike as well as advanced fighter aircraft, and the commissioning of the first Chinese aircraft carrier, the *Liaoning*. China also maintains a nuclear arsenal of approximately 50 to 75 intercontinental ballistic missiles and is developing a new generation of mobile missiles equipped with multiple independently targetable re-entry vehicle warheads. It will soon complete operational deployment of some submarine-launched, long-range nuclear systems (United States Department of Defense 2013a: 30–31). Beijing maintains that it adheres to a deterrence strategy that emphasizes a 'no first use' policy for nuclear weapons. Still, Chinese leaders have periodically indicated that their view of deterrence includes all the components of national military power and is intended to compel an opponent to submit. Further, it is part of the avowed goal of China's defence policy, which includes constraining or limiting wars (Cheng 2011: 94). These developments raise serious questions for Washington in terms of the pivot. How should the American extended deterrent posture evolve, and what actions should be taken by Washington and its allies to confront these emerging threats?

The desire of countries in Southeast Asia such as Malaysia, Myanmar, the Philippines, Singapore, Thailand and Vietnam, as well as Australia and New Zealand, to expand bilateral security ties with the United States are indicative of their concerns about the challenge posed by China in the South China Sea. Japan has also welcomed the American pivot to the Pacific and has shown a genuine desire to improve relations with the United States in light of its concerns about North Korea as well as its territorial disputes with Beijing in the East China Sea. The election of the conservative Prime Minister Shinzō Abe in December 2012 and the subsequent landslide victory of his Liberal Democratic Party (LDP) in the July 2013 parliamentary elections appear to herald a potential major shift in Japanese security thinking. A senior LDP lawmaker who heads the party's national defence division cited China's intrusion into areas that Tokyo firmly believes to be its sovereign territorial waters, as well as North Korea's missile programmes, as reasons 'to rebalance our basic policy' (Hayashi 2013). The LDP leadership issued new National Security Strategy and National Defense Program Guidelines in December 2013 which included building an increasingly integrated defence force in response to growing Chinese military power and activities, accelerating alliance cooperation with the United States in such fields as anti-piracy operations, maritime security, cyberspace and counterterrorism, and loosening previous restrictions for exporting defence equipment (such as coastguard vessels) to the Association of Southeast Asian Nations (ASEAN) members (Wilkins 2014). In July 2014, the Abe government imposed a landmark 'reinterpretation' of its post-war 'peace constitution', authorizing Japan to exercise the right of 'collective self-defense' to a limited extent for the first time in the post-war era. While Japanese Self-Defense Force contingents would not be deployed to fight in distant overseas conflicts, they could now be dispatched in response to an attack on a close Japanese ally (i.e. the United States) if the survival of that ally were threatened. Japanese defence forces could also provide logistical support to 'wider areas' if such locales were not directly involved in combat operations (*Yomiuri Shimbun* 2014).

It is likely that Washington is pleased by the efforts of its Asian allies and partners to expand security relationships and enhance their own defence capabilities. This is particularly true as the Pentagon faces unprecedented reductions in military spending. These efforts by regional actors, coupled with Washington's rebalancing of forces and commitment to accord the Asia-Pacific top priority in its strategic planning, may have reassured allies and friends about American security commitments. However, the ambiguity of America's extended deterrence could lead to a potential 'Georgia scenario' and a 'side-taking' dilemma. The 'Georgia scenario' refers to a situation where a state in a region takes American reassurances and security commitments too seriously and 'takes on a bigger fight than it can handle itself, only to find out that Washington had no intention of going to war in its defense over that particular issue' (Logan 2013: 14). This part of American extended deterrence must be managed carefully. It is undoubtedly true that Washington is not interested in becoming embroiled in a conflict with China over territorial issues that are not vital to American national security interests. However, the United States cannot be too explicit about its lack of interest in a confrontation that may pose a direct threat to one or more of Washington's regional friends or allies.

Some experts have argued that Air–Sea Battle is the logical next step in a campaign to bolster America's extended deterrence in the Asia-Pacific region. Other experts, however, view Air–Sea Battle as overly provocative and warn that it will ultimately lead the United States into confrontations with China (see Etzioni 2013). This is probably true, absent other corresponding diplomatic, economic and political efforts. Consequently, American policymakers should revise frequently their assessments of Chinese military forces. For example, some experts have argued that expansions in Chinese naval power are in reality more 'the natural progression of a developing power as it moves from seeing itself as a land power primarily concerned with internal convulsions to seeing itself as a maritime power' that has appropriate concerns about its sovereign boundaries (Le Mière 2013). As a result, the Obama Administration should pursue every opportunity to conduct military-to-military talks with the Chinese that seek to dampen down fear and uncertainty on both sides.

Reassurance

The final aspect of deterrence to be considered is 'reassurance'. As Sir Michael Howard noted, the 'object of reassurance is to persuade one's own people, and those of one's allies, that the benefits of military action, or preparation for it, will outweigh the costs' (Howard 1982/83: 317). Howard warned that during the Cold War, the defence of Europe was eventually perceived not as the responsibility of the Europeans themselves, but increasingly in terms of a system of extended deterrence manipulated by the United States in accordance with strategic concepts that few in Europe fully understood. In many ways he was describing what had become known as the 'Healey Theorem' which was formulated by former British Defence Minister Dennis Healey during the 1960s. Healey argued that it took 'only five per cent credibility of American retaliation to deter the Russians, but ninety-five per cent credibility to reassure the Europeans' (quoted in Murdock and Yeats 2009: 2–3). Some argued that if this was true for the Cold War, then it is even more true today.

While 'reassurance' must be an aspect of the evolution in American deterrence thinking, it may be different in the Asia-Pacific region in the twenty-first century from during the Cold War in Europe. As the *Nuclear Posture Review Report* observed, '[t]oday, the reassurance mission remains, but the deterrence challenge is fundamentally different' (United States Department of Defense 2010: 45). NATO allies were periodically disturbed by American deployments of additional nuclear weapons capabilities on their soil. This led to debates over the stationing of Pershing 2 missiles and ground-launched cruise missiles in the 1980s. Many Europeans were terrified by what seemed to be arcane debates in American policy circles about fighting 'limited nuclear' war or 'prevailing' in a prolonged nuclear exchange with the Soviet Union. Howard noted that no matter how 'much sense this may make in the military grammar of deterrence', it was 'not persuasive in the political language of reassurance' (Howard 1982/83: 321). There were also no territorial disputes between individual NATO members and the Soviet Union that could have sparked a crisis. While crises occurred over Berlin, this was quite different due to its unique post-Second World War status.

As previously mentioned, Washington must ensure that its oft-repeated security commitments, increased military deployments, and joint military exercises are not misinterpreted by its allies and friends in the region as a willingness to defend disputed waterways or small islands. Yet, many ASEAN members fear that the American pivot may also put them in a position where they have to take sides and choose between good relations with Washington or Beijing. At present, most Asian governments prefer close security ties to the United States and have deep-seated historical concerns about China, but they also recognize the current and growing economic influence of that country. The situation is further complicated in Southeast Asia by an essential component of the ASEAN identity, which involves 'being neutral and independent rather than a victim in power confrontation and conflict' (Ling 2013: 152).

Ironically, 'reassurance' as an aspect of the pivot in the Asia-Pacific region must also be focused on the American and Chinese people. The United States will be confronted by difficult choices in terms of military capabilities and needs in the coming years due to emerging fiscal requirements. Furthermore, during the Cold War, the economic relationship between the United States and the Soviet Union was nearly meaningless. At its height, the Soviet Union achieved the economic strength of Belgium, and was variously known as a banana republic with nuclear weapons.

This is not the case with the relationship between the United States and China. Almost all economists will agree that Chinese influence will continue to grow and, within 20 years, likely supplant the United States as the leading global economic power. Some have suggested that by 2030, China's share of the world's gross domestic product (based on purchasing power parity) will be 23.5 percent, while the US share will be 11.8 percent. By that point, China will account for 15 percent of world trade and the United States will account for only 7.3 percent. It is also possible that a convertible Chinese renminbi could become the world's premier reserve currency (Elder and Ayson 2012: 7).

The Sino–American relationship is further compounded by the ongoing challenge of the US deficit. In the aftermath of the American credit downgrade in 2011, a Hong Kong newspaper published a front-page story that argued that Washington owed every single Chinese citizen 5,700 yuan (roughly US$900). One expert has argued that the Chinese–American economic relationship is one of 'mutual dependence'. Beijing needs access to American markets to sell its goods, while Washington needs China to continue to finance its debt. It is 'globalization's equivalent of the nuclear age's Mutual Assured Destruction' (Zakaria 2009: 124; see also Barnett 2004: 224–31).

Consequently, criticisms that Washington has excessively emphasized the military aspects of the pivot are deserved. Still, senior American policymakers have stressed the importance of good relations with China and repeatedly stressed that the United States has not abandoned efforts to cooperate with Beijing. As mentioned earlier, Secretary of State Clinton (2011: 58) stated that one of the key components of the pivot was 'deepening our working relationships with emerging powers, including with China'. In his 2013 speech at the Shangri-La Dialogue, Secretary of Defense Hagel (2013: 8) noted that '[b]uilding a positive and constructive relationship with China is also an essential part of America's rebalance to Asia'. However, balancing the rise of China as a global power at the least possible cost will demand a continued effort to modernize US capabilities while reassuring China's and America's friends and allies in the Asia-Pacific region in order to avoid unnecessary and costly conflict. The former is a military challenge while the latter is a political and economic challenge (Ross 2013: 25).

Conclusions and recommendations

Determining the ends, ways and means of the pivot strategy and articulating the proper role of America's deterrent posture in that strategy will be one of the biggest challenges that the United States will face in the twenty-first century. Military deterrence remains an important component of American national security strategy and of the pivot to the Asia-Pacific region. It also has a special emphasis for those Asian countries (particularly China and North Korea) that are nuclear powers as well as those American allies whose national security is dependent on the American 'nuclear umbrella'. It will continue to be a function of America's force capabilities and the credibility obtained through announced policies and actions. Washington's deterrent posture has undergone significant evolution over the past decade based on changes in the international system as well as emerging threats. Such developments will continue as the United States more fully develops its rebalancing to the Pacific, and several recommendations are appropriate.

First, careful consideration of military deterrence will be important for the American pivot to the Pacific. However, in order for the pivot to succeed, it must be more than solely a military effort. It must better synergize all of the elements of American national power.

Second, US policymakers and experts must make a concerted effort to improve their understanding of the requirements for effective deterrence in the twenty-first century. Such a reassessment of deterrence must address not only traditional challenges from nuclear and non-nuclear nations, but also new threats such as terrorism, proliferation of weapons of mass destruction, cyber warfare and so on. This should result in new policies as well as a further refinement of America's national security strategy. The Cold War produced major thinkers like Herman Kahn, Bernard Brodie, Thomas Schelling and many others who were instrumental in the development of deterrence, but there has not been a corresponding renewal in thinking about deterrence among American policy-makers or academics in the twenty-first century. Some analysts have noted that despite efforts since 2006, the 'deterrence approach remains a poorly understood and underutilized element of US counterterrorism strategy', despite the fact that it offers 'great potential for helping to thwart future terrorist attacks' (Kroenig and Pavel 2012: 22). Surprisingly, deterrence is rarely discussed in American graduate institutions; it has also almost completely disappeared from the curriculum at American service academies and war colleges. As a matter of priority, this must be rectified, and the United States should pursue discussions on deterrence with its primary Asian allies.

Third, the Obama Administration should carefully consider the role of arms control, nuclear security and enhanced transparency as aspects of deterrence. Such efforts not only provide a clear picture of the American deterrent to potential adversaries, but could also serve to forestall friction with China. The Obama Administration's announcement that during the second term it intended to push for final Senate ratification of the Comprehensive Nuclear-Test-Ban Treaty could also serve to enhance its overall non-proliferation posture and the continued adherence to the NPT by many countries in the Asia-Pacific region (see Pifer and O'Hanlon 2013: 139–61).

Fourth, the United States must pursue policies with China that strike a balance between deterrence and cooperative security. The meeting between President Obama and President Xi Jinping underscored that both countries have common threats such as climate change and terrorism, but the meeting also highlighted real points of dispute over such issues as Chinese cyber attacks on American intellectual property and Chinese support for North Korea. Solutions to most, if not all, of these problems cannot be found without cooperation between Washington and Beijing. Thomas Friedman (1999) described the Cold War as sumo wrestling. It is important to recall that the initial opening between Communist China and the United States began with ping-pong during Richard Nixon's Administration in 1971. Relations between these two great powers today are both complex and multi-faceted. It is far more like billiards.

Fifth, American policymakers must conduct frequent discussions with their principal allies in the Asia-Pacific region about questions of extended deterrence and their ongoing national security concerns. Washington must be very clear in private discussions with allies and partners about American commitments and expectations in the region. Every effort must be made to avoid the 'Georgian scenario' with allies and partners in the Asia-Pacific.

Sixth, the United States should also continue bilateral security efforts throughout the Asia-Pacific region to encourage intra-Asian security discussions. As individual states improve their individual security capabilities, their cooperation with the United States should serve to provide greater regional stability and deter conflict. American assistance should primarily focus on advising, training and equipping. The United States should not seek to expand significantly US bases in the region in an effort to enhance its overall deterrent posture.

Finally, in considering the pivot to the Asia-Pacific, American policy-makers and military leaders should accept that the debate over the relevance of nuclear deterrence will continue in the future and will 'survive several premature interments' (Dougherty and Pfaltzgraff 1981: 408). In conducting a careful consideration of the role of deterrence in the pivot, Washington may also need to remember a Chinese aphorism: 'may you live in interesting times'.

References

Barnett, Thomas P. (2004) *The Pentagon's New Map: War and Peace in the Twenty-First Century*, New York: Berkeley Books.

Burns, Robert (2013) 'MIAs and Troops Abroad Remain Korean War Legacies', Associated Press, 27 July.

Cheng, Dean (2011) 'Chinese Views on Deterrence', *Joint Force Quarterly*, 60(1st Quarter): 92–94.

Clinton, Hillary (2011) 'America's Pacific Century', *Foreign Policy* 189(November): 56–63.

Colby, Elbridge (2013) 'Nuclear Deterrence Still Matters', *Politico*, 23 April, www.politico.com/story/2013/04/nuclear-threat-north-korea-cold-war-90515.html (accessed 14 November 2013).

Denmark, Abraham M. (2011) 'Proactive Deterrence: The Challenge of Escalation Control on the Korean Peninsula', Korea Economic Institute (KEI) Academic Paper Series, Washington, DC: Korea Economic Institute of America, December.

Dougherty, James E. and Pfaltzgraff, Jr, Robert L. (1981) *Contending Theories of International Relations*, 2nd edn, New York: Harper & Row.

Elder, Chris and Ayson, Robert (2012) 'China's Rise and New Zealand's Interests: A Policy Primer for 2030', Discussion Paper No. 11, Wellington: Centre for Strategic Studies: New Zealand, Victoria University of Wellington.

Elleman, Michael (2013) 'Prelude to an ICBM? Putting North Korea's Unha-3 Launch Into Context', *Arms Control Today*, 43(2): 8–13.

Etzioni, Amitai (2013) 'Who Authorized Preparations for War with China?' *Yale Journal of International Affairs*, 8(2): 37–51.

Flynn, Michael T. (2013) 'Annual Threat Assessment', Statement before the Senate Armed Services Committee, United States Senate, Washington, DC, 18 April, www.armed-services.senate.gov/imo/media/doc/Flynn_04-18-13.pdf (accessed 14 November 2013).

Forsyth, Jr, James W., Saltzman, B. Chance and Schaub, Jr, Gary (2010) 'Minimum Deterrence and its Critics', *Strategic Studies Quarterly*, 4(4): 3–12.

Friedman, Thomas L. (1999) *The Lexus and the Olive Tree: Understanding Globalization*, London: HarperCollins.

George, Alexander L. and Smoke, Richard (1974) *Deterrence in American Foreign Policy: Theory and Practice*, New York: Columbia University Press.

Hagel, Chuck (2013) 'The US Approach to Regional Security', Shangri-La Dialogue, 12th IISS Asia Security Summit, Singapore, June.

Hayashi, Yuka (2013) 'Japan's Military Moves Toward Pre-Emptive Strike Capability', *Wall Street Journal*, 30 May.

Hoare, Jim (2013) '"Long Live the Dear Respected Marshal Kim Jong Un!" North Korea Since the Death of Kim Jong Il', *Asian Affairs*, 44(2): 188–201.

Howard, Michael (1982/83) 'Reassurance and Deterrence: Western Defense in the 1980s', *Foreign Affairs*, 61(2): 309–24.

IISS (International Institute for Strategic Studies) (2013) *The Military Balance 2013*, London: IISS.

Kehler, C. Robert (2012) 'Statement of General C.R. Kehler, Commander, United States Strategic Command, before the Senate Committee on Armed Services', Washington, DC, 27 March, www.stratcom.mil/files/2012_Posture_Statement.pdf (accessed 18 November 2013).

Kim, Duk-Ki (2012) 'The Republic of Korea's Counter-Asymmetric Strategy: Lessons from ROKS *Cheonan* and Yeonpyeong Island', *Naval War College Review*, 65(1): 55–74.

Kim, Hyung-Jin (2013) 'North Korea May be Preparing to Test Missile', Associated Press, 8 April.

Kim, Sam and Kim, Hyung-Jin (2013) 'S Korea: North Korea Moved Missile to East Coast', Associated Press, 4 April.

Klug, Foster and Kim, Hyung-Jin (2013) 'North Korea's Parliament Meets Amid Nuclear Tension', *Boston Globe*, 1 April.

Krepinevich, Andrew, Watts, Barry and Work, Robert (2003) 'Meeting the Anti-Access and Area-Denial Challenge', Washington, DC: Center for Strategic and Budgetary Assessments.

Kroenig, Matthew and Pavel, Barry (2012) 'How to Deter Terrorism', *Washington Quarterly*, 35(2): 21–36.

Le Mière, Christian (2013) 'China's Unarmed Arms Race', *Foreign Affairs*, 29 July, www.foreignaffairs.com/articles/139609/christian-le-miere/chinas-unarmed-arms-race (accessed 14 November 2013).

Ling, Wei (2013) 'Rebalancing or De-Balancing: US Pivot and East Asian Order', *American Foreign Policy Interest*, 35(3): 148–54.

Logan, Justin (2013) 'China, America, and the Pivot to Asia', Policy Analysis No. 717, Washington, DC: Cato Institute, 8 January.

Lowery, Todd (2012) 'Deterrence in the 21st Century', Presentation to the Office of the Secretary of Defense for Policy, United States Department of Defense, Washington, DC, 19 January.

McDevitt, Michael (2011) 'Deterring North Korean Provocations', Brookings East Asia Commentary No. 46, Washington, DC: Brookings Institution, February.

Moran, Daniel J. and Russell, James A. (2009) 'Special Issue on Extended Deterrence, Security Guarantees, and Nuclear Proliferation: Strategic Stability in the Gulf Region', *Strategic Insight*, 8(5): 1–4.

Murdock, Clark and Yeats, Jessica (2009) 'Exploring the Nuclear Posture Implications of Extended Deterrence and Assurance', Washington, DC: Center for Strategic and International Studies, November.

Naroll, Raoul, Bullough, Vern and Naroll, Frada (1974) *Military Deterrence in History: A Pilot Cross-Historical Survey*, Albany, NY: State University of New York Press.

Office of the Secretary of Defense (2012) 'Military and Security Developments Involving the Democratic People's Republic of Korea', Annual Report to Congress Pursuant to the National Defense Authorization Act for Fiscal Year 2012, Washington, DC: United States Department of Defense.

Perlez, Jane (2013) 'Calls Grow in China to Press Claim for Okinawa', *New York Times*, 14 June, p. A4.

Pifer, Steve and O'Hanlon, Michael (2013) *The Opportunity: Next Steps in Reducing Nuclear Arms*, Washington, DC: Brookings Institution Press.

Rapp-Hooper, Mira and Waltz, Kenneth (2011) 'What Kim Jong-Il Learned from Qaddafi's Fall: Never Disarm', *The Atlantic*, 24 October.

Rhee Sang-Woo (2011) 'From Defense to Deterrence: The Core of Defense Reform Plan 307', Washington, DC: Center for Strategic and International Studies, 7 September.

Robinson, Charles (1957) *Selections from Greek and Roman Historians*, New York: Holt, Rinehart and Winston.

Rosecrance, Richard (1975) *Strategic Deterrence Reconsidered*, Adelphi Paper Number 116, London: International Institute for Strategic Studies.

Ross, Robert S. (2013) 'US Grand Strategy, the Rise of China, and US National Security Strategy for East Asia', *Strategic Studies Quarterly*, 7(2): 20–40.

Sherbo, Andrew (2012) 'Perspectives on the Defense National Security Budget and President's Budget FY2013', Paper presented at the Reiman School of Finance and Daniels School of Business, University of Denver, Colorado, 21 October.

Stueck, Jr, William W. (1981) *The Road to Confrontation: American Policy Toward China and Korea, 1947–1950*, Chapel Hill, NC: University of North Carolina Press.

Taylor, Marcus and Collina, Tom Z. (2013) 'Key Senator Questions Plans for B61 Bomb', *Arms Control Today*, 43(4): 27–29.

Thielmann, Greg (2013) 'Sorting Out the Nuclear and Missile Threats from North Korea', Threat Assessment Brief, Washington, DC: Arms Control Association, 21 May.

Tow, William T. (1991) *Encountering the Dominant Player: US Extended Deterrence Strategy in the Asia-Pacific*, New York: Columbia University Press.

United States Department of Defense (2010) *Nuclear Posture Review Report*, Washington, DC: United States Department of Defense, April.

——(2012) 'Sustaining US Global Leadership: Priorities for 21st Century Defense', Washington, DC: United States Department of Defense, January.

——(2013a) 'Annual Report to Congress: Military and Security Developments Involving the People's Republic of China 2013', Washington, DC: United States Department of Defense.

——(2013b) 'Report on Nuclear Employment Strategy of the United States Specified in Section 491 of 10 USC', Washington, DC: United States Department of Defense, 19 June.

——(2013c) 'Statement by Press Secretary George Little on North Korea's Nuclear Capability', News Release, 11 April, www.defense.gov/releases/release.aspx?release id=15929 (accessed 14 November 2013).

Wilkins, Thomas S. (2014) 'Japan's Grand Strategy and New Strategic Partnerships', Tokyo Foundation, 28 May, www.tokyofoundation.org/en/articles/2014/japan-grand-strategy (accessed 3 July 2014).

Yomiuri Shimbun (2014) 'New Defense Era for Japan/Collective Right OK'd in Severe Security Environment', 1 July, the-japan-news.com/news/article/0001394249 (accessed 3 July 2014).

Yun, Joseph (2013) 'Rebalance to Asia II: Security and Defense: Cooperation and Challenges', Testimony of the Acting Assistant Secretary of State, Bureau of East Asian and Pacific Affairs, before the Senate Committee on Foreign Affairs, Subcommittee on East Asian and Pacific Affairs, Washington, DC, 25 April, www.state.gov/p/eap/rls/rm/2013/04/207981.htm (accessed 14 November 2013).

Zakaria, Fareed (2009) *The Post-American World*, New York: W.W. Norton and Company.

Part II
Northeast Asian partners and allies

5 US rebalancing to the Asia-Pacific

A Japanese perspective

Ken Jimbo

Introduction

In November 2011, US President Barack Obama announced that the United States would increase its strategic focus on the Asia-Pacific region by rebalancing US engagements, activities and resources (Obama 2011). The US Department of Defense followed in January 2012 with the publication of its 'Strategic Guidance', which also reiterated the necessity of rebalancing towards the Asia-Pacific region on the grounds that US economic and security interests are inextricably linked to developments in the arc extending from the Western Pacific and East Asia into the Indian Ocean region and South Asia (United States Department of Defense 2012c).

Tom Donilon (2013), then national security advisor to President Obama, further articulated the concept of rebalancing. In his view, there was a key geographic imbalance in the projection and focus of US power: the Asia-Pacific region was underweighted and the Middle East was overweighted. To accomplish the necessary rebalance, US policymakers recognized that they would have to implement a comprehensive, multidimensional strategy: strengthening alliances, deepening partnerships with emerging powers, building a stable, productive and constructive relationship with China, empowering regional institutions, and helping to build a regional economic architecture that can sustain shared prosperity. Washington would have to accord much more time, attention and resources to the Asia-Pacific region.

As a linchpin of the US-sponsored regional alliance network, and as a country whose national security architecture is deeply embedded in the US-Japanese security alliance and the US forward presence, Japan generally welcomes the concept of a US rebalance to the Asia-Pacific (White House 2014). Not only does the concept clearly demonstrate America's security and diplomatic commitments to the region, but it also signals to China, the region's core emerging power, that the United States has the capability and the will to maintain the status quo and to continue to provide the stabilizing foundation for regional cooperation. The rebalance concept came at a time when regional strategic trends – dramatic change in the Sino–Japanese strategic balance, threatening North Korean nuclear and missile developments, the re-emergence of a stronger Russia, and growing concerns about maritime security – were fuelling a growing sense of insecurity among Japanese defence planners. Under these circumstances, it is not surprising that Tokyo was attracted to any American policies that involved both military and diplomatic reassurance and recommitment.

While welcoming the idea of a US rebalance to the Asia-Pacific, Japanese defence planners nonetheless recognize that many questions still need to be answered in order to accomplish a true rebalancing of the US-Japanese alliance relationship. What specific military policies does the United States intend to pursue in the name of a regional rebalance, and what role does the United States expect its regional friends and allies to play in the development of a new regional deterrence architecture? How does the concept of rebalancing address the rise of Chinese military power in general, and the People's Liberation Army's (PLA) growing anti-access/area-denial (A2/AD) capability in particular? What impact will rebalancing have on the stability–instability paradox in Northeast Asia? What effect will the rebalance have on Tokyo's concerns about defending remote islands? Will the rebalance reassure Japan and South Korea about the threat posed by North Korea? Will an enhanced American military presence in the Asia-Pacific result in increased security cooperation between Japan, Australia and the nations of Southeast Asia? What about the prospects for Japan–South Korea military-to-military relations?

The military dimension

The military dimension of the rebalancing strategy was illustrated in the aforementioned US 'Strategic Guidance'. As US Defense Secretary Leon Panetta mentioned at the time, '[t]he US military will increase its institutional weight and focus on enhanced presence, power projection, and deterrence in Asia-Pacific' (United States Department of Defense 2012a). This assertion was followed by his statement during the Shangri-La Dialogue in June 2012 that 'by 2020 the Navy will re-posture its forces from today's roughly 50/50 percent split between the Pacific and the Atlantic to about a 60/40 split between those oceans. That will include six aircraft carriers in this region, a majority of our cruisers, destroyers, Littoral Combat Ships, and submarines' (Panetta 2012). Subsequently, Panetta stated that the United States would modernize and strengthen its alliances and partnerships in the region. While enhancing relations with traditional allies such as Australia, Japan, the Philippines, South Korea and Thailand, the US government has invested in new forms of security cooperation with India, Indonesia, New Zealand, Singapore and Vietnam. Among the most significant developments to date have been the rotational deployment of US Marines to Darwin, the deployment of littoral combat ships to Singapore, and the enhancement of Washington's military relationship with the Philippines.

The US Department of Defense's version of rebalancing emphasizes the role of existing alliances as a vital foundation of regional security and the importance of expanding networks of security partnerships with emerging partners throughout the Asia-Pacific to 'ensure collective capability and capacity' for securing common interests. The main agenda of rebalancing efforts is clearly aimed at enhancing regional connectivity among US allies and partners to bolster regional capacity. From a US-Japanese alliance perspective, the military dimension of rebalancing may bring about new opportunities and challenges.

Other key US policy statements, including the *Ballistic Missile Defense Review Report*, the *Nuclear Posture Review Report*, and the *Quadrennial Defense Review Report*, have emphasized the importance of crafting 'tailored regional deterrence architecture' to enhance regional order (United States Department of Defense 2010c: 14, 2010a, 2010b). This Department of Defense approach assumes that US extended deterrence has to correspond to the unique characteristics of the regional strategic environment, while at the same time being adapted to the special strategic priorities of America's regional friends and allies. The major elements of this tailored regional deterrence architecture includes nuclear deterrence, effective missile defence, counter-weapons of mass destruction capabilities, conventional power-projection capabilities, and integrated command and control – all underwritten by strong political commitments and diplomatic activity.

One important challenge that the Obama Administration has faced has been to reconcile its goal of enhanced extended deterrence in the Asia-Pacific with its commitment to reducing the role of nuclear weapons in the US national security strategy. The tension between these two goals was highlighted by the *Nuclear Posture Review Report*'s commitment to retire the Tomahawk Land Attack Missile/Nuclear (TLAM/N), a nuclear-equipped, sea-launched cruise missile that constituted an important pillar of America's nuclear extended deterrence in Northeast Asia during the Cold War (United States Department of Defense 2010b). Not surprisingly, this announcement generated a certain amount of concern in the Japanese policy community that the retirement constituted a visible reduction in the US nuclear commitment in Asia. To reassure its regional partners, Washington asserted that TLAM/N was one of a number of nuclear weapons that could be employed in the event of a regional crisis. Specifically, the *Nuclear Posture Review Report* mentioned that the role of TLAM/N could be substituted by the forward deployment of heavy bombers and dual-capable fighters, as well as by intercontinental ballistic missiles and submarine-launched ballistic missiles. In spite of American efforts at reassurance, the US nuclear commitment in Northeast Asia in a non-TLAM/N environment will continue to be a source of concern for key allies like Japan and South Korea. Under these circumstances, periodic displays of the US ability and willingness to forward deploy nuclear-capable assets such as the B2 and B52 (as demonstrated in the US–South Korea Foal Eagle training exercise in March 2013) will be an increasingly important requirement of US post-*Nuclear Posture Review Report* nuclear extended deterrence in the Asia-Pacific.

The second component of the new US-sponsored regional deterrence architecture is an effective missile defence system. Japan has steadily strengthened its ballistic missile defence (BMD) system since the Cabinet decision to do so in December 2003. By March 2012, Japan had deployed four Aegis-equipped destroyers armed with the SM-3 missile and 16 Patriot PAC-3 missile-firing units, and radar capabilities were strengthened by the installation of four FPS-5 and the upgrading of seven FPS-3 radar sites. The Ministry of Defense continues to develop the BMD system, and its current objectives include the enhancement of BMD capabilities through two new Aegis-equipped destroyers and improvements to one PAC-3 missile-firing unit. American and Japanese headquarter organizations have also strengthened BMD cooperation with the relocation of the Air Defense Command Headquarters (completed in March 2012) from Fuchu to the US Air Base at Yokota, and the establishment of the Bilateral Joint Operations Coordination Center.

US-Japanese joint research and development of the next-generation interceptor, the SM-3 Block II/IIA (with a 530mm diameter), will have additional capability to deal with incoming missiles with a longer range than the North Korean Nodong (which has a maximum range of 1,300 km). This provides an opportunity for Japan to intercept missiles that fly over Japanese territory, including those that target the US forward bases and the US mainland. Before Tokyo can deploy the new generation BMD interceptor it still needs to overcome the legal constraint that prohibits exercising the right of collective self-defence. The current official interpretation does not allow the use of force against a target for reasons other than individual self-defence. According to some experts, this means that Japan may be prohibited from using its BMD interceptors in order to help defend the US mainland from a long-range missile attack. This issue was specifically highlighted in a report by the Advisory Panel on Reconstruction of the Legal Basis for Security (the so-called Yanai Commission), which was published in April 2008 and May 2014 (see Advisory Panel on Reconstruction of the Legal Basis for Security 2008, 2014).

Projecting power despite A2/AD challenges: implications for the US-Japanese alliance

The modernization of China's air and naval power and of its missile capability is heightening China's anti-access capability with regard to areas where China's core interests are involved, while also heightening its area-denial capability in theatres where US forward deployed forces had previously been able to assume uncontested supremacy.[1] China's A2/AD capabilities and strategies to employ them combine to make US power projection increasingly risky, and in some cases prohibitive, while enabling the PLA to extend its coercive strength well beyond China's borders. In the most challenging of scenarios, the United States may not be able to employ forces in the way that it has in the past: by building up combat power in an area, performing detailed rehearsals and integration activities, and conducting operations when and where desired.

As explained in the 2012 'Strategic Guidance', US military planners have increasingly focused on 'Project[ing] Power Despite Anti-Access/Area Denial Challenges' (United States Department of Defense 2012c: 4). The Pentagon formulated the Joint Operational Access Concept (JOAC) in January 2012 to ensure that the US joint forces would achieve the ability to project military force into an A2/AD environment (United States Department of Defense 2012b). Its central theme, which is highly conceptual, is the attainment of cross-domain synergy, described as 'the complementary vice merely additive employment of capabilities in different domains such that each enhances the effectiveness and compensates for the vulnerabilities of the others – to establish superiority in some combination of domains that will provide the freedom of action required by the mission' (United States Department of Defense 2012b: ii). JOAC reiterates the importance of establishing conditions prior to the onset of combat operations. These essential preconditions include US forward deployment forces, bases and facilities, access and support agreements, prepositioning of supplies, and bilateral multinational exercises. To ensure operational access, US joint forces will need to achieve a higher degree of integration and additional operational capabilities, including the ability to disrupt an enemy's surveillance and reconnaissance efforts, attack an enemy's A2/AD defence in depth, and exploit surprise to complicate an enemy's targeting.

In July 2009, the US secretary of defense directed the Departments of the Navy and the Air Force to address these challenges by means of a new operational concept called Air–Sea Battle (ASB). This controversial concept finally took shape in May 2013, with the establishment of an Air–Sea Battle Office (United States Air–Sea Battle Office 2013). ASB is the supporting concept of JOAC. At the low end of the conflict spectrum, ASB is designed to help US policymakers engage with regional allies and partners in order to assure access, maintain freedom of action, conduct shows of force and, if necessary, engage in limited strikes. At the high end of the conflict spectrum, the ASB concept is designed to preserve the ability to defeat aggression and maintain escalation dominance despite the challenges posed by advanced weapons systems.

The US-Japanese alliance is already characterized by various aspects that support the US projection of power in accordance with the concept of ASB. Japan provides more than 90 US bases across the nation, including core US overseas bases in Northeast Asia that ensure US operations in the Asia-Pacific. These include the headquarters and home base of the US Navy 7th Fleet and aircraft carrier battle groups in Yokosuka, the Kadena Airbase in Okinawa which is a hub of US airpower in the Pacific, and the US Marine Corps III Marine Expeditionary Force headquarters in Okinawa. In an expanding A2/AD environment, these forward deployed bases and facilities are becoming increasingly vulnerable to an adversary's attacks, especially by ballistic and cruise missiles. A report published by the Center for Strategic and Budgetary Analysis describes China's military options as follows:

> Conduct ballistic missile salvo attacks, complemented by LACMs [land-attack cruise missiles] launched from various platform types, against US and Japanese air and naval bases. Attacks on Japanese targets could be supplemented by air strikes. Key targets would include forward air bases including those at Andersen, Kadena and Misawa; major logistics nodes such as Guam (airfields and port facilities); and key logistics assets such as fuel storage tanks. The PLA's objective would be to deny US forces the ability to generate substantial combat power from its air bases in the Western Pacific.
>
> (van Tol *et al.* 2010: 21)

The PLA's growing A2/AD capabilities challenge America's ability to engage in 'in-theatre operations' off the coast of the Chinese mainland and, more specifically, inside China's first-island chain. The possible options for the United States under such scenarios include withdrawal of the US forces from bases in Northeast Asia and diversification of its force presence in the outer range of the A2/AD environment. This scenario would be consistent with the concept of offshore balancing, but it would also be interpreted by many Japanese as a strategic abandonment of Japan (see Layne 1997).

Policymakers in Tokyo and Washington would not agree to such a scenario for three reasons: the US force presence in Japan constitutes the core component of America's extended deterrence strategy in the Asia-Pacific; no other countries or bases in East Asia could substitute for the US bases in Japan; and the possible cost of re-entry into the theatre would be too high during a contingency. According to Japanese expert Sugio Takahashi (2012: 18):

> [G]iven their combat radius, both current and next generation ground based tactical aircraft (i.e., F-15, F-16, F-22, and F-35) needs in-theater air base for effective operations. Therefore, for both the US Navy and Air Force, stand-off strike from outside A2/AD range is not a viable option, simply because of the lack of such assets.

However, the United States and Japan are aware of the need to deal with vulnerable bases and facilities that are increasingly threatened by A2/AD attacks (Takahashi 2012). Some of the measures that are required include fighter-based air defence, missile defence, hardening of facilities, construction of underground facilities, and tactical dispersion among multiple in-theatre bases. The United States and Japan have also decided to review the Guidelines for Japan-US Defense Cooperation by the end of 2014, in order to 'enable seamless bilateral cooperation in all situations', including the new roles and missions that are envisioned in JOAC and ASB (Security Consultative Committee 2013: 3).

US-Japanese strategic cooperation: facilitating the rebalancing?

The United States must also assist Japan in its efforts to adapt its military strategy to the demands of a rapidly changing security environment. Japan's National Defense Program Guideline (NDPG), adopted on 17 December 2010, provided a new concept called 'dynamic defence' (*doh-teki boei ryoku*) (Ministry of Defense, Japan 2010). This concept replaced the Self-Defense Force's (SDF) long-standing 'basic-defence force concept' (*kiban-teki boei ryoku kohso*) which was formulated in the 1970s. The previous concept emphasized securing Japan's minimum requirements for defence in order to avoid being regarded as a vulnerable target in the region. This policy led to the placement of SDFs across Japan, including the deployment of a major Ground SDF battalion in Hokkaido.

The new 'dynamic defence' and 'dynamic deterrence' concepts, in contrast, focus on the 'operational use of the defense force such as demonstrating the nation's will and its strong defense capabilities through timely and tailored military operations under normal conditions' (Ministry of Defense, Japan 2012: 115). These concepts are designed to enhance the SDF's operational readiness in dealing with situations surrounding Japan by reinforcing intelligence, surveillance and reconnaissance (ISR) capabilities; Japan's ability to respond quickly and seamlessly to various contingencies; and the promotion of multi-layered cooperative activities with foreign countries.

As a geographical focus, the NDPG called for greater defence preparedness in the southwestern regions of Japan, in response to China's growing activities both in the air and at sea, which threatened to create a sea change in the military balance of power in that sub-region. Risks and threats in the southwestern region can be classified as low intensity, involving violations of Tokyo's maritime interests by the intrusion of fishing boats and marine observation vessels, and medium/high intensity, involving the destruction of bases (US forces and SDF) and logistics infrastructure (ballistic/cruise missiles, special forces and cyber attack), and attacks on (and invasions of) Japan's numerous islands. Tokyo recognizes that accomplishing the goals set out in the NDPG will require both the management of its own 'dynamic defence', and new forms of joint action with Washington in support of US extended deterrence.

On 25 October 2011, the Japanese Minister of Defense Yasuo Ichikawa and US Secretary of Defense Panetta agreed to 'promote dynamic defense cooperation, which aims to enhance activities of units of the SDF and US forces and demonstrate the presence and capabilities of both countries' (Ministry of Defense, Japan 2012: 269). At the core of this plan for enhanced defence cooperation is a joint commitment to the development of forces capable of 'swift and seamless cooperation both at ordinary times and in emergency situations' (National Institute for Defense Studies 2013: 114). This dynamic defence force is expected to improve the regular operational capabilities of unit, while at the same time enhancing mutual trust and confidence between the two governments. Dynamic defence is also expected to make it easier for Japan to pursue new forms of security with other regional actors. This may take the form of trilateral defence cooperation among Japan, the United States and South Korea, or Japan, the United States and Australia. In some cases, it may also take the form of US-Japanese cooperation in a multinational framework.

Specific measures for US-Japanese dynamic defence cooperation consist of three pillars: timely and effective joint exercises and training; joint surveillance and reconnaissance operations; and joint use of facilities. US-Japanese joint exercises and training (the first pillar) have been conducted frequently between and among the three services in both countries. However, these activities have become increasingly robust, mission oriented and multi-lateralized. For example, in May–June 2013, the SDF participated for the first time in the joint US exercise Dawn Blitz, in which training is carried out for a series of operations relating to coordination with the US forces and responses to attacks on offshore islands areas. Held off the West Coast of the United States, this was the first US-Japanese bilateral joint exercise held abroad (Ministry of Defense, Japan 2013: 152). In July 2011, Japan, the United States and Australia conducted a joint naval exercise off the coast of Brunei. This was the first time that a trilateral exercise was conducted in the South China Sea. Japan, the United States and South Korea also conducted a series of naval exercises in the waters south of the Korean peninsula in June 2012, in Hawaii in August 2012, and in the waters west of Kyushu in May 2013, to strengthen coordination among the three countries (Ministry of Defense, Japan 2013: 236).

The second pillar, joint surveillance and reconnaissance operations, has also gained greater importance in past bilateral meetings. The two countries agreed to establish a bilateral defence ISR Working Group in February 2013 consisting of director-level defence officials from Tokyo and Washington. The importance of the ISR Working Group was reiterated at the Japan-US Joint Consultative Committee (2+2) meetings in October 2013, to facilitate the mission of encouraging closer alliance interoperability and information sharing between US forces and the SDF. Such joint ISR operations include peacetime intelligence sharing, coordination of intelligence gathering platforms, and investment in future technologies such as unmanned aerial vehicles.

The third pillar of US-Japanese dynamic defence cooperation is the joint use of facilities. The relocation of the Air SDF Defense Command to Yokota in April 2012, and the relocation of the Ground SDF Central Readiness Force Headquarters to Zama in March 2013, are important developments that enhance bilateral coordination and joint operations between the two forces. Tokyo and Washington also confirmed their plan to develop training areas in Guam and the Northern Mariana Islands as shared-use facilities. The primary significance of this plan is to secure training areas for offshore island defence. Although SDF training and exercises related to offshore island defence have been increasing in recent years with the strengthening of the defence posture of the southwestern islands, sufficient Japanese locations have not been secured for amphibious exercises that are indispensable for remote island defence (National Institute for Defense Studies 2013: 117). This provides wider options for the SDF to conduct its own exercises and opportunities for intensified joint operations with the United States and other friendly nations like Australia.

Japan's expanded security partnerships: the case of Southeast Asia

Another Japanese response to the US rebalance to Asia is a diversification of Japan's strategic partnerships in the Asia-Pacific and beyond. Preserving the stability of two vital seas – the South China and East China Seas – for Japan's sea lanes of communication has become an increasingly important priority for Tokyo in its engagement with the nations of Southeast Asia. Japan has significant commercial and security interests in the South China Sea, as well as a large stake in how the rules for maritime security are interpreted and obeyed. However, the current stand-off in the South China Sea raises doubts about the prospects for continued cooperation between China and the Association of Southeast Asian Nations (ASEAN). Three issues bear special mention.

First, the maritime capability gap between China and ASEAN is growing quickly. China's rapid procurement of patrol ships, surveillance vessels and aircraft, submarines and new-generation fighters is bound to enhance its maritime and air superiority vis-à-vis its Southeast Asian neighbours. Second, the ongoing efforts to generate an ASEAN-led, rules-based maritime order in the South China Sea have not achieved visible success. The negotiations over establishing a legally binding code of conduct for the South China Sea have foundered on the fact that China has not shown an accommodative stance toward multilateral discussions. Third, although ASEAN accepts the importance of the US 'rebalance to Asia', the majority of ASEAN members are reluctant to support publicly the US role as an external balancer against China, in part because of the high level of ASEAN-China economic interdependence.

Enhancing ASEAN's resilience

In dealing with these difficult conditions, ASEAN needs to contribute to a favourable balance of power by a campaign of rapid capacity building. From the Japanese perspective, ASEAN's strength and resilience in the face of China's growing maritime pressure is an important element of any campaign to challenge China's creeping expansion to the contested territorial waters. Strength and resilience are also essential preconditions for the success of ASEAN's diplomatic relations with Beijing.

Under these circumstances, helping to build ASEAN's maritime security capacity has become a key policy focus of the Japanese government. First,

Japan is more actively engaged in joint military exercises and training in Southeast Asia. In the past several years, Japan has increased its profile, participating in joint exercises, humanitarian assistance, disaster relief and non-combatant evacuation operations. The Japanese SDF has been participating in the US-Thai Cobra Gold joint/combined exercises since 2005 and joined the US-Philippine Balitakan series for the first time in March–April 2012. Japan has also been an active participant in the Pacific Partnership, a dedicated humanitarian and civil assistance mission in Southeast Asia.

With increased participation in multilateral joint military exercises and training, Japan is significantly increasing its networking, communications and security cooperation with regional states. Since fiscal year 2012, the Ministry of Defense has embarked on an assistance programme for security capacity building in ASEAN members in such fields as humanitarian assistance, disaster relief and counter-piracy operations. Although the current budget is rather small, it is expected to expand over the longer term.

Second, Japan has become more publicly supportive of ASEAN's security capacity by boosting its official development assistance (ODA). During the Japan-ASEAN summit meeting in November 2011, then Prime Minister Yoshihiko Noda pledged US$25 billion to promote flagship projects for enhancing ASEAN connectivity. At the Japan-Mekong summit in April 2012, Japan also pledged US$7.4 billion in aid over three years to help five Mekong states with critical infrastructure projects, such as airports, ports, roads, power generation stations and electricity supply, communications and software development. All of these projects have important security implications, and are compatible with Foreign Minister Koichiro Genba's promotion of the 'strategic use of ODA' to seek connectivity between Japan's aid and regional security. If Japan's financial assistance is more strategically oriented to support these functions, it can serve as a major tool for ASEAN to build its defence infrastructure.

Capacity building in Southeast Asia is also indispensable for the development of an effective US military presence in the Asia-Pacific region. If ASEAN coastal states are able to perform effective ISR operations and develop their capabilities for low-intensity operations, escalation management at the initial level of tension would be dramatically improved. An enhanced ASEAN security infrastructure could also provide potential alternative access points for US forces in Southeast Asia. In pursuing a 'geographically distributed, operationally resilient, and politically sustainable' presence, capacity building in Southeast Asia would bolster regional security in ways that are valued by both Tokyo and Washington.

Contributing to maritime security

The Japanese government is seeking to promote direct arms exports to support the defence infrastructure of ASEAN members. In December 2011, Japan decided to ease the restrictions imposed under its 'Three Principles on

Arms Exports'. While maintaining the basic philosophy of restraining exports, overseas transfers of defence equipment are now allowed in principle in circumstances that contribute to peace and advance international cooperation. For example, Japan is providing the Philippines with patrol vessels for its coastguard and maritime communications systems through ODA in the coming years. Building upon the relaxed restrictions, Japan is also considering the export of patrol vessels, aircraft and multipurpose support ships to enhance ASEAN's maritime security capabilities. If this hardware assistance is coupled with technical support and training by the Japan Coast Guard and the Maritime SDF, Tokyo will make a valuable contribution to maritime security.

Helping to build ASEAN's defence capacity while avoiding any unnecessary conflicts with China requires Japan to perform a delicate balancing act. Tokyo will need to develop a clear strategy supported by close coordination among domestic institutions, such as the Ministry of Defense and the SDF, the ODA strategies of the Ministry of Foreign Affairs and the Japan International Cooperation Agency, and the financial functions of the Japan Bank for International Cooperation. This will be challenging, as each institution has a different perspective on capacity building in ASEAN. If managed properly, however, the coordinated use of joint military exercises/training, ODA and arms exports will constitute important pillars of Japan's policy toward ASEAN.

Conclusion

This chapter clarifies the emerging Japanese perspectives on and responses to the US rebalance to Asia. As a cornerstone of the US alliance network in the Asia-Pacific, Japan welcomes the American decision to maintain and strengthen its military and diplomatic commitment to the region. However, eastward expansion of China's A2/AD capabilities challenges the premise of US uncontested preponderance in the military domain as well as a stable US forward presence. Joint development of tailored regional deterrence architecture and the review of the Guidelines for Japan-US Defense Cooperation to facilitate dynamic defence cooperation are the key for alliance management under the US rebalancing.

The US rebalancing to Asia also needs regional support. Japan's increasing efforts to build security ties and networks among like-minded states such as Australia, South Korea and ASEAN members would have great potential to connect Washington's and Tokyo's strategic interests in the Asia-Pacific. Japan's upgrade of security relations with these countries indicates both attempts to hedge collectively against the rise of China and to promote a stable US presence in Asia. The new dimension of such partnerships includes the capacity building of ASEAN coastal states, especially towards the Philippines. With expanded participation in joint training and exercises, provision of 'strategic use' of ODA, and arms exports to such states, Japan's security engagement in Southeast Asia has become an important asset for the US rebalancing to Asia.

Notes

1 Anti-access, or A2, refers to action intended to slow deployment of friendly forces into a theatre or cause forces to operate from distances further from the locus of conflict than they would otherwise prefer. A2 affects movement to a theatre. Area-denial, or AD, refers to action intended to impede friendly operations within areas where an adversary cannot or will not prevent access. AD affects manoeuvre within a theatre (see United States Air–Sea Battle Office 2013). According to the 'Strategic Guidance', sophisticated adversaries, such as China and Iran, would use asymmetric capabilities, to include electronic and cyber warfare, ballistic and cruise missiles, advanced air defences, mining and other methods, to complicate US operational calculus (see United States Department of Defense 2012c).

References

Advisory Panel on Reconstruction of the Legal Basis for Security (2008) 'Report of the Advisory Panel on Reconstruction of the Legal Basis for Security', 24 April, www.kantei.go.jp/jp/singi/anzenhosyou/report.pdf (accessed 25 February 2014).

——(2014) 'Report of the Advisory Panel on Reconstruction of the Legal Basis for Security', 15 May, www.kantei.go.jp/jp/singi/anzenhosyou2/dai7/houkoku_en.pdf (accessed 17 June 2014).

Donilon, Tom (2013) 'The United States and Asia-Pacific in 2013', Speech to the Asia Society, New York, 11 March, www.whitehouse.gov/the-press-office/2013/03/11/remarks-tom-donilon-national-security-advisory-president-united-states-a (accessed 20 February 2014).

Layne, Christopher (1997) 'From Preponderance to Offshore Balancing', *International Security*, 22(1): 86–124.

Ministry of Defense, Japan (2010) 'National Defense Program Guideline for FY2011 and Beyond', 17 December, www.mod.go.jp/e/d_act/d_policy/pdf/guidelinesFY2011.pdf (accessed 25 February 2014).

——(2012) *Defense of Japan 2012*, Tokyo: Ministry of Defense.

——(2013) *Defense of Japan 2013*, Tokyo: Ministry of Defense.

National Institute for Defense Studies (2013) *East Asian Strategic Review 2013*, Tokyo: The Japan Times.

Obama, Barack (2011) 'Remarks by President Barack Obama to the Australian Parliament', 17 November, www.whitehouse.gov/the-press-office/2011/11/17/remarks-president-obama-australian-parliament (accessed 20 February 2014).

Panetta, Leon (2012) 'Shangri-La Security Dialogue: As Delivered by Secretary of Defense Leon E. Panetta', Singapore, 2 June, www.defense.gov/speeches/speech.aspx?speechid=1681 (accessed 25 December 2013).

Security Consultative Committee (2013) 'Toward a More Robust Alliance and Greater Shared Responsibilities', Joint Statement, 3 October, www.mofa.go.jp/mofaj/files/000016028.pdf (accessed 17 June 2014).

Takahashi, Sugio (2012) 'Counter A2/AD in Japan–US Defense Cooperation: Toward Allied Air–Sea Battle', *Futuregram* 12-03, Arlington, VA: Project 2049 Institute, project2049.net/documents/counter_a2ad_defense_cooperation_takahashi.pdf (accessed 17 June 2014).

United States Air–Sea Battle Office (2013) 'Air–Sea Battle: Service Collaboration to Address Anti-Access and Area-Denial Challenges', Unclassified Summary, May, navylive.dodlive.mil/files/2013/06/ASB-ConceptImplementation-Summary-May-2013.pdf (accessed 25 February 2014).

United States Department of Defense (2010a) *Ballistic Missile Defense Review Report*, Washington, DC: United States Department of Defense, February.

——(2010b) *Nuclear Posture Review Report*, Washington, DC: United States Department of Defense, April.

——(2010c) *Quadrennial Defense Review Report*, Washington, DC: United States Department of Defense, February.

——(2012a) 'Defense Strategic Guidance Briefing from the Pentagon', 5 January, www.defense.gov/transcripts/transcript.aspx?transcriptid=4953 (accessed 20 February 2014).

——(2012b) 'Joint Operational Access Concept (JOAC)', Version1.0, 17 January, www.defense.gov/pubs/pdfs/JOAC_Jan%202012_Signed.pdf (accessed 25 February 2014).

——(2012c) 'Sustaining US Global Leadership: Priorities for 21st Century Defense', Washington, DC: United States Department of Defense, January.

van Tol, Jan, with Gunzinger, Mark, Krepinevich, Andrew and Thomas, Jim (2010) *Air–Sea Battle: A Point-of-Departure Operational Concept*, Washington, DC: Center for Strategic and Budgetary Assessments, 18 May.

White House (2014) 'Joint Press Conference with President Obama and Prime Minister Abe of Japan', Akasaka Palace, Tokyo, 24 April, www.whitehouse.gov/the-press-office/2014/04/24/joint-press-conference-president-obama-and-prime-minister-abe-japan (accessed 17 June 2014).

6 South Korea's adaptation to the US pivot to Asia

Changsu Kim

Introduction

The Barack Obama Administration has officially implemented a new strategy in Asia, initially known as the 'return to Asia', rebranded as a 'pivot to Asia', and more recently referred to as a 'rebalancing' policy towards the Asia-Pacific region. The US interest in maintaining its leadership and primacy in the face of a rising China serves as the backdrop for this policy. The winding down of overseas contingency operations has allowed US forces stationed in Afghanistan and Iraq to be relocated to other parts of the world, most notably East Asia and the Pacific. The South Korean political elite, opinion leaders and public have watched these changes in the US national strategy, as reported by the media and responded to by the South Korean government. Not surprisingly, these sources of information have generated a wide array of differing perceptions and assessments concerning the pivot policy.

In this chapter I survey the evolving South Korean policy debate regarding the American pivot strategy and summarize the official position of the South Korean government regarding the pivot. I place the pivot in the context of six decades of US-South Korean bilateral defence cooperation, and then offer some comments on South Korean concerns about the implications of the American pivot for US-Chinese relations and for China's relationship with North Korea. Finally, I provide a South Korean perspective on some of the changes that are taking place in the Asia-Pacific region, with particular emphasis on US-Japanese defence cooperation.

South Korean perceptions of the US pivot

Statements delivered by high-ranking officials of the Obama Administration have been analysed, translated and reported by South Korean media outlets, often misleading the general public on the details and implications of the strategy for the nation and the region. It is understandable that the public have an interest in the American rebalance, given the impact that this strategy might have on domestic, political and economic issues, and in light of the continued security challenges posed by North Korea in recent years.

American statements regarding plans to deploy 60 percent of US naval assets and 60 percent of the US Air Force in the Pacific by 2020 have generated particular interest.

Many South Koreans have accepted and understand the new pivot strategy largely in the manner and context that it has been delivered to them. Most of the South Korean media coverage has focused on security and military matters to the exclusion of economic and diplomatic ones, despite frequent assertions by members of the Obama Administration regarding the multi-faceted nature of the rebalance.[1] This raises questions regarding the success of Washington's strategic communications campaign with its Asia-Pacific friends and allies. It also highlights the extent to which the United States and its Asian partners are being guided by differing national interests, distinctive security situations, and country-specific public agendas.

US officials have expressed concerns regarding the misunderstandings and misinterpretations of the rebalance strategy by allies and foes alike. Indeed, recently delivered speeches by US policymakers have spent as much time outlining what the new strategy is *not* as they have on what it *is*. Assertions that the rebalance is a form of encirclement or containment of China by the United States and its allies and partners has been undeniably the most commonly heard theme. Furthermore, details regarding US military plans – an essential subject that requires long-term expertise and professional knowledge – are often ignored and dismissed as secondary by commentators on the American rebalance.

For a number of reasons, Obama's rebalance strategy has generally been seen as not very different from what has already occurred on the peninsula. First, from the South Korean perspective, the United States has already pivoted toward the Korean peninsula in response to North Korea's security challenges and military provocations. South Korea's media coverage of these issues has heightened awareness of the importance of national security among the general public, political elite and opinion leaders, and they already feel familiar with the American military presence.

Second, evolving relations between the United States and China has led many South Koreans to perceive the 'pivot to Asia' as truly a 'pivot to China'. It is argued that Washington is strengthening and deepening its regional alliances and partnerships as part of a campaign to keep a rising China in check. Whether this is indeed the case has been the focus of considerable debate in South Korea. The perception that the US pivot to Asia is actually about China has become so widespread in South Korea and many other nations that it tends to eclipse official US claims to the contrary. Despite official denials of such intentions by the US government, concern about American containment or encirclement of China has become increasingly prevalent across the Asia-Pacific.

Third, Australian and Japanese active and visible responses to the US rebalance strategy have led many South Koreans to wonder why these countries appear to be more accommodating and adaptive to the strategy than their own nation. The 2011 decision to deploy US Marines to Darwin on a rotational training basis has been perceived by many South Korean experts as an intentional contrast to existing plans to relocate US ground troops within South Korea. The comparison has caused confusion and scepticism on the Korean peninsula. Moreover, South Korean policymakers have observed Canberra and Tokyo co-hosting a number of workshops and seminars on the US pivot in collaboration with their American counterparts.

Fourth, renewed attention on Southeast Asian nations and India has encouraged an increased South Korean interest in these countries. Again, because of the continued and long presence of American troops in South Korea, even these relatively small steps in US security policy loom large in the eyes of many South Koreans. The protection of sea lines of communication in the Indian Ocean and the South China Sea have also gained more prominence in the strategic thinking of the South Korean government and businesses.

Fifth, the South Korean political elite and opinion leaders understand what the US pivot strategy is designed to accomplish in the economic, diplomatic and military fields.[2] They believe the new strategy intends to lead the world in the 'right' direction, under US leadership, while simultaneously relying more on its allies and partners for contributions to preserving the 'global commons' in response to a rapidly changing security environment and severe budgetary constraints. Many conservative South Koreans have tacitly welcomed the new strategy as a credible path proposed by their closest ally, the United States. They perceive the rebalance as complementing South Korean strategies toward North Korea and surrounding powers, and they believe there are no better alternatives available for the present or future.

Policymakers' and security experts' assessments

It is not easy to distinguish South Koreans' perceptions of national security from their assessments of the US rebalancing strategy. Perceptions and assessments are related to one another and the rebalance policy can be seen from a number of different vantage points. At the risk of generalization, perceptions often represent the appearance of a matter and its message, while assessments focus on its substance. I focus on the official and publicized assessments of the strategy.

From the perspective of the South Korean military, and the security and defence standpoint, the 'rebalance' is no different from what the United States has already been doing in South Korea. The Korean peninsula has remained one of the two major anchor points (along with the Middle East) for US forces stationed in the Asia-Pacific since the end of the Korean War in 1953. While the chances of all-out war on the peninsula have gradually decreased, the military standoff between the two Koreas across the demilitarized zone has intensified as the North has developed its nuclear weapons and longer-range ballistic missiles programmes.

South Korean experts believe that the US rebalance has both positive and negative implications (as can be seen in its changing relations with China and Japan) for South Korea's national security. Although a strong security relationship already exists between the United States and South Korea, the rebalance provides government officials and security experts with continued assurance that the United States intends to remain a power presence in the region. This is of utmost importance to South Korea as the United States provides essential extended deterrence in terms of nuclear deterrence, conventional strike capabilities and missile defence systems.

In more general political terms, the rebalance has been received favourably by the South Korean government as a timely and proper policy for the Asia-Pacific century, which can contribute to peace and stability on the Korean peninsula. Rebalance serves not only American national interests, but also the interests of South Korea in an increasingly interdependent global community.

The South Korean official assessment of the US rebalance and its impact on the US-South Korean alliance can be found in the Ministry of National Defense's *2012 Defense White Paper*. It describes the US rebalancing strategy in the following context:

> In 2011, the United States issued a foreign policy related to politics, economy, and strategies that focuses on the Asia-Pacific region. In accordance with this policy, the United States is strengthening its traditional security cooperation relationships with five key allies including the ROK [Republic of Korea], Japan, Australia, the Philippines, and Thailand, while constructing a more effective system of multilateral security in the region ... in the form of two trilateral arrangements (ROK, United States, and Japan/United States, Japan, and Australia), centering on humanitarian assistance and disaster relief.
>
> (Ministry of National Defense, South Korea 2013: 14–15)

> The United States is currently pursuing a new military strategy in order to meet the demands of a changing strategic environment, characterized by defense cuts, end of war in Iraq, ongoing drawdown of US forces from Afghanistan, and the increase of China's influence and Asia's importance ... the new 'Defense Strategic Guidance', ... lays out the strategy for each region in order to maintain its global leadership ... the United States noted its intention to maintain or increase the level of US forces in the Asia-Pacific region, as it evaluated the Asia-Pacific region as the top priority region in its global strategy.
>
> (Ministry of Defense, South Korea 2013: 17)

> The US Department of Defense, evaluating China's A2/AD [anti-access/ area-denial] capability as a key challenge, is continuing to strengthen its naval and air force capabilities that can execute new operational concepts such as 'Air–Sea Battles' in order to effectively counter such capability. It

plans to operate a maximum of six aircraft carriers in the Asia-Pacific by 2020, while maintaining its existing aircraft carrier strike groups and carrier air wings. Moreover, the US Navy plans to deploy more than half of its submarine force, including the new Virginia-class strategic nuclear submarines, to the Asia-Pacific region. The Air Force is continuing to enhance its long-range strike capabilities and is steadfastly pursuing the transition of its forces in the direction of unmanned platforms, while additionally deploying the newest fighters, strategic airlifters, aerial refueling aircraft, and unmanned reconnaissance vehicles to key force projection bases in the Asia-Pacific: Guam and Hawaii.

(Ministry of Defense, South Korea 2013: 17–18)

Compared to the Ministry of National Defense, the Ministry of Foreign Affairs has touched less frequently or explicitly on the new US strategy, presenting its arguments at a rather high level of abstraction. Indeed, only a few diplomatic speeches and articles written by South Korean officials have discussed the new US strategy in any real depth. Rather, the rebalance is mentioned largely in diplomatic and economic terms, with trade volumes and economic statistics cited.

A similar pattern emerges in the United States. The sheer volume of speeches and statements by high-ranking officials of the US Department of Defense and the joint chiefs of staff dwarfs the volume of comments on the rebalance by US Department of State officials. Under these circumstances, it is not surprising that the concepts and connotations of the US rebalance have been introduced and discussed in South Korea and other Asian countries more in security and military terms than along diplomatic or economic lines. This is especially true in China, where questions about the intentions of the Obama Administration's rebalance have been addressed primarily by military experts. These comments have, in turn, influenced the debate among policy experts in South Korea. South Korean liberal commentators tend to take issue with what they perceive as problems for South Korea's national interest that are created by the Park Geun-hye Administration's support for the rebalance strategy. Some of these commentators have also shown a keen interest in sharing information about the US-led missile defence programme, in addition to related military capabilities and technologies among the United States, Japan and South Korea.

Not surprisingly, most South Korean commentary about the US rebalance has centred on the strategy's implications for specific aspects of South Korea's defence posture, rather than on the actual contents of the strategy itself. For example, when detailed plans to withdraw US forces from Afghanistan and Iraq and other troop reductions were made public in the 2010 *Quadrennial Defense Review Report* and through the speeches of high-ranking US officials, initial South Korean reactions focused on whether or not the US troops stationed in South Korea would be reduced as well. Debates on the next steps of US force management, or 'strategic flexibility' on the Korean peninsula and in the Asia-Pacific region, led to serious discussions about the allocation of future defence budgets among the three services of the South Korean armed forces as part of its defence reform.

Additionally, many South Korean security experts have paid close attention to the political and economic background to the rebalance strategy, including America's severe budgetary problems and the debates surrounding the sequester. The possible impact of defence budget cuts, including US demands for more defence burden sharing on the part of Washington's allies and partners, has been discussed routinely at security and defence forums held in Seoul. How much more support South Korea will be asked to provide, and under what circumstances, remains one of the pressing issues facing South Korea's political elite and public.

Impact on alliance politics

China continues to register high economic growth and has displaced Japan as a member of the Group of Two (China and the United States). Based upon the claim that a stable environment is an essential facet of sustained economic growth, China has strengthened its defence capabilities to counter what it perceives as a containment strategy led by the United States and supported by Japan and other allies and partners. Despite numerous attempts by Washington to reassure Beijing, this view is widely held in China, and Chinese public opinion supports tougher stances against the United States and Japan.

Seeing that North Korea and some Southeast Asian countries, such as Myanmar and Cambodia, have the ability to contribute to a campaign of counter-encirclement, Beijing has developed closer ties with these countries and provided them with diplomatic, military and other support. The Chinese embrace of North Korea in the wake of the sinking of the South Korean naval ship *Cheonan* on 26 March 2010 represents a typical example of this behaviour. However, Beijing's attitude toward Pyongyang changed following North Korea's third nuclear test on 12 February 2013, which was conducted despite direct opposition and warnings by Chinese officials. This tactical, if not strategic, change in China's policy toward North Korea can be interpreted within the broader context of US-Chinese relations and especially in terms of the US rebalance to Asia.

Faced with the possibility of a downturn in US-Chinese relations, the Obama Administration appears keen to expand and strengthen its regional alliance network. One key component of this US strategy is the assertive encouragement of improvements in trilateral security and military cooperation, based on America's long-lasting bilateral alliances with Japan and South Korea. Washington has also encouraged new forms of bilateral security cooperation between Tokyo and Seoul, including the proposed General Security of Military Information Agreement, which is designed to facilitate the sharing of technology and intelligence.

The US-Japanese alliance has played an important role in America's rebalancing strategy toward Asia. It would be safe and reassuring to assume that, despite their severe economic problems, the United States and Japan will continue their efforts to pursue detailed initiatives and action plans to enlarge and deepen their security cooperation. The rise of China has certainly put the two allies into a situation where they need to work together to prepare for future contingencies. However, Washington must also consider the delicate trilateral relationship between China, Japan and South Korea, as well as a number of historical and territorial issues that could undermine Washington's bilateral and trilateral initiatives in Northeast Asia.

First, from the South Korean perspective, enhancing US-South Korean-Japanese trilateral security cooperation and South Korean-Japanese bilateral cooperation are considered some of the major tasks facing the US-South Korean alliance. With regard to US-initiated proposals for a trilateral security cooperation agreement, Seoul has sustained a rather reserved position due to historical and domestic political reasons. Some commentators in Washington and Tokyo perceive this as intentionally ambiguous, designed to avoid antagonizing Pyongyang and Beijing. There is a risk, however, that if South Korea, a long-time ally of the United States and a friendly neighbour of Japan, continues to participate in the trilateral security cooperation only in a minimal fashion, the result will be a weakening of the US-South Korean alliance. This would be particularly true if the United States and Japan continue to exhibit a downward trend in their economies and in their national competitiveness, in stark contrast to a rising China.

At the core of this seeming disconnect between South Korea and Japan is a long list of historical rivalries and myths. For example, Prime Minister Shinzō Abe's Cabinet's distortion of history may have a seriously negative impact on US-South Korean-Japanese trilateral cooperation. This could in turn undermine efforts to sustain cooperative mechanisms to achieve the denuclearization of North Korea. North Korea has been very vocal in its criticisms of Abe's handling of certain historical issues, particularly the so-called 'comfort women' issue. Fortunately, however, there is recognition among political professionals in South Korea and Japan of encouraging cooperation rather than conflict. These security experts understand that bilateral security cooperation between Seoul and Tokyo is essential in order to expand trilateral cooperation among the three nations as part of Washington's new rebalance campaign.

Second, South Korea has also developed further interest in other forms of trilateral and multilateral security cooperation among the United States, Japan, South Korea, Australia, India and, most recently, China (White House 2013). In recent years, there has been an increase in interaction among members of various think tanks from South Korea and China. This is in stark contrast to the stalled relationship between South Korea and Japan. Also, recent proposals for advancing US-South Korean-Chinese cooperation over North Korean weapons of mass destruction merit special international attention. As James Przystup (2013: 1) aptly indicates, 'North Korea is now in the bull's eye of a slowly constricting US–ROK–China triangle of strategic cooperation. Pyongyang's policy options are narrowing daily, even as its economic prospects continue to deteriorate and relations with its sole, erstwhile ally have come under increasing strain'.

Third, while at times there have been setbacks, multilateral exercises, training for humanitarian assistance and disaster relief, and the sharing of information on security challenges in the region have become routine among Asia-Pacific allies. Reforms that were outlined in President Lee Myung-bak's and President Obama's joint vision statement of June 2009 have led to a reset of allied priorities and an upgrade of the bilateral security relationship in order better to reflect and adapt to an increasingly complex security environment and significant leadership changes in most nations in the Asia-Pacific region. Furthermore, the Park–Obama summit talks in May 2013 yielded a renewed emphasis on security cooperation in response to various types of transnational, non-conventional challenges at the regional and global levels (Kim 2013). Currently, important global issues that require expanded cooperation between the United States and South Korea include counter-proliferation of nuclear weapons and counterterrorism, development assistance to countries such as Afghanistan and Iraq, joint responses to climate change and other environmental challenges, and peace in the Middle East through efforts that include supporting Syrian opposition forces.

Fourth, securing support from the United States, China and other neighbouring countries to replace the existing armistice with a new peace regime on the Korean peninsula is of high importance to the South Korean public. South Korea has maintained its commitment to a robust alliance with the United States as the most reliable basis for a campaign designed to replace the current North–South standoff with a new peace regime on the peninsula. From the South Korean perspective, the US pivot to Asia represents a positive step toward this ultimate goal.

Impact on South Korean defence and military planning

As previously stated, the US pivot policy is not seen as a new phenomenon by the South Korean government or public, particularly in terms of its military implications for Seoul. However, the pivot has added some new elements to the existing US–South Korean security alliance. To South Korean security experts, US plans to rebalance its resources, operations and troop deployments (as laid out in United States Department of Defense 2010, 2012a, 2012b) may have a direct impact on South Korean defence plans.

First, American efforts to bolster the assurance/reassurance provided by US extended deterrence have been the most important element of the new rebalance strategy in the eyes of South Korean security and defence planners. The participation of US strategic bombers and submarines in the 2013 annual combined military exercises Key Resolve and Foal Eagle has enhanced the credibility of the rebalance, and the US extended deterrence guarantee, vis-à-vis South Korea.[3] On the other hand, Washington's ability to continue such activities has been questioned by South Korean experts in light of recent Pentagon budget cuts and the acrimonious disputes over sequestration.

Second, China's so-called A2/AD capabilities and US responses in the form of Air–Sea Battle have captured the attention of South Korean defence and military planners. These experts are seeking to understand where the Air–Sea Battle concept fits into the context of the broader rebalance strategy. Some have also asked if there are alternatives to Air–Sea Battle that better serve South Korea's national and security interests.

Third, the pivot strategy has also begun to have an impact on the defence and military posture of the South Korean armed forces. In addition to the recent weight placed upon the new military doctrine referred to as 'proactive deterrence' against North Korea's military provocation,[4] there has been a renewed focus on how better to coordinate different elements of South Korea's defence posture on and off the peninsula. These debates relate to a wide range of increasingly important security challenges including humanitarian aid and disaster relief, maritime security, sea lines of communication protection, defence against latent territorial disputes over Dok-do and Ieo-do islands, climate change and cyber security.

Fourth, the pivot may indirectly change the content and format in which Washington and Seoul discuss issues of defence burden sharing and cost sharing. Although these issues are not new, they will have an impact on the revision of the Special Measures Agreement due later in 2014. In 2013, many US senior military officials testified that there would be no drastic reduction in funding for US troops and military facilities in South Korea. While security and defence planners in Seoul understand the budgetary pressures that their American counterparts are experiencing, they are also reminded of their own budgetary constraints and domestic politics. A pressing issue for South Korea is how to agree on a new Special Measures Agreement that will satisfy the two allies in an era of what Hans Binnendijk (2013) has called US 'forward partnering' in the Asia-Pacific region.

Fifth, South Korean military and security experts are examining the pivot's impact on the transfer of wartime operational control scheduled for December 2015. In February 2007, the Pentagon agreed to provide the South Korean armed forces with a number of 'bridging and enabling capabilities', most notably in intelligence, surveillance and reconnaissance, to facilitate a smooth transfer of wartime operational control and a consolidation of the new combined defence system. However, whether this agreement still holds true has been questioned by South Korean counterparts, who want to make sure that the scheduled transfer of the wartime operational control does not leave a vacuum in combined defence capabilities in peacetime (armistice), wartime, and during a crisis.

Sixth, the US pivot to Asia has also influenced South Korea's defence reform debate. The force structure, the armed forces end strength, its weapons systems and procurement policy, and especially the upper-tier command structure, have been reviewed and revisited in light of the US rebalance strategy as it applies to the Korean theatre.

Conclusion

The South Korean political elite, opinion leaders and public have welcomed and gradually adapted to the idea of the Obama Administration's pivot to Asia strategy. They have wanted to maintain a close and robust alliance with the United States in their defence primarily against North Korean security and military threats. The pivot strategy is not seen as something particularly new or inventive on the Korean peninsula, since a military pivot to South Korea has existed for decades, and has been particularly pertinent in recent years in response to the increased nuclear and missile threats from North Korea. The rebalance has nonetheless provided the two governments with an impetus to strengthen and deepen their alliance. It is worth noting, however, that many in South Korea have begun to take an interest in the improvement of US-Chinese relations and the enhancement of security cooperation with the nations of Southeast Asia and with India. The challenge for South Korea and the United States is to adapt the rebalance to the demands of extended deterrence without damaging these positive regional developments.

At the risk of over-simplification, it appears that the impact of the US pivot toward the Asia-Pacific region has been most directly felt in Australia and Japan, where the new strategy has been the subject of numerous speeches, seminars, forums and dialogues. These two close allies of the United States have obvious reasons to welcome and support the rebalance. Concerns about rapidly changing power politics in the region and, in particular, the rise of China, have provided Australia and Japan with incentives to support the policy.

This has not necessarily been the case with South Korea. Ever since the Korean War ended with an armistice in 1953, South Korea's foremost defence priority has been to deter and manage North Korea's military threats and provocations. Six decades since the signing of the armistice agreement, the core of the US-South Korean alliance remains nearly unchanged. Therefore, from Seoul's perspective, the pivot to Asia is hardly new. Consequently, South Korea has not played as active a role as Australia and Japan. Furthermore, South Korea is a medium-sized power with a growing economic stake in China. Many South Koreans also believe that unification of the two Koreas will not be achieved if China objects to it. These factors help to explain why South Korea finds itself in a different position from other nations that have intensified their security cooperation with the United States.

The US rebalance will continue to evolve in response to the policies of major powers in the Asia-Pacific region. Indeed, the rebalance has two faces: positive and negative, light and dark, myth and reality, true and false. Such duality is normal for a very large and ambitious policy. Ideally, over time it will be better understood and supported throughout the region, but South Korea cannot wait until the rebalance has matured. It has been adapting quietly to the American strategy, while at the same time positioning itself to enhance its own regional and global strategy and manage its relations with Pyongyang and other governments in its neighbourhood.

As with any political strategy, perceptions matter, often more than facts. This is true with regard to the US rebalance strategy. In a rapidly changing world, the American strategic focus toward the dynamic Asia-Pacific region appears reasonable and understandable. Nevertheless, until the new strategy becomes more than mere political rhetoric, and moves beyond existing policies, America's friends and allies will continue to encourage Washington, but will stop short of making strategic commitments.

Notes

1 Major tenets of the new rebalance strategy can be found in many documents, statements and speeches. See, for example, United States Department of Defense 2010, 2012b; Clinton 2010, 2011; Panetta 2012; Carter 2013; Donilon 2013; Hagel 2013; Lippert 2013.
2 Author interview with James Przystup and Thomas X. Hammes of the Institute for National Strategic Studies, US National Defense University, at the Korean Institute for Defense Analyses, Seoul, 2 November 2012.
3 Deployment at a proper time of additional strategic weapons to assure South Korea has reportedly been on the agenda for the South Korea–US Extended Deterrence Policy Committee, which constitutes an element in the broader Korea–US Integrated Defense Dialogue, an official dialogue channel between the US Department of Defense and South Korea's Ministry of National Defense.
4 The doctrine gained the full support of the South Korean Ministry of National Defense after the *Cheonan* episode and the shelling of Yeonpyeong Island in 2010.

References

Binnendijk, Hans (2013) 'Rethinking US Security Strategy', *New York Times*, 24 March.
Carter, Ashton (2013) 'The US Defense Rebalance to Asia', Speech, Center for Strategic and International Studies, Washington, DC, 8 April.
Clinton, Hillary (2010) 'Leading Through Civilian Power: Redefining American Diplomacy and Development', *Foreign Policy*, November/December.
——(2011) 'America's Pacific Century', *Foreign Policy*, 189 (November): 56–63.
Donilon, Tom (2013) 'The United States and the Asia-Pacific in 2013', Speech at The Asia Society, New York, 11 March.
Hagel, Chuck (2013) 'The US Approach to Regional Security', Shangri-La Dialogue, 12th IISS Asia Security Summit, Singapore, 1 June.
Kim, Changsu (2013) 'Recommendations to Further Strengthen and Deepen the ROK–US Alliance at 60: Rebalancing Security Focus and Resetting Priorities', Paper presented to the Korea Research Institute for Strategy–Brookings International Seminar, Seoul, 24 January.
Lippert, Mark (2013) Luncheon and Keynote Address to 'The US Rebalance to Asia – A One Year Assessment: Where Have We Been and Where Are We Going?' Georgetown University, Washington, DC, 27 February.
Ministry of National Defense, South Korea (2013) *2012 Defense White Paper*, March, www.mnd.go.kr/user/mnd_eng/upload/pblictn/PBLICTNEBOOK_20130814100521 9260.pdf (accessed 21 November 2013).

Panetta, Leon (2012) 'Shangri-La Security Dialogue: As Delivered by Secretary of Defense Leon E. Panetta', Singapore, 2 June, www.defense.gov/speeches/speech.aspx?speechid=1681 (accessed 27 August 2013).

Przystup, James J. (2013) 'Triangulation and Trustpolitik', *PacNet* #43, Honolulu: Pacific Forum CSIS, 17 June.

United States Department of Defense (2010) *Quadrennial Defense Review Report*, 1 February, www.defense.gov/QDR/ (accessed 21 November 2013).

——(2012a) 'Joint Operational Access Concept', 17 January, www.defense.gov/pubs/pdfs/joac_jan2012_signed.pdf (accessed 26 November 2013).

——(2012b) 'Sustaining US Global Leadership: Priorities for 21st Century Defense', Washington, DC: United States Department of Defense, January.

White House (2013) 'Remarks by President Obama and President Park of South Korea in a Joint Press Conference', Washington, DC, 7 May, www.whitehouse.gov/the-press-office/2013/05/07/remarks-president-obama-and-president-park-south-korea-joint-press-confe.

7 The US pivot to Asia

Taiwan's security challenges and responses

Fu-Kuo Liu

In January 2012, President Barack Obama officially announced the new US defence strategic guidance, which emphasizes a rebalancing and reform of its global military deployment, and a redistribution of its defence resources. The United States will maintain a global reach while emphasizing its commitments to the Asia-Pacific region and the Middle East. The strategy is built around three military adjustments: a change of force structure, upgrades of technologies, and the relocation of US forces (see United States Department of Defense 2012). For many, the new American strategic guidance raised more questions than it answered. Why does the United States need to rebalance to Asia? At whom is the rebalance targeted? Will the pivot intensify strategic competition in the region? How should regional players respond? The most common question, however, is: how serious is the United States this time?

The terms 'pivot' and 'rebalancing' have now taken a central place in the policy debate in the Asia-Pacific region. The context of the pivot to Asia is clear. Washington has been trying to wind down its 'war on terror' in Iraq and Afghanistan, while at the same time coping with the global financial crisis and America's economic downturn. The United States can no longer afford its decade-long, global counterterrorism strategy. Under these circumstances, Washington needs to readjust its global military deployments in order to continue to protect its interests and those of its allies. With specific reference to the Asia-Pacific, China's growing military capability and its rising influence in the region has become a strategic concern and a challenge to the United States. The American pivot is also designed to make up for decades of strategic neglect of the Asia-Pacific region, which the US government defines as an 'underweighted' region in terms of America's national security interests (Donilon 2013).

To date, America's pivot has been quite successful. As a result of Washington's use of economic, diplomatic and military instruments of power, the United States is garnering new momentum to strengthen alliances and re-establish partnerships in order to recover its leadership in the region. The United States began the process of the pivot by committing to the facilitation of regional multilateralism. With regard to the security aspect, the United States has made a clear commitment to Asia and is reallocating its military resources to the Pacific region. Taiwan is hopeful that America's military efforts, including its redeployment of troops in the region, will encourage new forms of security cooperation with allies and partners. Washington has also pressed for a new economic architecture through the Trans-Pacific Partnership (TPP), which was designed to develop close ties with members of the Association of Southeast Asian Nations (ASEAN)-plus framework, while at the same time providing an alternative to the China-oriented ASEAN+3 (China, Japan and South Korea) trade agreement (known since 2011 as the Regional Comprehensive Economic Partnership).

In spite of the progress that the United States has made, however, many commentators question whether the pivot can be sustained. In light of America's difficult financial situation, it is doubtful how much it will be able to accomplish in the region, and it remains to be seen whether Washington's rhetoric will translate into specific long-term policies.

This chapter considers both the prospects for the American pivot strategy and the implications of this strategy for one of Washington's key strategic partners in the Asia-Pacific, Taiwan. Partly in response to the American pivot, but also in response to developments across the Taiwan Strait and in the East China and South China Seas, Taipei is revising and broadening its national security strategy. The success or failure of America's pivot will be determined, at least in part, by Taiwan's success at revising its national security strategy in ways that contribute to Asia-Pacific security.

Taiwan's perceptions of, and responses to, the US pivot to Asia

Taipei recognizes the value of the US pivot as a source of national and regional security, but it also appreciates the challenges that Washington will face as it seeks to implement the pivot. Taiwan's general perception of the pivot also reflects concerns about US-Chinese strategic competition. According to one expert, 'the US' strategy of refocusing to the Asia-Pacific region was aimed at countering the continued rise of China's economic and military power' (Edward Chen, quoted in Shih 2012). Discussions and assessments of the US pivot in Taiwan tend to emphasize American challenges to China's interests in the region. The pivot strategy is interpreted as either a US campaign to regain its superior position in the region, or as an attempt to push China into sharing a leadership role.

For more than six decades, Taiwan has relied on its security relationship with the United States to withstand threats from China. As the pace of Chinese military development has accelerated, however, Taiwan has come to accept that it will not be able to compete with China's military hard power. Instead, over recent years, Taiwan has concentrated more on developing asymmetric military capabilities and wielding soft power as a way to deter and discourage Chinese hostility.

Like many other countries in the region, Taiwan must develop its policies around the reality that China has already become its number one trading partner, at the same time that the United States remains its most important security guarantor. Whether managed well or badly, US-Chinese strategic competition will affect regional security and prosperity. While it continues to improve its relationship with the United States, Taiwan also intends to continue to deepen relations with China so that both security and prosperity can be sustained. The United States recognizes that recent progress in cross-strait relations is helpful to regional security, but Washington has also reiterated its commitment to the security of Taiwan and the 'one China policy' framework as pillars of the pivot strategy (Panetta 2012; Hagel 2013). Ideally, Taiwan will be able to reciprocate by developing even closer cooperation with the United States in order to enhance its capabilities and bolster its confidence.

While positive progress continues across the Taiwan Strait, Taiwan is carefully assessing what the pivot implies for the region, and is looking for ways to take advantage of the pivot to facilitate closer relations with the United States. Like its Asian neighbours, Taiwan is also looking for ways to avoid the strategic dilemma of having to choose sides.

The critical security elements of the pivot include, first, a re-allocation of military assets to the Asia-Pacific region; second, investment in the development of platforms and capabilities in the Asia-Pacific; third, investment in human resources, including language and cultural skills; and fourth, a revitalization of US defence partnerships across the region (Carter 2013). Taiwan is carefully observing the implementation of all these elements, in conjunction with its regional neighbours.

Taiwan has been a 'non-recognized' ally of the United States since the severance of diplomatic recognition in 1979. Because military cooperation between the United States and Taiwan runs much deeper than is generally revealed, Taiwan's response to the pivot basically follows along the lines of US military planning. Taiwan is currently going through the process of military transformation from a conscription to a voluntary system, and is facing financial constraints similar to the pressures imposed on the US military by the sequester reductions. Taiwan intends to restructure its force to become smaller, leaner, smarter and stronger, in order to be prepared for a rapidly changing security environment. A key element of this reform will be a reduction in the size of its military from 275,000 to 215,000 personnel by 2016. As the Chinese People's Liberation Army is rapidly increasing its modern weapons and platforms, and has largely eliminated Taiwan's conventional military superiority, Taiwan needs to rebuild its forces around advanced platforms and upgraded capabilities in order to implement an asymmetric strategy (Office of the Secretary of Defense 2013). The momentum of the US pivot will influence Taiwan's force restructuring planning and its changing defence posture.

Taiwan is also looking to engage fully in the process of regional security cooperation. The United States has invested in platforms and capabilities that could be applied throughout the region. Building on these platforms and capabilities, America is boosting its presence while also helping to link up with, and reassure, regional partners. By building the long-range, early-warning radar system capabilities, Taiwan and the United States are intensifying their cooperation on intelligence, surveillance and reconnaissance systems, which may help to foster regional joint defence linkages. Taiwan's and the United States' monitoring of the North Korean missile test in 2013 illustrate cooperation at the operational level between Taipei and Washington.

Taiwan and its neighbours recognize that financial constraints on the United States means it may not be able to maintain as powerful a presence in the region. Therefore, it is likely that the United States will need its regional allies and partners to share responsibilities. In responding to the pivot, regional security challenges and new cross-strait realities, Taiwan has been pressed to re-examine its defence strategy in order to play a greater role in this changing regional security environment.

Impacts of the pivot strategy

Three dimensions of the US rebalancing strategy – diplomatic, military and economic – were highlighted by Tom Donilon, a former national security advisor to President Obama, in March 2013:

> [T]he US is implementing a comprehensive, multidimensional strategy: strengthening alliances; deepening partnerships with emerging powers; building a stable, productive, and constructive relationship with China; empowering regional institutions; and helping to build a regional economic architecture that can sustain shared prosperity.
>
> (Donilon 2013)

Although US officials repeatedly emphasize that the core of the rebalancing strategy is the economic dimension, the region pays much more attention to the military dimension (regarding the economic dimension, see Nides 2012; for the military dimension, see Carter 2013). Because the US-Chinese relationship is critically important in the pivot to Asia, senior US officials repeatedly suggest that 'the rebalance is not a zero-sum game with Beijing or a contain China strategy' (Lippert 2013). Indeed, Washington has taken a proactive approach to engage fully with China, but the region is still prone to view the situation in terms of evolving conflict.

Regional security hinges upon the settlement of maritime territorial disputes in the East China and South China Seas, and upon North Korean denuclearization. A number of issues have contributed to maritime territorial disputes in East Asia, but recently the pivot has exacerbated these disputes. At the 2010 ASEAN Regional Forum, then US Secretary of State Hillary Clinton stated that the United States 'has a national interest in freedom of navigation, open access to Asia's maritime commons, and respect for international law in the South China Sea' (quoted in Kaufman 2010). This statement indicated that the United States was formally making its way back to the region and was directly challenging China. Since then, the United States has accelerated security cooperation with the Philippines and Vietnam. The political showdown in the South China Sea between the United States and China came as a shock to other claimants. Both the Philippines and Vietnam have taken a somewhat aggressive approach, encroaching on some areas within China's nine-dashed line in the South China Sea by sending more fishing boats and oil survey ships to the area. China has responded assertively against the exploitative activities of Vietnam and the Philippines in the region. The South China Sea dispute continues to escalate.

Given these circumstances, it is highly unlikely that the South China Sea claimants will back down on their sovereignty claims now or in the near future, especially if there are no influential regional mechanisms to facilitate direct dialogue among all involved parties. Furthermore, the US pivot to the region has encouraged Washington's allies and partners to assert their interests at the expense of others. In the case of the Diaoyu/Senkaku Islands dispute in the East China Sea, US policy is tied to the US-Japan Security Treaty, which is at the centre of the pivot strategy. As a result, the Japanese government is skilfully utilizing the US policy position on the Diaoyu/Senkaku Islands to compete against both China and Taiwan. The Chinese continuously criticize the United States for being prejudiced in favour of Japan's claims and against China (*People's Daily Online* 2013). While the United States is trying to deter and deny any possible challenge (read China) to alter the status quo in the Diaoyu/Senkaku Islands, it is at the same time discouraging allies (read Japan) from taking adventurous and provocative action. The Chinese official media has continuously criticized these US actions as an attempt at 'containment' or 'encirclement' of China.

As part of the pivot, the United States is closely working behind the scenes to ensure that the Diaoyu/Senkaku Islands dispute among China, Taiwan and Japan is manageable and does not escalate into a full-blown conflict. On the one hand, the United States has appealed to all parties to use only peaceful means to achieve a solution. On the other hand, Washington has made it clear to China that the US-Japan Security Treaty covers the Diaoyu/Senkaku Islands. In other words, in the event of a conflict, it will become a US defence obligation to engage in any Diaoyu/Senkaku Islands contingency. The United States is trying to press Japan's right-wing-oriented government to avoid a conflict with China.

Washington also hopes to contribute to cooperation between Taiwan and Japan in the East China Sea. Maintenance of stability in the Asia-Pacific region is central to the US pivot. As such, it would not be in US interests to have to deal with two strategic partners fighting each other. On 10 April 2013, Taiwan and Japan broke a political deadlock by signing an agreement regulating fishing activities and fishing zones surrounding the Diaoyu/Senkaku Islands and some parts of the East China Sea. This agreement had been under negotiation for more than 17 years without any appreciable progress. Although observers in the region have commented that Japanese Prime Minister Shinzō Abe gave the green light to signing the agreement based on

Japan's strategic interests, it has been speculated that the United States was operating behind the scenes, pushing Tokyo to make the concession to Taiwan in order to secure a peaceful environment between the two 'allies'. Whichever explanation is correct, the agreement can be interpreted as the United States and Japan jointly taking a pre-emptive step to discourage Taipei from leaning towards possible cross-strait cooperation. As part of its response to the US pivot, Taiwan has committed to the bilateral fishery agreement with Japan, and to earning the trust of both Washington and Tokyo.

Taiwan recognizes that a US military presence in the region not only provides stability and assurance by making conflict less likely in the East China Sea, but also might meet the conditions defined by the 'East China Sea Peace Initiative' proposed by Taiwan in 2012, thus increasing the chances of its implementation.

New cross-strait relations

In May 2008, Ma Ying-jeou assumed the Taiwanese presidency and began his rapprochement campaign with China, establishing institutional links with Beijing and successfully easing tensions in the Taiwan Strait. Over five years, with Ma now in his second term in office, China and Taiwan have signed 19 agreements to facilitate cooperation across the Taiwan Strait. Two-way communication is rapidly increasing. Taiwanese visitors to mainland China have reached more than 5 million per year since 2010, and the number of Chinese visitors to Taiwan reached a new high of 2.58 million in 2012 (up from 1.78 million in 2011) (see Shanghai Taiwanese Service Center 2011; Lee 2013). While Taiwan is increasing contacts and links with China, China has become Taiwan's largest trading partner. These efforts have gradually changed the atmosphere of hostility between the two countries, but many complex political and security issues have yet to be tackled.

In late June 2013, honorary Kuomintang (KMT) Chairman Wu Poh-hsiung met with Chinese Communist Party Chairman Xi Jinping, in Beijing. During the 'Wu–Xi summit', for the first time the 'one China' framework was clearly declared to be common ground between the two sides, which will help to regulate the future course of cross-strait relations (*Global Times* 2013). This agreement indicates the potential for future cross-strait dialogue.

As the cross-strait relationship shifts from one of hostility to one of trust building, Taiwan has to maintain a balanced policy between China (for market reasons) and the United States (for security). In addition, every inch forward in cross-strait progress could stir up concerns at home. In order to push forward, Taiwan's government needs to balance between domestic politics and its mainland policy. Unless it gains the necessary support at home, the KMT government will almost surely be unable to push through any new initiatives. Nevertheless, the new cross-strait relationship offers Taiwan a fresh chance to review its international and security policy.

The improved cross-strait relationship also complicates Taiwan's defence reform process, however, as increasing internal social pressures demand resource reallocation to reduce defence expenditure. Although the security risk from China remains, the rapprochement has had a great impact on Taiwan's efforts at defence modernization. Leaving aside the financial difficulties, public opinion in Taiwan shows a preference for cutting the defence budget and sustaining the cost of social welfare programmes. As rapprochement has developed between the two old enemies, Taiwan has been under pressure to review its existing national security strategy, which many view as unbalanced, unrealistic and overwhelmingly preoccupied with the Chinese security threat.

Despite frequent interaction across the Taiwan Strait, China has not changed its coercive strategy toward Taiwan. Indeed, new challenges in the form of maritime territorial disputes have awakened Taiwan's long-standing conservative and passive strategic thinking regarding national security threats. The provocative actions taken by the Philippines and Vietnam in the South China Sea have also sounded alarm bells in Taipei. Finally, while the US pivot is pushing the region toward new forms of cooperation, it also serves as a strong inducement to Taiwan's defence restructuring. Under such difficult circumstances, Taiwan has to reshape its force structure and develop an asymmetric strategy against China. In the *ROC 2013 Quadrennial Defense Review*, the government committed to establishing 'innovative and asymmetric' capabilities and maintaining 'fundamental warfighting capabilities while focusing on the development of asymmetric capabilities' (Ministry of National Defense, Taiwan 2013: chapter 2).

Taiwan is also broadening its definition of national security to include not just the threat posed by China, but also threats from neighbouring countries and from non-traditional security issues. In particular, the *Guang Ta-Shin 28* incident of 9 May 2013, in which a Philippines coastguard ship attacked a Taiwanese fishing boat, killing a fisherman, has had profound implications for Taiwan's national security thinking. Unsettled maritime disputes between the Philippines and Taiwan include fishing in overlapping exclusive economic zones and overlapping claims for sovereignty in the South China Sea. The Philippines attack on the Taiwanese fishing boat seriously challenged Taiwanese national security. Calls for the strengthening of Taiwan's military presence in those troubled waters have become common in Taipei, and since the fishing boat incident, Taiwan has been more organized and persistent in conducting law enforcement and military drills in the northern tip of the South China Sea. After the *Guang Ta-Shin 28* incident, Taiwanese public opinion supported the government strengthening its military capability in order to protect its maritime interests. After three months of tension, Taiwan and the Philippines reached a deal to compensate the victim's family, but related issues still linger, and Taiwanese public resentment against the Philippines is likely to persist.

At the same time, it is also a great challenge for the KMT government to reinforce bilateral relations with the United States – particularly with regard to economic and security cooperation – after all these years of relative inactivity. There is always pressure within Taiwan to push for closer relations with the United States. While cross-strait relations have dramatically improved over the last five years, the drive for more robust relations between the United States and Taiwan has also accelerated. The US pivot has contributed to this mood. However, the bilateral relationship will have to be framed in accordance with both the one China policy framework and the Taiwan Relations Act. This should be manageable, as Taiwan's policies in support of cross-strait cooperation are consistent with America's goals for the pivot, and clearly serve US interests (Ministry of National Defense, Taiwan 2013: 10).

Taiwan's role

In a hearing held by the US House Committee on Foreign Affairs in October 2011, former US Assistant Secretary of State Kurt Campbell testified that, '[a] critical part of that over-arching [pivot] strategy is building a comprehensive, durable, and unofficial relationship between the United States and Taiwan' (United States House Committee on Foreign Affairs 2011: 9). Although there has not been further elaboration on how the United States defines the terms of its bilateral relationship with Taiwan in the context of the pivot, its profound importance is widely recognized.

In regard to the military aspect of the pivot, Taiwan's defence establishment reckons that, in spite of defence cuts, the United States 'will continue to enhance air force and naval capabilities in the Asia Pacific region, demonstrate its military power, and step up military cooperation with friendly and allied countries' (Ministry of National Defense, Taiwan 2013: 14). Therefore, Taiwan takes the US pivot into account as it develops its plans further to strengthen its air force and naval capabilities.

US-Taiwanese defence cooperation could be disrupted, however, by territorial disputes in the South China and East China Seas. These destabilizing disputes have become the largest challenge to the pivot, as instances of strategic competition between American security partners – Taiwan and the Philippines in the South China Sea, and Taiwan and Japan in the East China Sea – have surfaced. Maintaining peace in the region is in the best interests of the United States, but this becomes very difficult when national insistence over sovereignty issues complicates relations between American friends and allies. With long-standing claims of sovereignty over the disputed islands, Taiwan is at the centre of such maritime territorial disputes. Under these circumstances, it would be natural for Taiwan to take effective action to protect its national interests. The implications of such action for US-Taiwanese relations, and for the American pivot strategy, are hard to predict.

Conclusion

The US pivot strategy has great importance for Asia-Pacific security and for Taiwan's national security strategy. Since the pivot was announced, Taiwan has gradually shifted its strategy more towards the United States, in particular with regard to security, but the crucial determinant of Taiwan's future policies will be the extent to which the pivot continues to serve the best interests of Taiwan, based on Taipei's reading of five indices of future progress:

1 The pace of US-Chinese relations. Taiwan is encouraged that this bilateral relationship has taken a positive turn. President Obama met with his counterpart Chinese President Xi in California in June 2013. The summit was critical, and set a hopeful tone for the region.
2 America's handling of its economic challenges. The US sequestration has encouraged many policymakers to doubt whether US military capabilities and presence can be maintained at current levels.
3 Washington's ability to cope with a transformation of the cross-strait relationship. The policymaking community in Taiwan will continue to monitor the US comfort level with progress in cross-strait relations.
4 US management of its campaign to make the TPP a key element of its pivot to Asia. Taiwan will rely very much on the future course of the TPP and the Regional Comprehensive Economic Partnership to develop further economic links with other countries.
5 America's capacity to instil regional confidence in its ability to balance China's influence while avoiding a military confrontation with Beijing. On the one hand, the United States has sufficient security capabilities to help deter China's advances in Asia and keep order in the region. On the other hand, it could also establish a constructive and even cooperative relationship with China in order to avoid conflict.

Today, the United States is facing unprecedented serious challenges. Its power is relatively weaker, while China's is much stronger. Its financial problems, as illustrated by the sequestration, are likely to pose the most critical challenge to the implementation of the US pivot in the region. China, meanwhile, is trying to shape a new big power relationship with the United States, and is requesting more respect on equal terms. America's handling of these Chinese demands may have a profound impact on the cross-strait relationship and, ultimately, on Taiwan's response to the American pivot.

References

Carter, Ashton (2013) 'The Rise of Asia and New Geopolitics in the Asia-Pacific Region', Speech at the Jakarta International Defence Dialogue, Jakarta, 20 March, www.defense.gov/speeches/speech.aspx?speechid=1761 (accessed 7 January 2014).

Donilon, Tom (2013) 'The United States and the Asia-Pacific in 2013', Remarks to the Asia Society, New York, 11 March, iipdigital.usembassy.gov/st/english/texttrans/2013/03/20130311143926.html#axzz203Tny83j (accessed 7 January 2014).

Global Times (2013) 'Xi Meets with KMT Honorary Chairman, Calling Nat'l Rejuvenation a "Common Goal"', 13 June, www.globaltimes.cn/NEWS/tabid/99/ID/788574/Xi-meets-with-KMT-honorary-chairman-calling-natl-rejuvenation-a-common-goal.aspx (accessed 7 January 2014).

Hagel, Chuck (2013) 'The US Approach to Regional Security', First Plenary Session, Shangri-La Dialogue, Singapore, 1 June, www.iiss.org/en/events/ shangri%20la%20dialogue/archive/shangri-la-dialogue-2013-c890/first-plenary-sessio n-ee9e/chuck-hagel-862d (accessed 7 January 2014).

Kaufman, Stephen (2010) 'Clinton Urges Legal Resolution of South China Sea Dispute', 23 July, iipdigital.usembassy.gov/st/english/article/2010/07/20100723154256 esnamfuak4.879177e-03.html#axzz2pfxES54s (accessed 7 January 2014).

Lee, Joy (2013) 'Mainland Chinese Visitors Jump by 40 Percent in 2012', *China Post*, 17 January, www.chinapost.com.tw/taiwan/china-taiwan-relations/2013/01/17/ 367640/Mainland-Chinese.htm (accessed 7 January 2014).

Lippert, Mark (2013) 'The Rebalance: One Year Later', Remarks at the CSIS-Georgetown-US Studies Center Conference, 27 February.

Ministry of National Defense, Taiwan (2013) *ROC 2013 Quadrennial Defense Review*, Taipei: Ministry of National Defense, March, qdr.mnd.gov.tw/encontent.html (accessed 7 January 2014).

Nides, Thomas R. (2012) 'Remarks', at the APCAC US-Asia Business Summit, Tokyo, 1 March, Embassy of the United States, Tokyo, japan.usembassy.gov/e/p/tp-20120302-01.html (accessed 7 January 2014).

Office of the Secretary of Defense (2013) 'Military and Security Developments Involving the People's Republic of China 2013', Annual Report to Congress Pursuant to the National Defense Authorization Act for Fiscal Year 2000, Washington, DC: United States Department of Defense.

Panetta, Leon (2012) 'The US Rebalance Towards the Asia-Pacific', First Plenary Session, Shangri-La Dialogue, Singapore, 2 June, www.iiss.org/en/ events/shangri%20la%20dialogue/archive/sld12-43d9/first-plenary-session-2749/leon-panetta-d67b (accessed 7 January 2014).

People's Daily Online (2013) 'Experts Slam US Report Regarding China's Diaoyu Islands Baseline Announcement', 10 May, english.peopledaily.com.cn/90883/82404 25.html (accessed 7 January 2014).

Shanghai Taiwanese Service Center (2011) 25 February, www.tbfw.org/Fanti/General. aspx?id=843&tupian=9 (accessed 7 January 2014).

Shih, Hsiu-chuan (2012) 'Taiwan Should Aim to be US' Asia Partner: Experts', *Taipei Times*, 8 November.

United States Department of Defense (2012) 'Sustaining US Global Leadership: Priorities for 21st Century Defense', Washington, DC: United States Department of Defense, January.

United States House Committee on Foreign Affairs (2011) *Why Taiwan Matters, Part II*, Hearing Before the Committee on Foreign Affairs, House of Representatives, 112th Congress, 4 October, Washington, DC: US Government Printing Office, archives.republicans.foreignaffairs.house.gov/112/70584.pdf (accessed 7 January 2014).

Part III

Southeast Asian partners and allies

8 Strategic communication

US-Philippines relations and the American rebalancing strategy

Charmaine G. Misalucha

From 2011, the Barack Obama Administration made a series of announcements that the United States was shifting its attention away from Iraq and Afghanistan and towards Asia (Obama 2011). This rebalancing, it has been argued, is a 'natural trend' that focuses on the up-and-coming, dynamic region of the world (Cronin 2012: 12). At the same time, this new policy was seen as a counter-narrative to American decline, as well as a way to balance the rapid growth, strength and influence of China in the region (McDevitt 2012). While the strategy was multi-faceted, tensions in the South China Sea overshadowed its diplomatic and economic rationale and made it, at least insofar as the Philippines is concerned, 'a decidedly *military* effort' (Bitzinger 2012: 35, emphasis in original).

The American rebalancing strategy is much broader than a mere resuscitation of the US-Philippines security relationship. American strategic moves that are hallmarks of the rebalancing strategy include the deployment of 2,500 US Marines for training purposes in Darwin, the stationing of four new littoral combat ships at the Changi Naval Base in Singapore, plans for temporary basing access in the Philippines, and an increase in the number of ships in the Pacific Fleet. Such moves, however, do not definitively pin down the strategy's overall meaning and content (Glosserman 2013). I argue that until that is accomplished, the US rebalancing strategy will remain cloaked in ambiguity.

Interestingly, despite the ambiguity surrounding the rebalancing strategy and its motivations, the United States has been able to implement successfully its basic concept. If we strip away the diplomatic, economic and military aspects of the rebalancing strategy, we are left with several basic premises: that the United States is 'back' in the region, that it is prioritizing Asia, and that it has a stake in helping to shape the region's future security architecture. A good measure of the persuasiveness of this idea is not just that it was 'sold' in a narrative that is both cohesive and shaped against the backdrop of an empirical reality, but also that it was 'bought' by the Philippines, a renowned American treaty ally. The selling and buying of ideas in international relations is a paramount requirement for effective international security relations. In this case, that requirement seems well on its way to being fulfilled.

In this context, several questions are especially pertinent and will be considered in more detail below: how did the United States 'sell' the idea of a rebalancing strategy, and why did the Philippines 'buy' it? The focus here is on the methods used in the transaction, not the evidence that a sale has actually taken place. The United States' application of communication strategies – employed for framing the rebalancing concept – will be privileged over any quest to establish a causal link between the rebalancing strategy and a perceptible and tangible change in the beliefs and/or perceptions of the Philippines.

The reasons behind adopting this analytical framework of assessing communication strategies are twofold. First, despite some instances of resistance, it is commonplace to argue that Southeast Asia in general, and the Philippines in particular, have generally accepted the rebalancing strategy. Second, previous studies on Southeast Asian-US relations have noted a discernible shift in the American stance – that is, that the United States is 'back' in the region and is now more committed to regional security efforts (United States Department of Defense 2012; Manyin *et al.* 2012; Misalucha 2011, 2012). However, little systematic analysis has been offered on the tools that the United States has utilized to convince its Southeast Asian allies and partners of the validity and necessity of the rebalancing strategy. Moreover, strategic communication can be usefully evaluated by focusing on the use of linguistics, language and rhetoric as communications tools for promoting a specific strategy. Such an approach is incorporated into this chapter.

Ideas that parallel the American rebalancing initiative are, of course, not new in international relations. One can readily point to the post-11 September 2001 'war on terror' or, more historically, the Westphalian notion of state sovereignty (which has dominated state-centric international relations over the past half millennium). The recent emergence of constructivism as an analytical tool of international relations has illuminated the recognition that ideational factors 'matter' alongside material ones (Hopf 1998). Constructivist scholars have argued convincingly that ideas are the driving force of international relations (Katzenstein 1996; Wendt 1999). Ideas propel the development of the international system, and therefore engineer change. How ideas spread, according to extant literature, is dependent on an initiator. This presupposes, further, that ideas have clout if that initiator influences a targeted audience into believing that the ideas that it favours are important. Ideas are 'sold', therefore, only if someone accepts them. The US rebalancing strategy is one such idea. A central theme of this chapter, therefore, is how well the rebalancing strategy has fared as an international relations communication strategy. Indeed, the language and rhetoric that the United States and the Philippines have chosen to operationalize the effective communication of the rebalancing policy is a key element of the degree to which that strategy has been successful.

The rest of the chapter proceeds in the following manner. Initially, a framework that focuses on the methods of strategic communication is established that highlights the need to understand and explain American rebalancing strategy in Asia. Next, an assessment is made about how the rebalancing idea was conveyed and 'sold' by US security policy managers. Did the United States successfully 'sell' the policy idea by presenting a cogent version of it? To what extent has the Philippines really 'bought' the US vision? The chapter concludes by emphasizing that effective strategic communication can pave the way for successful policy changes and better ensure that appropriate courses of action are taken by both the 'seller' (the United States) and the 'customer' (the Philippines). However, it remains difficult to prove whether actors have made changes or taken action because they were forced, coerced or persuaded, or whether they have done so because they have internalized the idea that was communicated to them. Nevertheless, it is worth reiterating that the language and rhetoric that the United States and the Philippines have chosen to operationalize the effective communication of the rebalancing policy is a key element of the degree to which that strategy has been successful.

Ideas in international relations

To a significant extent, this chapter revolves around the capacity of ideas to shape power. An overarching concern is how to communicate ideas in international relations and convince audiences of their validity, as well as the necessity to take action based on their logic. This theme is situated within the theoretical literature provided in the field of international relations that details at least two ways in which the study of ideas has been applied (Klotz 1995; Finnemore 1996; Katzenstein 1996; Checkel 1998; Palan 2000; Björkdahl 2002). One focuses on *processes*: how certain ideas are given attention and thereafter take root in international relations. The other focuses on specific *methods* that actors utilize in order to spread ideas. Both classifications highlight ideational factors, although at no point do they neglect the tangible power and implications of material forces. If anything, both streams acknowledge that ideas spread wider and faster when material factors complement them.

Various international relations scholars and analysts have identified processes by which ideas are spread and, through regular practice and eventual institutionalization, become norms. Some of these processes include the 'norm life cycle', the 'securitization framework', and 'rhetorical contestation'. Despite their contributions to understanding international relations theory and behaviour, all these processes have serious shortcomings; however, these, in turn, can be rectified by focusing on the methods by which ideas spread.

The 'norm life cycle' is an idea developed by Martha Finnemore and Kathryn Sikkink (1998). According to their analysis, norm emergence begins when a 'norm entrepreneur' or advocate of a particular idea lobbies to place it within mainstream political thought. If such an effort succeeds, a 'tipping point' is reached where norms 'cascade' – the point at which ideas are generally accepted as norms after they emerge. Eventually, said norms win formal status and help to drive or shape policy. This model underscores how persuasive communication can be important to norm building (Payne 2001). When norms become 'internalized', the ideas underwriting them have been sufficiently persuasive to drive significant changes in both behavioural and rhetorical patterns of international relations. One must take care, however, in labelling how quickly such internalization occurs. Rodger Payne (2001: 41) observes that merely noticing changes in state practices is insufficient evidence that norms have become established or locked in as international behaviour. Observable changes in international relations, he asserts, are almost always due to some form of material or rhetorical coercion. In such instances, norm internalization can be assumed to have failed conclusively. Other critics, such as Diana Panke and Ulrich Petersohn (2012), focus more on the demise of norm life cycles rather than on their repetition. Their argument is that norms degenerate in unstable environments and if norms are very narrowly construed, they become inherently fragile and hence incapable of spreading or of being accepted. In this case, the 'death' of a norm becomes highly likely.

Another school of thought in international relations that emphasizes how ideas take root and become politicized is the 'Copenhagen School', spearheaded by such luminaries as Barry Buzan, Ole Wæver and Jaap de Wilde (1997; see also Buzan 1983). This approach is distinguished by its 'securitization framework', or the idea that governments can often control policy issues by categorizing them (justifiably or otherwise) as related to state security. The Copenhagen School argues that issues accede to a security agenda when a state government or other authoritative actor functions as a 'securitizing agent' (much like the norm entrepreneur in Finnemore's and Sikkink's model) and manages to convince an audience that an existential threat necessitates that extraordinary measures be taken to address a crisis. The securitization process, of course, is highly political and thus subject to the whims of the securitizing agent: self-interested actors (for example, governments) can ensure that certain issues constantly remain the top priority in the security agenda.

'Rhetorical contestation' is another example of a process of spreading ideas. It showcases the interface between a claimant, an opposing actor, and the general public (Krebs and Jackson 2007; Crawford 2009). The claimant's argument is framed based on a certain agenda, the implications of which can either be questioned or supported by the opposition, and thereafter accepted by the general public.

The above processes are very strong indicators of how ideas are plotted, traced and disseminated in international relations. However, focusing on processes alone may not be enough. What happens to the whole process, for instance, in the absence of a readily discernible policy initiator? Can the entire process still be launched without a norm entrepreneur, securitizing actor, or claimant? Further, what can possibly push an international relations actor to 'make the first move?' In other words, can ideas still spread, be sold, or take root without an external factor that triggers the first mover to spring into action? In response to these questions, it can be argued that the focus can instead be on the *methods* of strategic communication. These methods highlight the linguistic element in international relations, the rhetoric of actors, and the language games that states play. They revolve around what international relations theorists label the 'intersubjective' quality of interactions within the international realm: those understandings about an interaction that are either shared or differentiated between actors. Focusing on interactions in such a way allows one to trace nuances and textures that are not always readily apparent when one first looks at processes involved in assessing an issue of concern. Furthermore, examining the methods paves the way for centring how language and rhetoric facilitate the effective communication of ideas in international relations.

A method of strategic communication is the notion of frames or the act of framing an issue so that it has more clout in persuading others of its validity and necessity. Frames make apparent an issue and present it as a seamless, coherent portrait. Robert Entman argues: '[t]o frame is to *select some aspects of a perceived reality and make them more salient in a communicating text, in such a way as to promote a particular problem definition, causal interpretation, moral evaluation, and/or treatment recommendation* for the item described' (Entman 1993: 52, emphasis in original). Furthermore, like the securitization model, Entman highlights the very political nature of framing:

> [F]rames select and call attention to particular aspects of the reality described, which logically means that frames simultaneously direct attention away from other aspects. Most frames are defined by what they omit as well as include, and the omissions of potential problem definitions, explanations, evaluations, and recommendations may be as critical as the inclusions in guiding the audience.
>
> (Entman 1993: 54)

A frame, therefore, is a line drawn, albeit arbitrarily, to demarcate what is inside from what is outside – that is, what is relevant to the issue and what is not. In this sense, the method of framing is similar to the method of 'symbolic technologies', which highlights how certain courses of action become possible *because* of the way an issue is framed (Laffey and Weldes 1997). In this chapter, I posit the idea that the US rebalancing strategy was framed in a certain way, which made it persuasive enough to be accepted by the Philippines.

Admittedly, the ontological positions of most of the models discussed here are not entirely dissimilar from each other. However, it is the logic of frames and symbolic technologies and their epistemological commitments that make them highly appropriate for analysing the American rebalancing policy vis-à-vis the Philippines. Without discounting the significant contributions of the *processes* of how ideas spread that have been described above, focusing on the *methods* of strategic communication captures the dynamism of the interaction between the actor who sells the idea, and the actor to whom that idea is being sold. They also highlight the active participation of both actors in the creation of the structure of their relationship. This, however, begs the question of what constitutes a successful 'sale'. I pinpoint two criteria: that the seller can present a coherent and cogent version of the idea being sold, and that the seller and the buyer take coordinated action in response to the idea. The next part of the chapter explores this in the context of examining the US rebalancing initiative in the Asia-Pacific.

Selling an idea: rebalancing as an 'American story'

Effective strategic communication in international relations requires, first and foremost, a clear picture of an idea. In order to do this, the seller needs to justify the idea with the objective of convincing another to buy into it. A 'narrative' – a set of premises and assumptions that can serve as a convincing justification for an idea – is therefore required. In the case at hand, the United States' justification for its rebalancing initiative developed throughout 2011 and early 2012, is framed against the logic of needing to move alongside an increasingly dynamic Asia. This can only be achieved through a continued and deepened American engagement with the region. The so-called 'Asian century' is, after all, already afoot. Moreover, the Organisation for Economic Co-operation and Development notes that China's gross domestic product will soon exceed that of the United States (Cronin 2012). Hence, the rebalancing strategy is meant to refocus America's attention towards and sustain its economic and geopolitical influence within the growing centrality of Asia.

Two key policy statements spelling out the US rebalancing strategy are former US Secretary of State Hillary Clinton's November 2011 *Foreign Policy* article, and US President Obama's speech to the Australian Parliament, also in November 2011 (Clinton 2011; Obama 2011). In both, the message is clear: America is reprioritizing towards the Asian region. The main objectives are to sustain the United States' leadership, to secure its economic and national security interests, and to advance its values. The instruments required to achieve these objectives are strengthening bilateral security alliances, deepening working relationships with emerging partners, engaging with multilateral institutions, expanding trade and investment, forging a broad-based military presence, and advancing democracy and human rights. Crucial in the narrative of the rebalancing strategy is the demonstrated fact that the groundwork has already been laid; efforts and initiatives have already been taken towards closer ties between the United States and Asia.

First, in terms of strengthening bilateral security alliances, the United States aims to adapt to new challenges and opportunities by making its relationships with respective treaty allies 'nimble' – that is, ensuring that they have operational and material capabilities to address threats from either state or non-state actors. Insofar as the Philippines is concerned, the focus has been on counterterrorism after the 11 September 2001 attacks on America. However, efforts are underway to prepare for new challenges, such as the 2+2 meeting held in April 2012 and composed of the foreign and defence secretaries from both countries. The meeting became the venue for both sides to talk about increasing foreign military sales to the Philippines from US$11.9 million in 2011 to US$30 million in 2012 (Bower and Poling 2012). The meeting also resulted in a joint commitment to focus on training and increased rotational access. This would entail joint bilateral activities in non-traditional security areas such as humanitarian aid and disaster relief, addressing climate change, preventing deforestation, illegal fishing and poaching, as well as increasing anti-piracy efforts, cyber security and United Nations peacekeeping missions (Bower and Poling 2012). The recent incident involving the Moro National Liberation Front's seizure of parts of Zamboanga City brings to mind possible dents in the US-Philippines relationship, given that American counterinsurgency assistance is largely located in this geographic area. However, it seems apparent that this is an isolated incident and that the treaty allies were focused on other issues, such as Obama's scheduled visit to the Philippines in mid-October 2013 to discuss ways of expanding America's military presence there (Ager 2013; Fonbuena 2013; Quismundo and Ubac 2013).

Second, apart from working with treaty allies, another policy instrument the United States has applied to its rebalancing strategy is working with emerging partners. This was evident particularly in Obama's visits to Cambodia and Myanmar, and Clinton's visit to Laos. The US-Indonesian relationship also sees improved relations via the United States–Indonesia Comprehensive Partnership. Likewise, US-Vietnamese relations are on their way to greater normalization in regard to more coordination on maritime security issues and related measures.

Multilateralism, the third instrument of the rebalancing strategy, is known to avert the escalation of crises through bargaining (simple and complex) and via the elimination or lowering of reputational costs ('political cover') (Tierney 2011). The United States has made it clear that it wants to be an active member in selected regional multilateral organizations, as manifested in its accession to the Association of Southeast Asian Nations (ASEAN) Treaty of Amity and Cooperation. This initiative enabled Washington to justify its (successful) quest for membership in the East Asia Summit (EAS). The United States has also deepened its involvement in the Asia-Pacific Economic Cooperation grouping, as well as the ASEAN Regional Forum (Manyin *et al.* 2012), and it has appointed a full-time ambassador to the ASEAN Secretariat. Alongside these initiatives are minilateral meetings such as the Lower Mekong Initiative and the Pacific Islands Forum, as well as talks in forums like the Six-Party Talks, and functional efforts like the Proliferation Security Initiative and the ASEAN Maritime Forum. Trilateral opportunities likewise take place with Indonesia, Japan, Kazakhstan, Mongolia and South Korea. As Clinton (2011: 61) remarked:

> Even as we strengthen … bilateral relationships, we have emphasized the importance of multilateral cooperation, for we believe that addressing complex transnational challenges of the sort now faced by Asia requires a set of institutions capable of mustering collective action.

The rebalancing strategy's fourth component is expanding trade and investment. Efforts already undertaken include signing the US-South Korea Free Trade Agreement, hosting the US-ASEAN Business Council forum, launching the US-ASEAN Expanded Economic Engagement (E3) initiative, and formation of the Trans-Pacific Partnership, which could eventually lead to a comprehensive free trade area of the Asia-Pacific (Emmerson 2012).

The rebalancing strategy's economic aspects are perhaps overshadowed by the strategy's fifth instrument: the forging of a more broadly based US strategic presence in the region. Militarily, the rebalancing strategy entails developing an operational concept known as Air–Sea Battle, likely in response to China's 'counter-intervention operations' (McDevitt 2012). The Air–Sea Battle focuses on the disruption of enemy surveillance and launching systems, and the overpowering of enemy missiles and other weapons. Aside from this, within the next seven years, the US Navy is also set to increase the number of ships in the Pacific Fleet from its current 55 percent to 60 percent of total US naval assets. The plan is to build new ships instead of transferring those from the Atlantic Fleet. Meanwhile, the US Air Force will move some of its surveillance capacity from Afghanistan to the Asia-Pacific, including the MQ-9 Reaper, U-2 reconnaissance aircraft, and the Global Hawk (McDevitt 2012). These moves emphasize the importance of security interests like the freedom of navigation, counter-proliferation and military transparency. The role of Southeast Asia here is indeed significant: 'The United States needs cooperation with Southeast Asia to achieve these goals … But also important is that on its own terms Southeast Asia offers new opportunities for partnerships and is sending a strong demand signal for a US presence' (Limaye 2013: 44).

The sixth and final instrument of the rebalancing strategy is the advancement of democracy and human rights. While this has been at least somewhat obscured by the military, economic and diplomatic aspects of the strategy, it is nonetheless still a priority. The United States supported Myanmar's political opening-up, even if said democratization effort was partial at best, because it would rather engage than isolate any member states of the region (Limaye 2013). The motivations of Myanmar notwithstanding – that is, that the promotion of reforms 'reflected less a conversion to liberal ideology than a nationalistic wish to reduce the country's overdependence on China on the one hand, and a desire to catch up with the economies of the modern world on the other' – the United States sees these as 'opportunities for strategic access' (Emmerson 2012: 24).

In sum, the US rebalancing strategy provides a clear picture of renewed American commitment to Asia. Its internal logic emphasizes clear objectives, as well as comprehensive instruments needed to achieve them. Its framing is succinct and presents a coherent and cogent narrative of a justifiable American presence in the region. Taken in isolation, the US portrait of the rebalancing strategy is convincing. However, the China factor made it more persuasive for the Philippines to buy into the idea.

Buying an idea: the 'Philippines' story'

One cannot ignore the role of China in the US rebalancing strategy, although to single it out as the sole driving force of American decisions in the region is, at best, inaccurate. Still, China enriches the narrative of US-Philippines relations, particularly given its assertions in the South China Sea that have turned more vigorous and involve naval confrontations (Simon 2012). China claims historical precedence over these areas, while others, including the Philippines, rely on the United Nations Convention on the Law of the Sea's definitions of territorial waters and exclusive economic zones. Hence, the United States' framing of the rebalancing strategy coincides with China's rise, an emergence which, from the Philippines' perspective, is something of which to be wary. In this context, the United States' rebalancing therefore became a very attractive and persuasive idea for the Philippines.

Traditionally, the United States has been perceived to revive its relations with the Philippines every time a crisis occurred (de Castro 2009, 2010). In the mid-1990s, the Mischief Reef incident helped to revive US-Philippines military ties; in 1995, the US Navy Seals held a combined exercise with Philippines counterparts, and participated in a larger joint military combined exercise with air, land and naval operations the following year; and in 1996, negotiations on renewing the old Status of Forces Agreement between the United States and the Philippines began, which led to the ratification of the Visiting Forces Agreement between the two countries in 1999. Moreover, the United States dispersed military stations in the littorals of southern Mindanao and developed Cooperative Security Locations in the Philippines.[1]

However, the 2011 stand-off between the Philippines and China over Scarborough Shoal evoked a more measured American response. The United States is not a claimant in the South China Sea, and does not and cannot support one claim over another. Therefore, explicit US support for the Philippines on this issue cannot be forthcoming because the United States does not interpret the Mutual Defense Treaty Between the Republic of the Philippines and the United States as encompassing the Philippines' territorial claims. Interestingly, this is in contrast to the US interpretation of the Treaty of Mutual Cooperation and Security between the United States and Japan, where the United States is committed to defend an external attack on the Senkaku Islands because Japan has long exercised de facto 'administration' over the territory.

In March 2011, two Chinese patrol boats were said to have harassed a Philippines survey ship that was conducting oil explorations in Reed Bank. The Philippines immediately filed a protest with the Chinese embassy in

Manila. However, the embassy responded by insisting that China has sovereignty over the Nansha (Spratly) Islands and adjacent territories (de Castro 2012). By June, China had disclosed plans to construct an oil rig within the Philippines' exclusive economic zone. Any oil exploration activities required Chinese permission, Beijing insisted, even if said explorations were well within the Philippines exclusive economic zone. China's argument was based on a map it presented to the United Nations that highlighted a '9-dash line', which allows it to claim sovereignty over most of the South China Sea. At this point, the Philippines launched all possible diplomatic means to address the issue, including pursuing legal arbitration with the United Nations in January 2013. China's preference has always been to address issues bilaterally, and in February it rejected the Philippines' submission. Talks are now ongoing between ASEAN and China in order to begin discussions about a code of conduct. However, tensions remain high among the actors involved (Storey 2013a, 2013b).

In the wake of events in the South China Sea, the US rebalancing strategy appears very attractive and persuasive to the Philippines. Under the umbrella of a rebalancing strategy, the Philippines can work on a constructive relationship with China and, at the same time, be guaranteed of a US presence and engagement in the region. Choosing between the two therefore becomes irrelevant. This is similar to Satu P. Limaye's observation that:

> US primacy provides Asia the space to have confident and productive dealings with China and carry out nation and state-building activities. Neither the United States nor China have asked the region to make an exclusive choice. That is a straw man – or a 'fallacy of choice'. The region has already made a choice – and that choice is that it wants US ability to ensure order so that the region can have constructive and mutual benefits from relations with China.
>
> (Limaye 2013: 49–50)

The US's rebalancing strategy in Asia also permits the Philippines to align its own programme of territorial defence with America's agenda in the region.[2] While the Americans will not formally commit to defending the Philippines' territorial claims under the Mutual Defense Treaty, the US Navy has every interest in sustaining freedom of maritime access throughout Southeast Asia (Thayer 2013). In this sense, the Philippines' efforts to modernize its military forces dovetails nicely with the rebalancing strategy's emphasis on a continued and strengthened American strategic presence and with the notion that alliance burden sharing is being systematically pursued. The United States and Philippines' joint activities in this context include assistance in the establishment of the Coast Watch South project, which provides partial funding for 17 coast watch stations. Other discussions in the same assistance programme include establishing an additional 30 coast watch stations between the waters of Mindanao and Borneo to stop smuggling, drug trafficking and terrorism.

Between March and April 2012, joint exercises were conducted involving 1,500 US and Philippines Marines in the Philippines exclusive economic zone of Reed Bank in the South China Sea (Simon 2012).

Accordingly, a key reason why the US rebalancing strategy has become attractive to the Philippines relates to China's behaviour and enhancement of its military strength. The framing of the rebalancing strategy is set against what appears to be – at least from the Philippines perspective – China's objectionable activities in the South China Sea. In this sense, applying the logic of securitization, rhetorical contestation and framing allows the claim that Philippines acceptance and support of the US rebalancing strategy was possible largely because of China's actions. China thus becomes the variable that allows the successful trade (selling and buying) of the rebalancing strategy idea.

Conclusion

Effective strategic communication in international relations depends not just on the presence and interaction of both seller and buyer, but also on the actions they decide to take together. In the case of the rebalancing strategy, the United States sold the idea, and the Philippines bought it, as measured by their joint activities. Admittedly, the strategy is very new and it is perhaps too soon to conclude whether it will continue in the foreseeable future. Several challenges need to be overcome to make it more sustainable, but some policy options or avenues are open to both sides of the Pacific.

First, the United States needs to be more active in trying to reconcile the interests of the claimant states in the South China Sea. This could be done bilaterally or multilaterally. Bilaterally, it could continue to improve its relations with the ASEAN claimants (such as the Philippines and Vietnam), and also with China. More areas of cooperation need to receive as much attention as that given to the military, such as non-traditional security issues of disaster relief and management. Multilaterally, the United States could offer support to help ASEAN and China formalize a code of conduct in the South China Sea. Given the 2015 deadline for ASEAN's economic integration, the United States could assist in ensuring that the agendas of the various regional arrangements in Southeast Asia coalesce into achieving a more 'people-centred approach', which is at the heart of the integration ideal.

Second, Southeast Asian countries need to consolidate their voices under the ASEAN framework. As a corollary, ASEAN must be able to ensure that multilateral efforts produce concrete outcomes. By so doing, it will increase its credibility and strengthen its clout in the region and beyond. This directly relates to the objectives of Washington's rebalancing strategy, insofar as it will eventually need to 'sell' the same idea to ASEAN as a single entity or unit. This will remain difficult, if not futile, if ASEAN cannot make the voices of ten diverse members cohesive.

It is evident that the United States has been able to sell the idea of the rebalancing strategy to the Philippines. This, however, begs another question.

While effective strategic communication in international relations may pave the way for policy changes, and while it may ensure that appropriate courses of action are taken, it remains impossible to know whether actors have made changes or taken action because they were forced, coerced or persuaded by the seller or by circumstances in general. Or do actors simply buy into an idea and strategies that emanate from it because they have internalized the idea that was communicated to them to the extent that they form and adhere to a concrete norm? This matters because there are certain ideas prevalent in international relations that enjoy the status of inherent realities. Yet do we really know that ideas have changed – not just policies but also the thinking and values of international actors? Is there a way of knowing? Indeed, does it matter that we know? To echo the words of former US Secretary of Defense Donald Rumsfeld, 'there are known knowns; there are things we know we know. We also know there are known unknowns; that is to say we know there are some things we do not know. But there are also unknown unknowns – the ones we don't know we don't know' (United States Department of Defense 2002).

Notes

1 Cooperative Security Locations are heavy infrastructure bases that can accommodate larger forces and can be outfitted with supplies and equipment. See de Castro (2009).
2 Similarly, the Philippines is encouraging the evolution of its strategic relationship with Japan. See Amador (2013).

References

Ager, Maila (2013) 'Obama PH Visit will Press Ahead Despite Zamboanga Crisis – DFA Chief', *Inquirer Global Nation*, 19 September, globalnation.inquirer.net/85965/obama-ph-visit-will-press-ahead-despite-zamboanga-crisis-dfa-chief (accessed 19 September 2013).

Amador, III, Julio S. (2013) 'The Philippines' Security Cooperation with the United States and Japan', *Asia Pacific Bulletin*, 227(8 August), www.eastwestcenter.org/sites/default/files/private/apb227.pdf (accessed 25 August 2013).

Bitzinger, Richard A. (2012) 'Will the US Pivot Trigger a New Regional Arms Race?' *Global Asia*, 7(4): 34–37.

Björkdahl, Annika (2002) 'Norms in International Relations: Some Conceptual and Methodological Reflections', *Cambridge Review of International Affairs*, 15(1): 9–23.

Bower, Ernest and Poling, Gregory (2012) 'Implications and Results: United States–Philippines Ministerial Dialogue', Washington, DC: Center for Strategic and International Studies, 4 May, csis.org/publication/implications-and-results-united-states-philippines-ministerial-dialogue (accessed 22 August 2013).

Buzan, Barry (1983) *People, States, and Fear: The National Security Problem in International Relations*, Chapel Hill, NC: University of North Carolina Press.

Buzan, Barry, Wæver, Ole and de Wilde, Jaap (1997) *Security: A New Framework for Analysis*, Boulder, CO: Lynne Rienner.

Checkel, Jeffrey T. (1998) 'The Constructivist Turn in International Relations Theory', *World Politics*, 50(2): 324–48.

Clinton, Hillary (2011) 'America's Pacific Century', *Foreign Policy*, 189(November): 56–63.

Crawford, Neta C. (2009) '*Homo Politicus* and Argument (Nearly) All the Way Down: Persuasion in Politics', *Perspectives on Politics*, 7(1): 103–24.

Cronin, Patrick M. (2012) 'As the World Rebalances in the Asian-Pacific Century, So Must the United States', *Global Asia*, 7(4): 8–13.

de Castro, Renato Cruz (2009) 'The US–Philippine Alliance: An Evolving Hedge Against an Emerging China Challenge', *Contemporary Southeast Asia*, 31(3): 399–423.

——(2010) 'Engaging Both the Eagle and the Dragon: The Philippines' Precarious and Futile Attempt in Equi-balancing', *Pacific Focus*, 25(3): 356–75.

——(2012) 'The Philippines in 2011: Muddling Through a Year of Learning and Adjustment', *Asian Survey*, 52(1): 210–19.

Emmerson, Donald K. (2012) 'Challenging ASEAN: The US Pivot through Southeast Asia's Eyes', *Global Asia*, 7(4): 22–27.

Entman, Robert M. (1993) 'Framing: Toward Clarification of a Fractured Paradigm', *Journal of Communication*, 43(4): 51–58.

Finnemore, Martha (1996) *National Interests in International Society*, Ithaca, NY: Cornell University Press.

Finnemore, Martha and Sikkink, Kathryn (1998) 'International Norm Dynamics and Political Change', *International Organization*, 52(4): 887–917.

Fonbuena, Carmela (2013) '6 Killed, 24 Hurt in Zamboanga Clashes', *Rappler*, 9 September, www.rappler.com/nation/38432-mnlf-hostages-zamboanga-city (accessed 19 September 2013).

Glosserman, Brad (2013) 'Rhetoric and Reality of the US Rebalance', *East Asia Forum*, 30 July, www.eastasiaforum.org/2013/07/30/rhetoric-and-reality-of-the-us-rebalance (accessed 22 August 2013).

Hopf, Ted (1998) 'The Promise of Constructivism in International Relations Theory', *International Security*, 23(1): 171–200.

Katzenstein, Peter J. (ed.) (1996) *The Culture of National Security: Norms and Identity in World Politics*, New York: Columbia University Press.

Klotz, Audie (1995) *Norms in International Relations: The Struggle Against Apartheid*, Ithaca, NY: Cornell University Press.

Krebs, Ronald R. and Jackson, Patrick Thaddeus (2007) 'Twisting Tongues and Twisting Arms: The Power of Political Rhetoric', *European Journal of International Relations*, 13(1): 35–66.

Laffey, Mark and Weldes, Jutta (1997) 'Beyond Belief: Ideas and Symbolic Technologies in the Study of International Relations', *European Journal of International Relations*, 3(2): 193–237.

Limaye, Satu P. (2013) 'Southeast Asia in America's Rebalance to the Asia-Pacific', in Daljit Singh (ed.) *Southeast Asian Affairs 2013*, Singapore: Institute of Southeast Asian Studies, pp. 40–50.

Manyin, Mark E., Daggett, Stephen, Dolven, Ben, Lawrence, Susan V., Martin, Michael F., O'Rourke, Ronald and Vaughn, Bruce (2012) 'Pivot to the Pacific? The Obama Administration's "Rebalancing" Toward Asia', *CRS Report for Congress*, 28 March, www.fas.org/sgp/crs/natsec/R42448.pdf (accessed 23 September 2013).

McDevitt, Michael (2012) 'America's New Security Strategy Dimension and its Military Dimension', *Global Asia*, 7(4): 14–17.

Misalucha, Charmaine G. (2011) 'Southeast Asia–US Relations: Hegemony or Hierarchy?' *Contemporary Southeast Asia*, 33(2): 209–28.

——(2012) *The Problem of Describing Relations Between the United States and Southeast Asian Nations: A Study of Political Language Games*, Lewiston, NY: Edwin Mellen Press.

Obama, Barack (2011) 'Remarks by President Obama to the Australian Parliament', 17 November, www.whitehouse.gov/the-press-office/2011/11/17/remarks-president-obama-australian-parliament (accessed 22 August 2013).

Palan, Ronen (2000) 'A World of Their Making: An Evaluation of the Constructivist Critique in International Relations', *Review of International Studies*, 26(4): 575–98.

Panke, Diana and Petersohn, Ulrich (2012) 'Why International Norms Disappear Sometimes', *European Journal of International Relations*, 18(4): 719–42.

Payne, Rodger A. (2001) 'Persuasion, Frames and Norm Construction', *European Journal of International Relations*, 7(1): 37–61.

Quismundo, Tarra and Ubac, Michael Lim (2013) 'Obama Visit Seen to Boost Security Ties Mid China Row', *Inquirer Global Nation*, 15 September, globalnation.inquirer.net/85641/obama-visit-seen-to-boost-security-ties-mid-china-row (accessed 19 September 2013).

Simon, Sheldon W. (2012) 'Conflict and Diplomacy in the South China Sea: The View from Washington', *Asian Survey*, 52(6): 995–1018.

Storey, Ian (2013a) 'The South China Sea Dispute (Part 1): Negative Trends Continue in 2013', *China Brief*, 13(12) (7 June): 3–6.

——(2013b) 'The South China Sea Dispute (Part 2): Friction to Remain the Status Quo', *China Brief*, 13(13) (21 June): 2–5.

Thayer, Carlyle A. (2013) 'US Rebalancing: What Regional Support?' *Thayer Consultancy Background Brief*, 27 May, www.scribd.com/doc/152363766/Thayer-U-S-Rebalancing-What-Regional-Support (accessed 25 August 2013).

Tierney, Dominic (2011) 'Multilateralism: America's Insurance Policy Against Loss', *European Journal of International Relations*, 17(4): 655–78.

United States Department of Defense (2002) 'DoD News Briefing – Secretary Rumsfeld and Gen. Myers', 12 February, www.defense.gov/transcripts/transcript.aspx?transcriptid=2636 (accessed 19 September 2013).

——(2012) 'Sustaining US Global Leadership: Priorities for 21st Century Defense', Washington, DC: United States Department of Defense, January.

Wendt, Alexander (1999) *Social Theory of International Politics*, Cambridge: Cambridge University Press.

9 A reluctant ally?

Thailand in the US rebalancing strategy

Kitti Prasirtsuk and William T. Tow

Perhaps more than any other formal US ally in Asia, Thailand has been successful in striking a careful balance between sustaining cordial alliance relations with Washington and pursuing an intensifying and comprehensive relationship with China. Such a quest is hardly unique in Thai history. Thailand has survived as an independent state even during the years of Western colonization and the Japanese invasion by successfully 'bending with the wind' – identifying the correct timing and circumstances as to when it must deal with various great powers without incurring the long-term animosity of any one of them (Kislenko 2002).

Accordingly, the Barack Obama Administration's rebalancing initiative presents Thailand with a unique policy challenge. By implication, the United States is signalling that it is not only 'back' in Asia as a strategic player, but it is also expecting formal treaty allies such as Thailand to engage in greater 'capacity building' in order to facilitate a regional power balance designed to preclude growing Chinese power from transforming into Chinese regional hegemony. This at least implicitly contradicts Thailand's traditional strategic logic which rests on the assumption that it will be granted sufficient leeway by both the United States and China to shape its own form of alliance and strategic relations with them, and largely on its own terms. Such a contradiction may further intensify in the aftermath of the Thai military assuming power in the country during late May 2014 and the subsequent US levying of sanctions against Thailand. How Thailand responds to increased US pressure will be a key test case for how other US allies and various US security partners – each with their own version of reconciling the dichotomy of Sino–American influence and rivalries in the Asia-Pacific – might shape regional order building in accordance with their national security and broader policy interests.

This chapter argues that Thailand will only be a 'reluctant ally' of the United States if the rebalancing strategy evolves in ways that privilege the military and geopolitical dimensions of regional politics. If the Obama Administration and its successors are effective in cultivating a wide-ranging rebalancing posture and in modifying the American tendency to link Washington's own version of democratic politics with an insistence that Thai leaders conform to Western norms, Thailand will perceive, welcome and cultivate areas of policy convergence between the United States and itself. A broader approach to rebalancing will dovetail with traditional Thai preferences for creating 'room to manoeuvre' when dealing with great power politics and rivalries. In the Sino–American case, for example, Thailand can resort to nurturing viable and enduring avenues of cooperation in the economic, diplomatic and security sectors – often using its membership in the Association of Southeast Asian Nations (ASEAN) as a bridge for pursuing such interaction and, where possible, highlighting successful collaboration with both powers in relatively low-key or low-risk, non-traditional security sectors. Such an outcome would conform to both China's preference for dealing with its regional neighbours on a 'win–win' basis, and with the Obama Administration's stated preference to apply rebalancing across a wide range of policy areas.

This chapter initially provides a brief survey of developments in Thai-US security relations, both preceding and following US President George W. Bush's December 2003 announcement that Thailand would be regarded as a 'major non-NATO [North Atlantic Treaty Organization] ally'. In reality, the extent to which Thailand has conformed to Bush's original expectation of supporting US global security policy in return for continued US military assistance is debatable. Thailand's ongoing policy dilemma of adjudicating its traditional status as a US security treaty ally with its increasing propensity to adopt a 'hedging strategy' in its relations with great powers is then examined. This relates to the very difficult process of alliance transition in the post-Cold War era and to the extent that Thailand can still be considered a US 'ally' as opposed to a more qualified US security 'partner' for achieving selected policy objectives where the two interests coincide. The chapter concludes by offering a few policy observations on how the process of reconciling Thailand's national security imperatives with selected US regional security interests may already be under way, and how that process might be sustained despite recent bilateral tensions precipitated by Thailand's domestic politics.

Background

Prior to the winding down of the second Indochina War, Thailand was a staunch US ally, firmly embedded within the American sphere of influence. At the height of that conflict in 1969, Thailand had deployed nearly 12,000 troops in South Vietnam, while the United States Air Force deployed and operated from a number of Thai air bases, including Udorn, Korat, Nakhon Phanom, U-Tapao, Takli and Bangkok Airfields until 1976 – part of a complex that included nine US-Thai joint military bases in Thailand. The United States' military presence was initially justified by the 1954 Manila Pact that formed the Southeast Asia Treaty Organization (SEATO) and cemented by the March 1962 Rusk–Thanat Communiqué which reaffirmed Thailand's cooperation to prevent the communist domination of Indochina.

The Nixon Doctrine (announced in August 1969) combined with the de facto normalization of Sino–American relations prompted Bangkok to modify its traditional post-war collective defence relationship with the United States and to adopt a more 'evenhanded' security posture toward Beijing (Chinwanno 2004: 196). Indeed, Thai leaders came to view the American military presence as an increasing liability. Washington was clearly unwilling to maintain American troops on mainland Southeast Asia so it became politically impossible for the United States to send massive troops, as it did in Vietnam, to protect Thailand.

The end of the Thanom Kittikachorn regime and the brief establishment of a civilian-led Thai government in 1974 led to the eventual withdrawal of 27,000 US military personnel from March 1975 to mid-1976, Thailand's establishment of diplomatic relations with China in 1975, and initial efforts by Thai diplomats to cultivate reconciliation with the newly established bloc of Indochinese communist states that emerged in the aftermath of the US military withdrawal from Southeast Asia in 1975. Thailand also responded negatively to a May 1975 unilateral US decision to use American aircraft deployed at U-Tapao to assist in the rescue of the American container ship *SS Mayaguez* from a Khmer Rouge boarding party, by restricting US military access to Thai basing facilities.

Vietnam's invasion of Cambodia in December 1978 brought Thai and US interests at least partially back into alignment as those two countries, in conjunction with the other ASEAN members and China, opposed Hanoi's action. The major outcome of the Cambodian crisis, however, was the intensification of relations between Thailand and China, united by their mutual distrust of Vietnam. When the threat from Vietnam was looming large after its invasion and subsequent occupation of Cambodia in late 1978, Thailand increasingly relied on a tacit Chinese deterrent and Beijing's support of Cambodian resistance groups to ensure that Vietnamese troops would not probe too deeply into Thai border areas (Chinwanno 2008: 10–12). By 1983, moreover, China had reduced or discontinued its assistance to communist insurgency movements operating in Thailand and in other ASEAN member states. Vietnamese troops frequently attacked Khmer Rouge elements operating on the Thai side of the Thai-Cambodian border against Vietnamese occupation troops in Cambodia, with at least the tacit support of both Thailand and China. Meanwhile, the United States and Thailand initiated the annual Cobra Gold exercises in June 1982 (which have since grown to become the world's largest combined military drill), and reached a landmark agreement to create a 'war reserve stockpile' – the first of its kind outside NATO and South Korea (Stern 2009).

China countered this development by courting Thailand with an upgrade of its military sales/assistance programmes to the Thais in 1986. These included the transfer of armoured personnel carriers, artillery and missiles. Over the following decade, US sanctions were levied against Thai military governments on human rights grounds, and Cobra Gold exercises were temporarily suspended in mid-1992 following the 'Black May' massacre orchestrated by a military regime that had assumed power in Thailand the previous year. US-Thai security relations were further complicated by apparent inconsistencies in US arms sales programmes to Thailand (and throughout Southeast Asia), between restrictions on the transfer of new defence technologies imposed by Bill Clinton's Administration which was determined to defuse the arms race in Southeast Asia while simultaneously pressing for a Thai purchase of advanced air combat systems. Alternative Chinese, Russian or European sources of weapons supply, however, 'offered far less satisfactory packages, minimal follow up support, inferior training, and equipment that the Thai military was not at all prepared to embrace as a substitute for American-made military hardware' (Stern 2009: 2).

In a broader context, by the late 1990s, Thai policymakers were clearly shifting their overall assessments on the utility of the US alliance to Thailand's national security interests. Civilian government had returned to Thailand in September 1992 with Chuan Leekpai's election as prime minister. It had nevertheless become increasingly clear that a combination of economic, political and security differences emerging in the Thai-US bilateral relationship had sharpened to the point where the original rationales underlying postwar security collaboration between the two countries were becoming more strained. Thailand's rejection of a 1994 US request to pre-position American military supply ships in Thai territorial waters was indicative of this trend, as was Thailand's decision to join the Non-Aligned Movement in 1993. These developments exposed Bangkok's increasing tendency to interpret global geopolitics differently relative to how US policymakers viewed the world. It also underscored the Thai government's priority to cultivate more cordial ties with China and its Indochinese neighbours as part of Thailand's quest to make the newly established ASEAN Regional Forum a comprehensive dialogue forum for regional confidence building and conflict mitigation (Richardson 1994). The Bill Clinton Administration's qualified response to the 1997 Asian financial crisis appeared to be tepid and insensitive to Thailand's policymakers who were desperately endeavouring to manage their country's impossible financial situation. It may also have reflected Washington's displeasure over Thailand's adoption of a 'constructive engagement' posture toward Myanmar (later reversed when Thai-Burmese relations soured over refugee camps and narcotic flows, prompting the Myanmar military's incursion into Thai border areas) at the same time that the United States was advocating the imposition of sanctions against Rangoon. Tensions were further aggravated with the failure of the Thai and US governments to refinance Thailand's purchase of American F/18 aircraft at the same time as US executive and Congressional condemnations of Thailand's alleged human rights transgressions.

As the twenty-first century unfolded, US-Thai security relations evolved as a more qualified alliance. Differences over the two countries' economic relations, military commerce and Thai domestic politics 'spilled over' to affect the compatibility of their regional and international security postures. As one observer has since noted:

> In instances where Washington and Bangkok do not have a commonality of interest, or where Thailand does not see its defense equities as being at stake, it has indeed become harder to get Thailand to support US positions. The increasing complexity of regional relations, and growing political sophistication of the members of ASEAN in diplomacy, have combined to yield a Thailand that does not feel the compunction to automatically support US positions on regional and global challenges, to make contributions to international peacekeeping efforts at the level the United States feels is appropriate, to support US positions on regional arms procurement issues, or to accommodate US access and prepositioning requirements.
>
> (Stern 2009: 4–5)

It is important to remember that neither Washington nor Bangkok sought outright alliance dissolution. Rather, the growing policy fluidity actually generated opportunities for American security planners and their Thai counterparts to find new rationales for sustaining their long-standing bilateral security ties. Both sides still valued their enduring bilateral relations sufficiently to travel this path. US arms sales to Thailand intensified during the period 2000–01 – partially to counter what Washington viewed as increasing Chinese influence over Thailand – and a bilateral counterterrorism centre was founded even prior to the 11 September 2001 terrorist strikes in New York and Washington. Following those attacks, the Thaksin Shinawatra government allowed the United States over-flight rights and the right to re-fuel military aircraft at U-Tapao in support of Operation Enduring Freedom in Afghanistan. Thailand subsequently contributed engineering and medical teams to support reconstruction efforts in Afghanistan, dispatched troops to Iraq following the US invasion of that country in 2003 for peace-building missions, and allowed US access to its ports to reinforce both of those missions' logistical tails. It also joined the Container Security Initiative and captured Hambali, a major al-Qaeda figure who was hiding and planning future terrorist operations in the Thai city of Ayuthaya (background on these developments is offered by Chambers 2004).

The December 2004 Indian Ocean tsunami was one of the first instances where the US-Thai 'alliance adaptability' posture became clearly evident as Thailand's vulnerability to natural disasters combined with its geographic position to facilitate closer security cooperation. Thailand approved the United States' Combined Support Force (CS-536) access to U-Tapao and Sattahip naval base for transporting US forces stationed from Japan to Phuket, Sumatra, and other areas hard hit by the disaster. This experience underscored the extent to which Thailand remained unprepared to interact logistically with other parties in multilateral disaster relief and reconstruction efforts, and its need to work with the US Pacific Command and other relevant parties to strengthen such capabilities (Stern 2009: 7). Traditional 'threat-centric' rationales binding the alliance were being supplanted by more diffuse regional and international contingencies where sovereign principles and interests were less important. This trend was reinforced in 2008 when initial Thai efforts to assist Myanmar in the aftermath of Cyclone Nargis were rebuffed by the Burmese junta, which nevertheless allowed US relief operations to proceed in early May via the Office of US Foreign Disaster Assistance response team. A subsequent ASEAN relief effort was organized by Thailand and Singapore, but the lesson had been driven home that any substantial Thai capacity to deliver non-traditional security resources to Southeast Asian locales or beyond would only be developed in conjunction with greater training and support provided by Thailand's US ally. Since 2008, large components of the annual Cobra Gold exercises have been earmarked for training to respond to non-traditional security scenarios. In 2010, Thailand also contributed two naval ships to a peacekeeping operation in the Gulf of Aden off the coast of Somalia, and to a second peacekeeping mission in Darfur, Sudan.

Thailand continued to receive US Foreign Military Financing and International Military Education Training funds until the May 2014 military coup in Thailand. As a major non-NATO ally, it also had access to the Excess Defense Articles programme, which allows for the transfer of used US naval ships and aircraft (for a breakdown of US Foreign Military Financing assistance to Thailand from 2007 to 2013, see Chanlett-Avery and Dolven 2013: 13). Some of these programmes were cancelled or frozen following the Thai military coup in September 2006 to remove the Thaksin government, but were restored as Thailand moved back towards holding a democratic national election in December 2007 (Chanlett-Avery and Dolven 2013: 7). Following the May 2014 coup, the United States suspended US$3.5 million in funding and training for the Thai military (which totalled around US$10.5 million for 2013), and cancelled ongoing joint naval exercises that involved approximately 700 US forces. Scheduled visits by Thai police delegations to US federal law enforcement centres in Washington were also cancelled (*Bangkok Post* 2014b, 2014d). In late June 2014, in testimony to the US Congress, a US State Department official noted that the United States had increased its suspension of funds to US$4.7 million (*Bangkok Post* 2014c).

It is unclear what the future holds for US-Thai military collaboration. Cobra Gold has expanded to involve over 13,000 military personnel (around 9,000 US forces, 4,000 Thai forces, and other military contingents from Indonesia, Japan, Malaysia, Singapore and South Korea). These have recently included observers from Myanmar (in 2013), and even 17 People's Liberation Army personnel participated in its 2014 humanitarian relief component (Chan and Wee 2014). Intelligence cooperation and law enforcement training (largely geared toward counterterrorism and counter-narcotics operations) continue apace. However, in late June 2014, a US State Department spokesperson revealed that the United States was considering moving the 2015 Cobra Gold exercise from Thailand to Darwin (*Bangkok Post* 2014c). He announced that the small (if symbolic) contingent of Thai military personnel slated to participate in the 22-nation Rim of the Pacific 2014 maritime warfare exercise conducted out of Honolulu would also be excluded (Sky News Australia 2014).

At the time of writing, the US-Thai alliance remained a relatively viable instrument of Southeast Asian security cooperation, even though the focus and missions of that bilateral relationship has moved away significantly from the Cold War calculus that initially underpinned its founding. As will be discussed below, however, this situation, if not carefully managed by both Washington and Bangkok, could deteriorate markedly.

Thailand: ally or partner?

The 1962 Rusk–Thanat Communiqué remains the hallmark for defining US-Thai security relations, although it has been recently supplemented by the '2012 Joint Vision Statement for the Thai-US Defense Alliance'. The usual rationale for forming any alliance is to combine members' capabilities in ways that enhance their mutual military support 'against some external actor(s) in some specified set of circumstances' (Walt 1997: 157). The Rusk–Thanat Communiqué was clearly 'threat centric' and directed towards a commonly perceived adversary: communist forces operating in Indochina. It evolved from Thai concerns that SEATO was insufficient for deterring communist advances in Laos from spilling over to threaten Thailand's security and an American willingness to offer assurances it would defend Thailand from such a contingency if it were to materialize, even if SEATO were not activated (the American motivations behind the Rusk–Thanat Communiqué are discussed in Rusk 1961; see also van der Kroef 1976: 10). The joint vision statement, issued a half century later, was completely devoid of threat-centric language, focusing instead on such factors as 'regional and multilateral security cooperation', force modernization and 'shared values' (United States Department of Defense 2012).

Only the vision statement's shared values criterion appears to conform to traditional alliance characteristics. These are a security relationship: 1) that is defined by a formal treaty or agreement with a foreign state; 2) that is binding by international law; 3) that is designed to pursue mutual security interests and those common international values or norms to which the treaty's member states adhere against a clearly defined state-centric challenge to those interests and norms; and 4) that anticipates the application of member-state force assets in the defence of those interests in norms if challenged by an external hostile force.[1]

It is clear that despite US officials' references to Thailand, along with Australia, Japan, the Philippines and South Korea, as an alliance 'bedrock' of the US strategic balance in the Asia-Pacific, Thai strategic circumstances and interests diverge substantially from those of Washington (see Russel 2013). Apart from the primordial Manila Pact, there is no formal mutual defence treaty governing Thai-US security relations as is the case with America's other four 'formal' Asia-Pacific regional allies, and thus no bilateral collective defence treaty in place between Bangkok and Washington that enjoys the weight of international legal recognition. Nor is there any US-Thai equivalent of the US-Japanese and US-South Korean status of forces agreements or US-Philippines visiting forces agreement. Any US proposal for such an arrangement would certainly be rejected by the Thai public as undue interference in Thailand's sovereign affairs. However, the exchange of notes between US and Thai officials that accompanied the Rusk–Thanat Communiqué is recognized by the United States as a 'formal executive agreement' that the US Senate has affirmed other aspects of the United States' security relations with Thailand. Intermittent and informal US military access to Thai bases for relatively uncontroversial and largely non-traditional security-oriented missions is the best that Washington can now expect of its Thai 'ally'. This reality was underscored in June 2012 when the Yingluck Shinawatra government declined to meet the American deadline for approving the US National Aeronautics and Space Administration's (NASA) proposed Southeast Asia Composition, Cloud, Climate Coupling Regional Study. The study was to be conducted at U-Tapao but was delayed indefinitely by the Thais on the grounds that it was unclear if such atmospheric observation could have national security implications by at least indirectly linking Thailand to US intelligence surveillance operations directed against China or other regional targets (*Bangkok Post* 2012).

Another alliance criterion – a mutual will to defend commonly understood norms – has greater salience in the US-Thai security relationship. Both countries have a long history of generally adhering to democratic principles. Even here, however, tensions exist to the point where such compatibility remains conditional. Signs of intensifying tensions emerged during the first half of 2014. Although it was prepared prior to the May coup, a US Department of State Trafficking in Persons report released in late June 2014 demoted Thailand from a Tier 2 watchlist to Tier 3 – the lowest possible ranking. The Thai permanent secretary for foreign affairs expressed 'deep regret and disappointment' in disagreement with the US assessment (Ministry of Foreign Affairs, Thailand 2014; *Bangkok Post* 2014a).

Washington has criticized other aspects of Thailand's current policies. In a speech delivered to the Shangri-La Dialogue at the end of May, US Secretary of Defense Chuck Hagel (2014) warned Thai military leaders to release those who had been detained and to move their country towards free elections if they wished to avoid further suspension of US military assistance and engagement with Bangkok.

In reality, Thai politics is infinitely more complex than merely complying with broad generalizations about human rights violations or political liberalization by American and foreign press sources. It includes the rise of populist trends in the northern and northeastern parts of the country which arguably have historical equivalents in American history, and an intractable separatist insurgency in four southern Muslim provinces that have confronted Thai central governments of various persuasions. Western human rights advocates have been critical of Bangkok's management of the latter contingency, but disparate factions within the southern separatist movement have made negotiating long-term solutions an elusive and highly frustrating process (Chanlett-Avery and Dolven 2013: 11).

Finally, there is an evident disconnect between US and Thai perceptions on how to manage the 'rise of China' within the context of their own alliance relations. The logic underlying the US rebalancing initiative appears to be somewhat inconsistent to those Thai policy planners who have a problem reconciling US insistence that it wishes to engage with China or 'enmesh' within a new regional order, while simultaneously at least implying that an accelerated US strategic presence in Asia is necessary to achieve a desired 'balance' within any such order. Unlike during the Cold War, Bangkok no longer regards China as a probable national security threat and, unlike other ASEAN members, it neither shares a contiguous border with China nor does it entertain territorial claims that involve Chinese counter-claims. It has even entered into a 'comprehensive strategic cooperative partnership' with China when Prime Minister Yingluck and her top military chiefs visited Beijing consecutively in April 2012 (Prasirtsuk 2013: 34). While this initiative cannot yet match the depth and durability of the US-Thai alliance, it seems indicative of Thailand's determination to project a posture of strategic equilibrium toward China and the United States. This posture was further demonstrated when de facto Thai Defence Minister General Surasak Kanjanarat led a delegation to China in early June 2014 for annual talks on regional security and joint training. Meeting with Lieutenant-General Wang Guanzhong, the deputy chief of staff of the People's Liberation Army, the Thai contingent discussed 'closer cooperation in military affairs, training, and weaponry development' with its Chinese hosts. Just days before Surasak's departure, Thai coup leader General Prayuth Chanocha had observed that Thailand was now a partner of China 'at every level', while China had already made clear that it regarded Thailand's political problems as 'an internal issue' (Jory 2014).

The legacy of expensive US weapons systems has also weighed on the minds of Thai military planners, who remain determined to diversify their future military acquisitions. In mid-February 2014, reports were intensifying that the Poly Technologies and China Precision Machinery Import-Export Corporation was negotiating with Thai defence officials to sell Thailand the FD-2000 medium- to long-range surface-to-air missile, the FL-3000N ship-based surface-to-air missile system, and the FK-1000 mobile air defence system. Independent analysts are observing that 'it appears that the Thai government wants to strike a balance by encouraging its association with China … since Thailand's dependence on China economically is too strong to be overlooked' (Chansoria 2014). China is Thailand's largest trading partner and second largest foreign direct investor after Japan.[2]

If Thailand has not been a 'complete' US bilateral ally in the traditional sense that US post-war strategy would anticipate, could it at least be classified as a strong US security partner? This question is not only complicated by Washington's classification of Thailand as a 'major non-NATO ally' and by recent US–Thai political tensions but also by how an American security 'partner' should be perceived in the early twenty-first century.

One American analyst has attempted to differentiate between 'formal' US alliance relations and those conducted by the United States with countries designated as complying with 'major non-NATO ally' status. Larry Wortzel (2005) observes that the latter status is assigned to those states the United States wishes to 'engage in joint research and development on military systems and to cooperate on matters like counterterrorism'. Such states have built close working relations with the US Armed Forces over time and qualify for US military assistance and sales without the rigorous Congressional oversight that is normally exercised when the US government is contemplating such transactions. Thailand 'earned' such status when the Thaksin regime (belatedly) supported the US military interventions in Afghanistan and Iraq, but the momentum underlying this American recognition was stymied by Thaksin's removal from power three years later in September 2006. As Thitinan Pongsudhirak (2012: 76), a respected Thai analyst and professor at Chulalongkorn University, subsequently observed:

> The Americans have tried during the post-[2006] coup period to 'revitalise' this bilateral alliance, one of its five major bilateral treaty spokes in East Asia, in both Track I and II endeavours, but thus far to no avail, as neither side sees much urgency in this process. The Thai government is content to avoid the political controversy closer ties with US would likely generate domestically, and American policymakers are yet to coalesce around a shared diagnosis of the problem to underpin their strategic diplomacy. The Thai-US alliance is certainly not what it used to be, and appears in need of a complete revamp after more than two post-Cold War decades.

It may be, however, that an alliance 'revamp' is less relevant to shaping future Thai-American security relations than an exploration of how 'post-alliance' relations might evolve. Although it is not specifically defined in the literature dealing with Asia-Pacific security, or even commonly distinguished from the term 'ally', the concept of security 'partner' is applicable in this context. A security partner can be viewed as a state that is not fully committed to an alliance relationship but which has moved beyond the stage of 'coalition' – forging intermittent and short-term bilateral security ties with another state predicated on a single or specific issue area (the literature assessing coalitions is reviewed by Oest 2007: 21). Security partnership in an Asia-Pacific context is predicated not by a formal treaty document (which underpins or governs alliance rationales) but by 'clear and mutually understood expectations of the

United States and its partners' (Cossa *et al.* 2009: 65). A key precondition for effective partnership is for each state to have a distinct national security strategy that explains its interests and policies related to its perceptions of the region's evolving strategic challenges. The US government regularly produces such statements, but they usually do not move beyond characterizing Thailand as a long-standing *ally* helping to underwrite a 60-plus year-old bilateral alliance system, the relevance of which may be increasingly outdated. Thailand publishes occasional defence White Papers (in 2007, 2012 and 2013), but these documents have been preoccupied with repairing socio-political divisions in Thai society, tackling non-traditional security problems, and working with ASEAN. The most recent 2013 White Paper, for instance, spends much time discussing the maintenance of internal security, upholding the institution of the monarchy, and participating in peacekeeping, humanitarian assistance and disaster relief, particularly through ASEAN and the United Nations (Ministry of Defence, Thailand 2013).

The 2013 White Paper broadly outlines security cooperation as follows:

> Security cooperation can be defined as utilizing military resources to support the government by fostering with neighboring countries, Member States of ASEAN, friendly countries, and international organizations both at bilateral and multilateral levels.
>
> (Ministry of Defence, Thailand 2013: 8)

As such, relatively less attention has been directed toward forging a new consensus on how its US alliance and growing Chinese security tie can be rationalized and reconciled (Chachavalpongpun 2011: 60). This is hardly surprising given Thailand's historical preference to think about and express policy for its security relations with great powers tacitly rather than explicitly. Such a posture more readily coincides with its 'bend with the wind' legacy for cultivating external security relations.

Conclusion: points of policy convergence?

Semantics are less important than policy substance and to what extent the Americans perceive their Thai counterparts as 'allies' or 'partners' may ultimately prove to be a moot point. A more central concern is how Bangkok and Washington can identify and define points of security policy convergence with maximum effectiveness, especially in the post-May 2014 coup timeframe. The agenda for realizing this objective has been outlined in the aforementioned 2012 Joint Vision Statement for the Thai-US Defense Alliance, and in the Joint Statement of the Fourth United States–Thailand Strategic Dialogue that convened in Washington during June 2012 (United States Department of State 2012). Both sides have agreed to promote 'ASEAN centrality' in the Asia-Pacific's regional order-building politics. Both are inclined to link development politics with 'harder' regional security politics and to deem the former as a catalyst for greater democratization in such Southeast Asian states as Myanmar. Both assign a high premium to non-traditional security-centric concerns, with a particular focus on building greater infrastructure for humanitarian assistance and disaster relief, including the eventual creation of such a centre in Thailand. Interests also converge in maritime security (ensuring access to key sea lanes of communication and intensifying counter-piracy agendas), neutralizing the trafficking of people and narcotics, heightening counterterrorism capabilities and pursuing the non-proliferation of weapons of mass destruction. These common security interests remain viable, notwithstanding recent Thai efforts to forge closer ties with China in the aftermath of US criticism of the May 2014 military takeover in Thailand.

Many, if not all, of these policy components, moreover, supersede the threat-centric focus of traditional state-centric alliance politics. Most of them also are best managed by the harnessing of 'soft power' policy approaches where the Obama Administration has elected to place the emphasis in its rebalancing strategy. In this sense, the United States enjoys an advantage over China, if these two powers are indeed fated to become future rivals for regional influence. This is due to the inherent appeal of American and Western cultural approaches for encouraging risk, transparency and diversity in Southeast Asia's younger generations – notwithstanding challenges to this model by various strands of Confucian, Islamic and other forms of thought (Nye 2004).

However, US policy planners must learn from history and take special care not to be viewed as insensitive to the unique history, cultural practices and political challenges of Thailand and other ASEAN members. Pursuing those common objectives designated earlier constitutes a sound basis for defining a new Thai-American security relationship, whether it is one of alliance or partnership. More fundamentally, it is important for both countries to understand *why* their interests converge when they do, and to minimize both snap normative judgements about each other and hasty policy initiatives in response to short-term tensions when they do not.

Notes

1 Glenn Snyder (1997: 4) has incorporated these criteria in a more succinct way: 'formal associations of states for the use (or nonuse) of military force, in specified circumstances, against states outside their own membership'.
2 Sino–Thai trade topped US\$64 billion in 2011; by comparison, US–Thai trade was around US\$35 billion in the same year. See Trajano (2012).

References

Bangkok Post (2012) 'The Brouhaha Over U-Tapao', 20 June.
——(2014a) 'Downgrade Threatens Ties with US: Slavery Report Spurs Export Fears', 22 June.
——(2014b) 'US Cancels Military Exercises', 25 May.

——(2014c) 'US Cuts More Thailand Aid', 25 June.

——(2014d) 'US Suspends Military Aid for Thailand', 24 May.

Chachavalpongpun, Pavin (2011) 'Years of Living Dangerously: Thailand's Current Security Challenges', in National Institute for Defense Studies, *Security Outlook of the Asia-Pacific Countries and Its Implications for the Defense Sector*, Tokyo: National Institute for Defense Studies.

Chambers, Paul (2004) 'US-Thai Relations after 9/11: A New Era in Cooperation?' *Contemporary Southeast Asia*, 26(3): 460–79.

Chan, Minnie and Wee, Darren (2014) 'Chinese Troops Join US–Thailand Cobra Gold Military Exercises', *South China Morning Post*, 16 February.

Chanlett-Avery, Emma and Dolven, Ben (2013) 'Thailand: Background and US Relations', CRS Report 7-5700, Washington, DC: Congressional Research Service, 20 December.

Chansoria, Monika (2014) 'China Eyes Thai Arms Deal', *Sunday Guardian*, 16 February.

Chinwanno, Chulacheeb (2004) 'Thailand's Perspective on Security Cooperation in the Asia-Pacific', in See Seng Tan and Amitav Acharya (eds) *Asia-Pacific Security Cooperation: National Interests and Regional Order*, Armonk, NY: M.E. Sharpe, pp. 190–205.

——(2008) 'Thai-Chinese Relations: Security and Strategic Partnership', RSIS Working Paper 155, Singapore: S. Rajaratnam School of International Studies, 24 March.

Cossa, Ralph A., Glosserman, Brad, McDevitt, Michael A., Patel, Nirav, Przystup, James and Roberts, Brad (2009) *The United States and the Asia-Pacific Region: Security Strategy for the Obama Administration*, Honolulu and Washington, DC: Center for a New American Security, February.

Hagel, Chuck (2014) 'Secretary of Defense Speech', IISS Shangri-La Dialogue, Singapore, 31 May, www.defense.gov/Speeches/Speech.aspx?SpeechID=1857 (accessed 26 June 2014).

Jory, Patrick (2014) 'China is a Big Winner from Thailand's Coup', *East Asia Forum*, 18 June, www.eastasiaforum.org/2014/06/18/china-is-a-big-winner-from-thailands-coup/ (accessed 26 June 2014).

Kislenko, Arne (2002) 'Bending with the Wind: The Continuity and Flexibility of Thai Foreign Policy', *International Journal*, 57(4): 537–61.

Ministry of Defence, Thailand (2013) 'Defence White Paper', BE2556, Bangkok: Ministry of Defence.

Ministry of Foreign Affairs, Thailand (2014) 'Thailand Responds to the US Department of State's Placement of Thailand in Tier 3 in Its Annual Trafficking in Persons Report (2014)', Press Release No. 168/2557, 21 June, www.mfa.go.th/main/en/media-center/14/46952-Thailand-Responds-to-the-U.S.-Department-of-State'.html (accessed 26 June 2014).

Nye, Jr, Joseph S. (2004) *Soft Power: The Means to Success in World Politics*, New York: Public Affairs.

Oest, Kajsa Ji Noe (2007) 'The End of Alliance Theory?' Arbejdspapir 2007/3, Copenhagen: Institut for Statskundskab, March, polsci.ku.dk/arbejdspapirer/2007/ap_2007_03.pdf (accessed 27 February 2014).

Pongsudhirak, Thitinan (2012) 'Thailand's Foreign Policy in a Regional Great Game', in Nicholas Kitchen (ed.) *The New Geopolitics of Southeast Asia*, London: LSE IDEAS, November, pp. 74–79.

Prasirtsuk, Kitti (2013) 'The Implications of US Strategic Rebalancing', *Asia Policy*, 15(1): 31–37.

Richardson, Michael (1994) 'Thais Reject Proposal, While Indonesia and Malaysia Seem Negative: Asians Rebuff US on Basing Supply Ships for Crises', *New York Times*, 8 November.

Rusk, Dean (1961) 'Memorandum from Secretary of State Rusk to President Kennedy', 24 February, Document 397, *Foreign Relations of the United States 1961–1963*, Volume XXIII, *Southeast Asia*, history.state.gov/historicaldocuments/frus1961-63v23/d397 (accessed 26 February 2014).

Russel, Daniel R. (2013) 'Statement before the Senate Foreign Relations Committee', 20 June, www.foreign.senate.gov/imo/media/doc/Russel_Testimony.pdf (accessed 26 February 2014).

Sky News Australia (2014) 'Thailand Excluded from US Navy Event', 27 June, www.skynews.com.au/news/world/asiapacific/2014/06/27/thailand-excluded-from-us-navy-event.html (accessed 1 July 2014).

Snyder, Glenn H. (1997) *Alliance Politics*, Ithaca, NY: Cornell University Press.

Stern, Lewis M. (2009) 'Diverging Roads: 21st-Century US-Thai Defense Relations', *Strategic Forum*, No. 241(June).

Trajano, Julius Cesar I. (2012) 'Old Allies, New Dynamics in US Pivot', *Asia Times Online*, 31 August.

United States Department of Defense (2012) '2012 Joint Vision Statement for the Thai-US Defense Alliance', News Release No. 904-12, 15 November, www.defense.gov/releases/release.apsx?releaseid=15685 (accessed 26 February 2014).

United States Department of State (2012) 'Joint Statement of the Fourth United States–Thailand Strategic Dialogue', Washington, DC, 14 June, www.state.gov/r/pa/prs/ps/2012/06/192397.htm (accessed 27 February 2014).

van der Kroef, Justus M. (1976) 'The Lives of SEATO', ISEAS Occasional Paper No. 45, Singapore: Institute of Southeast Asian Studies, December.

Walt, Stephen M. (1997) 'Why Alliances Endure or Collapse', *Survival*, 39(1): 156–79.

Wortzel, Larry M. (2005) 'Change Partners: Who are America's Military and Economic Allies in the 21st Century?' Lecture # 886 on National Security and Defense, Washington, DC: Heritage Foundation, 6 June, www.heritage.org/research/lecture/change-partners-who-are-americas-military-and-economic-allies-in-the-21st-century (accessed 27 February 2014).

10 Security and power balancing

Singapore's response to the US rebalance to Asia

Ralf Emmers

Introduction

Singapore's innate sense of vulnerability has derived from its physical size, geostrategic location, history and its lack of natural resources (for a discussion on this sense of vulnerability's influence on foreign policy, see Leifer 2000). It has been a service centre, highly dependent on unimpeded air and maritime channels for its economic well-being. As a small state, it has traditionally adopted a holistic approach to its security. It has focused on deterrence and diplomacy as the twin pillars of its national security policy. The Singapore Armed Forces has provided a formidable physical deterrent while the state has sought, through its Ministry of Foreign Affairs and other ministries, to punch above its weight in international affairs, both in key bilateral relations and multilaterally at the United Nations, the Association of Southeast Asian Nations (ASEAN) and other international institutions (see Huxley 2000; Acharya 2007).

Singapore has traditionally relied on balance of power politics to prevent the dominance of a regional power that could ultimately undermine its own survival. The distinguishing feature of the policy of balance is a disposition to mobilize and employ military force, often in coalition, in order to affect the distribution of power. This city-state has historically followed two fundamental strategies, which may be identified as a balancing perspective. First, it has pursued a strategy of unilateral balancing by strengthening its military capabilities, the modernization of which is now second to none in Southeast Asia. Second, it has considered unilateral balancing as insufficient to fulfil its sense of relative security. Consequently, it has followed a policy of balancing through external association. This has involved strengthening its relative position through diplomatic and military alignments with the United States, and to a lesser extent the United Kingdom, Australia and other external powers (on cooperation with Australia and the UK, see Emmers 2012).

Indeed, Singapore has considered continued US strategic involvement in the region as essential to its security. The United States has been perceived as a benign hegemon and as an external balancer capable of preserving a stable distribution of power in Southeast Asia and the wider Asian region. The main function of the US security ties with Singapore has been to enhance the city-state's external defence in a changing regional security environment. In essence, this small Southeast Asian nation has balanced against potential external threats by bandwagoning with the United States' security policy. Yet, as Singapore is not a formal ally of the United States, an American military response to an external attack against it is not guaranteed. The special ties with Washington have, however, acted as a credible diplomatic and psychological deterrent. Security relations with the United States have over the years focused on traditional and non-traditional threats, most recently terrorism and maritime piracy.

With the United States' military withdrawals from Iraq and Afghanistan, US President Barack Obama has decided to refocus American diplomacy and military forces toward the Asia-Pacific, as part of a larger 'pivot' or rebalancing strategy. The chapter discusses how the US rebalancing toward Asia has been received in Singapore and whether this policy move fits in with its traditional reliance on balance of power politics to ensure its own security. It argues that Singapore has welcomed the rebalancing because it casts the United States as a 'resident Pacific power' and commits the pre-eminent economic and military power in the world to peace and stability in the Asia-Pacific. It is asserted, however, that despite its close defence relations with the United States, Singapore wants to preserve its independence of manoeuvre with China and to avoid a situation where it would eventually have to 'choose' between Washington and Beijing.

The chapter consists of two sections. Initially, Singapore's strategic outlook is reviewed and is linked to that country's defence ties with the United States since the 1960s. The second section focuses more specifically on Singapore's response to the US rebalancing strategy in Asia.

Singapore's defence relationship with the United States

The Singaporean military doctrine has evolved since independence in 1965 from a 'poison shrimp' deterrence strategy to a 'Total Defence' system (encompassing a military, socioeconomic, civil and psychological approach to national security), as well as subsequent forward defence postures based on credible deterrence and pre-emption. Central to Singapore's national strategy has been the preservation of its sovereignty and independence. This has led to consistent assertions of its sovereignty rights and national interests. For example, Singapore condemned Indonesia's annexation of East Timor in 1975 and also criticized the US-led invasion of Grenada in 1983 in an attempt to register its own sovereignty and independence as a small state.

In addition to building up its own military capabilities, Singapore first developed defence relations with the United States during the Vietnam War in the 1960s. Singapore's intensification of US defence ties was influenced by the British announcement in 1967 that it would withdraw its military troops from East of Suez, and the subsequent substitution in 1971 of the Anglo-Malayan

Defence Agreement and its commitment to the external defence of Malaysia and Singapore by the Five Power Defence Arrangements and its limited provision for consultation in the event of external aggression (Emmers 2012: 272–73). Singapore's traditional reliance on unilateral balancing and its special ties with the United States have been driven by its own history and perception of vulnerability. Its separation from the Federation of Malaysia in 1965 affected its ties with Kuala Lumpur, as the newly established city-state was often perceived as a Chinese enclave in a Malay world. In the decades that followed, recurrent tensions occurred due to a series of bilateral issues 'ranging from the denial of sand exports, the use of airspace to the island republic and a territorial dispute over a small atoll' (Saravanamuttu 2011: 43–44). Moreover, Singapore had suffered attacks during the period of *konfrontasi* against Indonesia and continued after 1965 to mistrust Jakarta. It also feared that Indonesia and Malaysia might adopt simultaneous assertive policies in their dealings with the dominantly ethnic-Chinese state of Singapore. Consequently, the latter country was left with a sense of vulnerability that still influences its strategic outlook today.

After the establishment of ASEAN in August 1967, Singapore remained fearful of absorption by Malaysia or Indonesia and perceived American involvement in the region as a means to preclude any such eventuality. While Indonesia has traditionally aspired to an autonomous security environment unaffected by external intervention, Singapore has continued to reject this conception of the regional order and relied on ties with external actors to ensure its security. It has never perceived ASEAN as a security arrangement that could replace existing bilateral links with the United States. This is arguably due to the fragility of ASEAN as a security provider in light of wider shifts in the power distribution in the Asia-Pacific. The partnership with Washington has over the years generated exclusive goods and benefits for Singapore both in terms of military ties and the provision of security, which ASEAN was never designed to provide as a cooperative security arrangement.

With the end of the Cold War era, the threat perception of Singapore moved away from its immediate neighbourhood to entail a rising China and the uncertain distribution of power in the Asia-Pacific. The cessation of Soviet–American and Sino–Soviet rivalries contributed to a sense of relief and optimism, but also to a feeling of strategic uncertainty in the region. The collapse of the Soviet Union and its own budgetary constraints obliged the United States to reconsider its military deployment in Asia. In addition, the United States had to withdraw from Subic Bay Naval Base and Clark Air Base in the Philippines by November 1992 after the Philippines Senate refused to sign a new base treaty with Washington in September 1991. In contrast, the influence of China became more significant. Singapore feared that a US military disengagement in Asia might encourage China to fill the 'power vacuum' left by retreating external powers (Buszynski 1996: 121).

Singapore's strategic calculations have often been translated into concrete policies. In response to the US withdrawal from the Philippines, it offered an agreement to Washington in November 1990, allowing its Navy and Air Force to use its military facilities more extensively. By offering the United States compensatory facilities, Singapore sought to mitigate the strategic consequences of the American departure from Subic Bay Naval Base and Clark Air Base. A US Navy logistics facility was also transferred in 1992 from Subic Bay to Singapore. In January 1998, the city-state declared that US aircraft carriers would have access to the Changi Naval Base after its completion in 2000. In more recent years, it has further developed strong military relations with the US Pacific Command, including through war games, map planning and manoeuvre exercises like Cobra Gold. Established in 1982, the Thai-US joint military exercise (Cobra Gold) now also involves Indonesia, Japan, Malaysia, Singapore and South Korea.

In terms of transnational security issues, Singapore has closely collaborated with the United States on the 'war on terror' since the 11 September 2001 terrorist attacks on America. Domestically, the arrest of *Jemaah Islamiah* militants in December 2001 and the discovery of bomb plots fuelled the country's sense of vulnerability. In particular, threats of piracy and maritime terrorism in the Strait of Malacca and Singapore were further securitized post-11 September (Emmers 2004: 39–49). Singapore has cooperated closely and shared intelligence with Washington. It was even the first Asian country to sign the Declaration of Principles for the Container Security Initiative with the United States in September 2002, and joined the Proliferation Security Initiative core group in March 2004. Moreover, it supported the US-led invasion of Iraq in 2003 and contributed troops to Iraq and medical teams and equipment to Afghanistan. It also joined the US-led naval task force to combat maritime piracy in the Gulf of Aden.

The bilateral ties maintained by Singapore with the United States have had a significant strategic impact in terms of strength and military involvement. Signed by Singapore Prime Minister Lee Hsien Loong and US President George W. Bush in July 2005, the Strategic Framework Agreement for a Closer Cooperation Partnership in Defense and Security recognized the Southeast Asian nation as a major strategic partner of the United States and provided a framework for bilateral defence cooperation. The Agreement also enabled the US deployment of littoral combat ships to Changi Naval Base. Washington further defined its ties with the city-state in the 2010 Quadrennial Defense Review (QDR), the first to be released by the Obama Administration. The QDR refers to three groups of security partners, namely, formal allies, strategic partners and prospective strategic partners (United States Department of Defense 2010). In Southeast Asia, the Philippines and Thailand are defined as US treaty allies. The QDR identifies Singapore as a strategic partner while Indonesia, Malaysia and Vietnam are classified as prospective strategic partners. Singapore has been more of a partner to Washington than its immediate neighbours as the city-state has been more comfortable with the adoption of a balancing strategy and less concerned with the military presence of external powers in Southeast Asia.

The Singapore Armed Forces has continued to train in the United States while US forces, especially the Navy, are the most frequent visitors to Singapore's military facilities. The Singapore and US armies have conducted the annual bilateral Tiger Balm exercises (alternately in Singapore and Hawaii) since 1981. Singapore also still purchases most of its military hardware from the United States (Chan 2012). Finally, successive US secretaries of defense have attended the Asia Security Summit, also known as the Shangri-La Dialogue, held annually in the city-state since 2002 and organized by the International Institute for Strategic Studies. Still, the close defence relationship that Singapore maintains with the United States is not exclusive. Singapore Ambassador Barry Desker notes that while American observers have often referred to that relationship as a 'quasi-alliance partnership', Singaporean policymakers 'do not regard such ties as mutually exclusive with the expansion of relationships with other rising powers in Asia, such as China' (Desker 2013: 27).

Singapore and US rebalancing in Asia

In 2010, US Secretary of State Hillary Clinton declared in a speech at the East–West Center in Hawaii that 'America's future is linked to the future of the Asia-Pacific region; and the future of this region depends on America' (Clinton 2010). At the East Asia Summit (EAS) in 2011, US President Obama declared that the United States would remain committed to the region. Besides deepening its military ties with the Philippines, Washington announced enhanced military relations with Indonesia, Malaysia, Pakistan, Singapore and Thailand. The United States also announced in late 2011 the rotational deployment of 2,500 US Marines in Darwin and, as noted above, the deployment of up to four of its littoral combat ships on a rotational basis in Singapore. Finally, in June 2012, US Secretary of Defense Leon Panetta stated that the United States would commit 60 percent of its naval capabilities to the Pacific Ocean by 2020 (Panetta 2012). That said, in light of fiscal constraints in the US federal budget, rebalancing in Asia 'may only mean that the United States maintains current levels of its military presence in Asia while significant declines occur in Europe' (Desker 2013: 26).

Beyond its military component, US rebalancing has also been characterized by a diplomatic and economic dimension. Under the Bush Administration, Washington was viewed regionally as disinterested in multilateral cooperation in the Asia-Pacific (Secretary of State Condoleezza Rice skipped two ASEAN Regional Forum meetings). The Obama Administration quickly reversed this perception by engaging more fully with regional bodies like ASEAN (Emmers *et al.* 2011: 29–34). The Administration acceded to ASEAN's Treaty of Amity and Cooperation by presidential decree in July 2009, which opened the door for the United States to join the EAS in November 2011. US Secretary of Defense Robert Gates also attended the first ASEAN Defence Ministers' Meeting Plus (ADMM+) in October 2010.

Finally, in the economic sphere, the United States 'wants to hitch its destiny to the more dynamic of the oceans it dominates' (Banyan 2013: 34). The Obama Administration therefore joined the Trans-Pacific Partnership (TPP) negotiations in November 2009 and it has tried to reinvigorate the Asia-Pacific Economic Cooperation (APEC) forum.

As a strategic partner of the United States, Singapore quickly welcomed the US pivot to Asia. It did, however, initially dislike the term 'pivot' as it suggested that the United States might in the future pivot away from Asia to another part of the world, and it therefore preferred the later rebranding of the US policy move as a 'rebalancing' of forces. Singapore has perceived the pivot as a wider balancing strategy involving the United States and China. Prime Minister Lee declared at the Central Party School in Beijing in September 2012 that 'Singapore believes that the US' continued presence in the region contributes to Asia's prosperity and security. The US has legitimate long-term interests in Asia, and plays a role in Asia which no other country can' (Lee 2012). As part of the Strategic Framework Agreement, the city-state has allowed four US littoral combat ships to use its facilities on a rotational basis. The first littoral combat ship, the USS *Freedom*, was deployed to Changi Naval Base in April 2013 for an eight-month period to participate in joint military exercises with Singapore and other Southeast Asian nations. During a visit to Washington in April 2013, Prime Minister Lee met President Obama and US Secretary of Defense Chuck Hagel, and reaffirmed the importance of a sustained American regional presence to enhance peace and stability in the Asia-Pacific. During their meeting in the Oval Office, Obama thanked Singapore 'for all the facilities that they provide that allow us to maintain our effective Pacific presence'. In response, Lee declared that 'Singapore will do our part to do what we can to help America engage the region constructively, productively, and in a way which fosters stability and prosperity for all the countries' (Obama and Lee 2013).

Singapore's support for the US rebalancing strategy in Asia should be examined in the context of an evolving strategic environment. China is a resurgent power and a competitor to US economic and military primacy in Asia. China's annual military budget is now second only to the United States and both countries have conflicting strategic interests in a series of regional security flashpoints including the Korean peninsula, Taiwan, and in the East China and South China Seas. External interference in the international relations of Southeast Asia is increasingly set by growing Sino-US competition and the two great powers' quest for regional influence. China's regional status has risen substantially over the last few years and its power projection and capability to sustain military force in Southeast Asia have strengthened, especially in the South China Sea. The emergence of an uncertain multipolar structure in the Asia-Pacific has encouraged Singapore to cultivate even closer ties with the United States with the aim of further deepening its benign involvement in regional security. Desker argues that the US rebalancing in Asia 'has the potential to check any tendency on the part of Beijing to create a China-centric order in the region and help nudge China to become a responsible power' (Desker 2013: 29).

The US regional presence continues to be viewed by Singapore as the best guarantor for a stable power distribution. Its support for an ongoing US presence in the region is not surprising. The bilateral relationship is based on a strong convergence of strategic interests with Washington. In an editorial, the *Straits Times* (Singapore's highest-selling newspaper) noted that interests 'remain highly complementary: Singapore desires and welcomes a counter-vailing American presence in the region, while the US needs friendly locations that will facilitate such a presence' (*Straits Times* 2013). Still, the city-state is concerned over the long-term viability of rebalancing. In the short term, it wonders whether President Obama will, in his second term, be equally committed to sustaining US influence in the region in light of American domestic priorities as well as turmoil and looming crises in the Middle East. Moreover, while former Secretary of State Clinton and Assistant Secretary of State Kurt Campbell paid significant attention to ASEAN and its member states (Chan 2012), questions remain regarding Secretary of State John Kerry and his commitment to Southeast Asia. In the longer term, Singapore fears like others that the United States might not be able to afford its ambitions in Asia, especially in light of automatic spending cuts and the constraints they impose on defence budgets. Michael Richardson (2013) writes that whether the US rebalance is sustainable is 'the question that most concerns Asian countries that want America fully engaged in the region to help keep the peace and discourage China from using force or intimidation to achieve its objectives'.

Furthermore, while supporting the military component of US rebalancing, Singapore still favours accommodation rather than competition between China and the United States and is concerned over the cycle of mistrust and rivalry between Washington and Beijing. Critically, it does not want to be forced to 'choose' between China and the United States. This is a key dimension of Singapore's 'partnership' status vis-à-vis the United States: collaborating where obvious security interests converge, but qualifying Singapore's actual commitment to defending US interests under all circumstances. In his speech to the Central Party School, Prime Minister Lee clearly stated that '[w]e hope China–US relations flourish, because we are friends of both countries. We do not wish to see their relations deteriorate, or be forced to choose one or the other' (Lee 2012).

Singapore views the rise of China both as an economic opportunity and as a major shift in the distribution of power. As the world's second largest economy, China has become a major trading partner and a key source of investment for the region. Singapore, like most other Asian nations, is becoming increasingly dependent on China for its own economic growth and prosperity. Strategically, the city-state seeks to engage Beijing and to socialize it into habits of good international behaviour through its active participation in ASEAN-led regional institutions. It would arguably reject any attempt at encircling China as a threatening rising power. Like other Asian partners of the United States, Singapore therefore wants to prevent the rebalancing of US troops from being perceived in Beijing as a renewed containment strategy (see Goh 2012). Instead, it is careful not to give China 'any impression of being stymied from rising peacefully to its full potential' (*Straits Times* 2013). In short, Singapore favours a scenario of an active US participation combined with an accommodative Chinese involvement in regional affairs.

Singapore is well aware that the strategic impact of the US rebalancing initiative in Asia remains rather minimal in light of modest US rotational military deployments and additional bilateral exercises with regional partners. A greater impact has been felt in the diplomatic realm, however. As part of its rebalancing strategy, the Obama Administration has paid close attention to regional multilateral diplomacy. By relying on the ASEAN-led institutions (ASEAN Regional Forum, EAS and ADMM+) to provide diplomatic substance to the rebalancing strategy, the United States has acknowledged the centrality of ASEAN in the institutional architecture emerging in the Asia-Pacific. Singapore has welcomed this renewed focus on diplomacy for two main reasons. First, the city-state favours a multi-level US engagement in the region that goes beyond security to include diplomacy, economics and other areas of cooperation. Second, it has traditionally been concerned over the possible marginalization of ASEAN in regional affairs, and has therefore sought to preserve its driving role in Asia-Pacific regionalism as a means to guarantee its long-term relevance.

As part of its renewed diplomatic focus, the United States has paid more attention to the South China Sea disputes and repeatedly raised this issue at international forums. It has also called on all the parties involved to negotiate a code of conduct for the South China Sea and expressed its commitment to a peaceful resolution of the sovereignty disputes based on the principles of international law. For example, Clinton openly supported attempts by ASEAN to negotiate a code of conduct for the South China Sea with Beijing. The US position on the South China Sea is similar to that adopted by Singapore. As a non-claimant state, the city-state has remained a neutral party in the sovereignty disputes and has limited its interest to the preservation of the freedom of navigation. It is an important user state, with vital economic and strategic interests in the disputed areas in light of its global trans-shipment port activities and the sea lanes of communication that cross the Strait of Malacca and the South China Sea. Singapore also perceives the sovereignty disputes as a reflection of a changing power distribution and a rising China. In particular, it views the disputes as a test case of whether China is more likely in the years to come to resolve its differences with its neighbours in accordance with international law or through the use of force.

Finally, beyond its strategic and diplomatic focus, Singapore is particularly keen on the economic dimension of US rebalancing in Asia. The US–Singapore Free Trade Agreement was already signed in 2003 and the Southeast Asian nation was the 15th largest trading partner of the United States in 2011. As previously observed, the Obama Administration has sought in recent years to accelerate the negotiation of a trans-Pacific free trade agreement (the TPP) and to reinvigorate APEC. Launched in 2005, the TPP negotiations involved 12 nations at the time of writing (Australia, Brunei, Canada, Chile, Japan, Malaysia, Mexico, New Zealand, Peru, Singapore, the United States and Vietnam), but not China.

Successive US Administrations have approached APEC as the core institutional mechanism in the Asia-Pacific. Established in November 1989 as a regional economic dialogue that includes Singapore and the United States, APEC is based on the concept of 'open regionalism', which means that the outcome of economic liberalization is applied both within the regional grouping and to non-APEC economies.

This American approach to economic regionalism continues to suit US interests in the Asia-Pacific. It also coincides with Singapore's own interests, as Prime Minister Lee has repeatedly argued that '[i]n Asia, trade is strategy' (Lee 2013). Its national economy is highly dependent on trade and is closely integrated into global financial and production networks. Like the United States, the Southeast Asian nation has an immediate interest in seeking a deepening of trade and financial integration in the Asia-Pacific. Both countries want a rapid conclusion of the TPP negotiations and a more successful APEC.

Besides these two institutions that include the United States, Singapore is also involved in the negotiation of a Regional Comprehensive Economic Partnership with the other ASEAN members as well as Australia, China, India, Japan, New Zealand and South Korea. Hence, just as in the case of its defence relations, Singapore's close economic ties with the United States do not exclude the city-state from developing deeper economic relations with other Asian states, especially China.

Conclusion

Singapore has welcomed the US rebalancing strategy in Asia. It continues to view the United States as a great provider of essential public goods such as a peaceful strategic environment, the preservation of the freedom of navigation, and an economic architecture that promotes free trade. In light of Chinese rising power and the emergence of an uncertain strategic environment, Singapore still perceives a strong American presence as the best guarantor for peace and stability in the Asia-Pacific. Its positive response to rebalancing has resulted from a strong convergence of strategic interests that defines its bilateral defence relationship with the United States. The most immediate impact of the American rebalancing of forces for Singapore has been the rotational deployment of US littoral combat ships to Changi Naval Base. The Southeast Asian nation also supports the US engagement policy to Asia as it cuts across security, diplomacy and economics. In short, American rebalancing fits in and contributes to Singapore's traditional reliance on balance of power politics to ensure its security.

Nevertheless, Singapore realizes that the US pivot to Asia is more likely to have a diplomatic and economic impact than a significant strategic influence in light of a modest US force alignment to the region. The Southeast Asian nation is concerned over the viability of the rebalancing strategy in the longer term due to fiscal constraints imposed on the US defence budget. In this context, Singapore is most comfortable remaining a US partner – but not its ally – as the Asia-Pacific order-building process matures two decades beyond the end of the Cold War. For now at least, the *modest* rebalancing of US military forces is favoured by Singapore, as it fears the great power competition that a more robust military approach might generate. While concerned over Chinese renewed assertiveness in regional affairs, Singapore prefers accommodation between the United States and China and, most fundamentally, does not want to be forced to 'choose' between Washington and Beijing. Within those parameters, it is likely that the partnership between Singapore and the United States will be sustainable and will contribute to overall regional stability.

References

Acharya, Amitav (2007) *Singapore's Foreign Policy: The Search for Regional Order*, Singapore: World Scientific.

Banyan (2013) 'Pivotal Concerns', *Economist*, 11 May.

Buszynski, Leszek (1996) 'Post-Cold War Security in the ASEAN Region', in Gary Klintworth (ed.) *Asia-Pacific Security: Less Uncertainty, New Opportunities?* New York: St Martin's Press, pp. 120–31.

Chan Heng Chee (2012) 'ASEAN's Growing Ties With US, Now and In Future', *Straits Times*, 22 October.

Clinton, Hillary (2010) 'Remarks on Regional Architecture in Asia: Principles and Priorities', Speech delivered at the East–West Center, Imin Center-Jefferson Hall, Honolulu, 12 January, www.state.gov/secretary/rm/2010/01/135090.htm (accessed 27 August 2013).

Desker, Barry (2013) 'The Eagle and the Panda: An Owl's View from Southeast Asia', *Asia Policy*, 15 (January): 26–30.

Emmers, Ralf (2004) *Non-Traditional Security in the Asia-Pacific: The Dynamics of Securitisation*, Singapore: Marshall Cavendish.

——(2012) 'The Five Power Defence Arrangements and Defence Diplomacy in Southeast Asia', *Asian Security*, 8(3): 271–86.

Emmers, Ralf, Liow, Joseph Chinyong and Tan, See Seng (2011) *The East Asia Summit and the Regional Security Architecture*, Maryland Series in Contemporary Asian Studies, Baltimore, MD: University of Maryland School of Law.

Goh, Evelyn (2012) 'US "Pivot" Should Not End Up Forcing Asia to Choose Sides', *Straits Times*, 18 July.

Huxley, Tim (2000) *Defending the Lion City: The Armed Forces of Singapore*, St Leonards, NSW: Allen & Unwin.

Lee Hsien Loong (2012) 'China and the World: Prospering and Progressing Together', Speech delivered at the Central Party School (English translation), Beijing, 2 September, www.pmo.gov.sg/content/pmosite/mediacentre/speechesninterviews/pri

meminister/2012/September/speech_by_prime_ministerleehsienloongatcentralpartysc
hoolenglish.m.html (accessed 27 August 2013).
——(2013) 'Speech by Prime Minister Lee Hsien Loong at Gala Dinner Hosted
by US Chamber of Commerce and US–ASEAN Business Council', Washington,
DC, 2 April, www.pmo.gov.sg/content/pmosite/mediacentre/speechesninterviews/
primeminister/2013/April/speech_by_prime_ministerleehsienloongatgaladinnerhoste
dbyuschamb.html (accessed 27 August 2013).
Leifer, Michael (2000) *Singapore's Foreign Policy: Coping with Vulnerability*, London:
Routledge.
Obama, Barack and Lee Hsien Loong (2013) 'Remarks by President Obama
and Prime Minister Lee of Singapore Before Bilateral Meeting', White House Office
of the Press Secretary, Washington, DC, 2 April, www.whitehouse.gov/the-
press-office/2013/04/02/remarks-president-obama-and-prime-minister-lee-singapore-b
ilateral-meeti (accessed 27 August 2013).
Panetta, Leon (2012) 'Shangri-La Security Dialogue: As Delivered by Secretary of
Defense Leon E. Panetta', Singapore, 2 June, www.defense.gov/speeches/speech.
aspx?speechid=1681 (accessed 27 August 2013).
Richardson, Michael (2013) 'The Mechanics of US Engagement in Asia', *Straits
Times*, 25 March.
Saravanamuttu, Johan (2011) 'Malaysian Foreign Policy and the Five Power Defence
Arrangements', in Ian Storey, Ralf Emmers and Daljit Singh (eds) *The Five Power
Defence Arrangements at Forty*, Singapore: Institute of Southeast Asian Studies, pp.
36–50.
Straits Times (2013) 'The Wisdom of Trade as Strategy', 6 April.
United States Department of Defense (2010) *Quadrennial Defense Review Report*, 1
February, www.defense.gov/QDR/ (accessed 27 August 2013).

Part IV
The wider Indo-Pacific region

11 Australia responds to America's rebalance

Brendan Taylor

Australia did not feature especially prominently during the early years of the Barack Obama Administration's 'pivot' to Asia. Much of the focus of the administration's energies during the period 2009–11 was on diplomatic re-engagement with Southeast Asia, arguably as a direct response to the perceived neglect of East Asian multilateralism that was seen to be a feature – and, indeed, a failing – of the preceding George W. Bush Administration. Canberra's place as part of the pivot strategy did not become fully apparent until Obama's first visit to Australia as president in November 2011. Obama used this opportunity to begin putting some military 'meat on the bones' of the pivot strategy by announcing during this visit that up to 2,500 US Marines would be rotated through facilities in north Australia for approximately six months each year.

This chapter tells the story of Australia's place in the American pivot. It is divided into three parts. The first details the Obama visit of November 2011 and the strong expressions of Australian support that were apparent during his short stay and which were reinforced in three key policy documents launched by the Australian government during the 18 months after it: statements of support which, as the chapter demonstrates, obscured deeper strains beginning to emerge in Australia's relationship with the United States.

The second part details the Australian public debate that emerged during the same period and which supports the view that the Australian posture on the US pivot is indeed less unified in its support than official pronouncements emanating from Canberra might initially suggest. Part three analyses Washington's reaction to these developments, and contends that it, too, reveals strains in the US-Australian alliance which will require careful monitoring in the years ahead.

Strong support?

The lack of explicit focus on Australia during the early days of the Obama Administration's pivot strategy seemed to do little to undermine Canberra's stated support for the strategy. Indeed, since Australia's 'turn to America' and the formal establishment of the US-Australian alliance in the aftermath of the Second World War, Australia has consistently favoured a strong American presence in the Asia-Pacific and has directly benefited from the security order this presence has created (for further reading on the history of this period, see Bell 1993). Epitomizing this support, Australian Prime Minster Julia Gillard addressed the US Congress in March 2011 during a visit to Washington marking the 60th anniversary of the US-Australian alliance. During this speech, Gillard observed that America has 'a true friend down under' and urged the United States to remain committed to the maintenance of peace and security in the Asia-Pacific – notwithstanding the economic difficulties that it had been experiencing as a consequence of the 2008–09 global financial crisis. Gillard's speech received no fewer than six standing ovations from a packed Congressional chamber, including a final ovation that lasted for four minutes (Franklin 2011). It was a speech that set the stage perfectly for Obama's November visit.

Further momentum was built in the lead-up to the Obama visit by the September 2011 Australia–United States Ministerial Consultations (AUSMIN). Held annually, the 2011 AUSMIN gathering was significant for two components of the resulting joint communiqué which also became a feature of Australia's response to the US pivot. First was the addition of cyber security issues to contingencies that could be encompassed under the terms of the 1951 Australia New Zealand United States (ANZUS) alliance treaty. Added to this, the communiqué also emphasized a new Indo-Pacific strategic construct. Whereas traditionally the United States and Australia had tended to refer to the region in 'Asia-Pacific' terms, reference to the Indo-Pacific represented a broadening in conceptualization of the region that some commentators took to suggest a paradigmatic rethink on the part of US and Australian policymakers – particularly in terms of the inclusion of rising India as a counterbalance to rising China – which was consistent with the thinking underpinning the pivot strategy (see, for example, Sheridan 2011; Medcalf 2012).

Twice postponed, Obama's visit to Australia lasted a short 28 hours when it finally occurred and only took in the Australian capital Canberra and the northern Australian city of Darwin. Yet the short duration of Obama's visit 'down under' should not detract from the significance of its key 'takeaways' in the context of the US pivot strategy. The centrepiece of the visit was the announcement by Obama and Gillard that up to 2,500 US Marines would be rotated each year through facilities in north Australia. During their six-month rotation period, it was envisaged that the Marines would spend half of that time based in Australia's north and the remainder undertaking cooperative engagement activities with other US security partners in the region. As part of this initiative, there was also to be increased US Air Force access to facilities in north Australia and US Navy access to the Royal Australian Navy base, HMAS Stirling, in Perth, Western Australia.

The announcement of the US Marine rotation proved controversial throughout the Asia-Pacific region. Indonesian Foreign Minister Marty Natalagawa – regarded by many as a friend of Australia – was particularly vocal in his criticism, observing that he would 'hate' to see the initiative 'provoke a reaction and counter-reaction that would create a vicious cycle of tensions and mistrust' (cited in Nusa Dua 2011). Somewhat more predictably, Beijing also responded critically to the announcement by characterizing it as a 'Cold War era' strategic move by Canberra and Washington during Australian Foreign Minister Bob Carr's May 2012 visit to Beijing (*Age* 2012). When Defence Minister Stephen Smith visited Beijing in June of that year, official Chinese criticism was somewhat more veiled in suggesting that Australia was trying to have 'its legs in two different boats' in its dealings with China and the United States (Garnaut 2012).

Despite such criticism, strong Australian support for the US pivot to Asia remained a feature of official pronouncements during the 18 months following Obama's visit. In October 2012, for instance, the Gillard government launched the first of three White Papers – *Australia in the Asian Century* – that would be released over the following 18 months with a view to lending a greater degree of coherence to Australian foreign, defence and national security policy. All three expressed a strong degree of support for the US-Australian alliance and the American 'rebalance', as the pivot was increasingly referred to. *Australia in the Asian Century*, for example, outlined that Australia 'will continue to support US engagement in the region and its rebalancing to the Asia-Pacific, including through deepening our defence engagement with the US and regional partners' (Australian Government 2011: 231).

In January 2013, the Gillard government subsequently produced *Strong and Secure: A Strategy for Australia's National Security*, which was equally supportive in its description of the US-Australian alliance, characterizing it as one of eight 'pillars' of Australia's national security and a relationship that was 'as strong as ever' (Department of the Prime Minister and Cabinet, Australia 2013: ii). In a similar vein, the May *Defence White Paper 2013* described the alliance as Australia's 'most important defence relationship', and observed that Canberra 'welcomes the shift in US strategic focus towards the region, and the US commitment to maintain its strong diplomatic, economic and security presence' (Department of Defence, Australia 2013: 56).

These effusive statements of support notwithstanding, a closer inspection of the Gillard government's three White Papers suggests that all may not have been as it seemed in the US-Australian alliance, and that Canberra's position on the pivot was not quite as unified as these policy documents evidently sought to imply. The very title of *Australia in the Asian Century*, for instance, might legitimately have been met with a degree of consternation in Washington, suggesting as it does a transition away from the so-called 'American Century' – a characterization that some commentators have employed with reference to the twentieth century. Likewise, some commentators detected a distinct softening in Canberra's position on China in the *Defence White Paper 2013* – in contrast to its 2009 predecessor, which adopted a more hard-line posture with reference to China's rising power – as evidenced by its coverage of the United States and China in a single subsection, and one containing reference to the fact that Australia does not face a choice between its leading trading partner (China) and its long-standing strategic ally (the United States) (see, for example, Nicholson 2013b). The announcement of a new 'strategic partnership' between Australia and China in the month prior to the release of the *Defence White Paper 2013* lent some credence to this view (Jakobson 2013).

Australia debates the rebalance

In some respects, the *Defence White Paper* seeming equivocation on Australia's position vis-à-vis the United States and China could be interpreted as a direct response to a heated public debate which predated the pivot and considered how Australia should respond to the rise of China. For the purposes of this chapter, the positions advocated by Australian commentators who have been party to this debate are categorized into three main camps. First, there are the doves, who have argued that four decades of US primacy in the Asia-Pacific are coming to an end as a result of China's rise. These commentators contend that Australia should be encouraging the United States to make space and thus 'accommodate' China's rise with a view to avoiding US-Sino strategic competition that has the potential for conflict. Juxtaposed against the doves is a group of more hawkish commentators, who argue that Australia should actively join with the United States and its allies in confronting China with a view to counter-balancing its rising regional power and influence. A third group of commentators might then be termed the owls, given their tendency to stake out more subtle positions between the stark postures advocated by the hawks and the doves.

Public debate over Australia's response to the US pivot, which has gathered momentum during the period since the Obama visit, can be read as a direct extension of this earlier China debate.

Doves

Hugh White, a former senior defence official and a central figure in Australia's earlier China debate, has been the most prominent amongst a handful of Australian commentators who have criticized the US pivot strategy and suggested that Canberra needs to convince its American ally to pursue a more accommodating posture vis-à-vis a rising China. In his analysis of the pivot, White has emphasized the historical significance of the strategy, suggesting that it is the most important shift in America's Asia strategy since the Harry S. Truman Administration implemented the containment strategy at the outset of the Cold War (White 2011b). During Obama's November 2011 visit to Australia, White argued that Canberra's acquiescence to the rotating Marines initiative demonstrated its 'willingness to join America's military coalition against China' (White 2011a). This was a mistake, according to

White, because Australia's 'highest diplomatic priority must be to help stem the escalating rivalry [between] America and China', not to facilitate and encourage it (White 2013).

A handful of current and former senior Australian political figures have joined White in adopting a similarly critical stance on the US pivot strategy. Former Prime Minister Malcolm Fraser (1975–83) has been a particularly prominent critic of the US pivot in terms that, initially at least, look deceptively similar to White's. Fraser, like White, accuses the United States of seeking to 'contain' China's rising power and criticizes Australia for its support of this strategy:

> Obama's inappropriate speech to the Australian Parliament in November 2011 implied that Australia fully supports American militarisation of the Western Pacific and the policies of containment that this implies.
>
> (Fraser 2012: 31)

Also in similar terms to White, Fraser suggests that the preservation of peace in the Asia-Pacific hinges upon America being 'prepared to come to an accommodation with China'. As his argument develops, however, it becomes apparent that Fraser's primary problem with the US pivot is Canberra's neglect of Australia's national interest and the sacrifice of its strategic independence to America. In his terms '[t]he Australian government has made us hostage to the politics of the US, to the machinations of the Pentagon, and the plans for continuing supremacy of the US in the Western Pacific'. Such an approach is misplaced, according to Fraser, because '[t]he imperative for Australia is to make sure that Australian governments place the interests of the people of Australia first. We must be subservient to no one' (Fraser 2012: 33).

Two other prominent Australian political figures can also be classified as members of the dovish school of thinking: former Prime Minister Paul Keating and former leader of the opposition (and current Minister for Communications) Malcolm Turnbull. Interestingly, White chose Keating and Turnbull to launch his book, *The China Choice*, in 2012. Speaking at that launch, Turnbull drew upon Thucydides's classic history of the Peloponnesian War to urge his fellow Australians to 'ensure that the Americans, unlike the Spartans, do not allow their anxiety about a rising power to lead them into a reflexive antagonism that could end in conflict' (Turnbull 2012: 55). Keating was less circumspect, rejecting the notion that 'Australia had no choice but to back US rivalry against a rising China', and asserting that 'the US and Australia needed to recognise the legitimacy of the current Chinese government and its prerogatives as a great power' (Earl 2012).

Hawks

Like the doves, the hawks in Australia's public debate over the US pivot also have strong political connections and, arguably, are gaining ascendancy in this debate following the election of a conservative Tony Abbott government in September 2013. Prominent amongst the hawks is Ross Babbage, founder of the Kokoda Foundation. Babbage was an adviser on Australia's hard-headed 2009 Defence White Paper and has famously expressed the view that Australia needs to develop the military capacity to 'rip an arm off' any threatening Asian power, namely a rising China (Babbage 2008: 18). Regarding the US pivot, Babbage has been supportive on the grounds that the strategy 'reassures US allies in the region and deters those who might want to interfere with them' (Robson 2013). He is unsympathetic to the views expressed by the more dovish camp who warn of Chinese sensitivities to deepening security cooperation between America and Australia. His blunt response to such concerns is a simple 'so what?' (see, for example, Kerin 2012). More recently, reflecting upon the evolution of the US pivot strategy, Babbage predicts a continuing deepening of the US-Australian alliance and the development of additional new elements of cooperation – particularly in air and naval operations to complement the US Marine rotation – in the years ahead (Slavin 2013).

Babbage could well be correct, given the influence reportedly held by some prominent hawks in the new Abbott government. For instance, notwithstanding his close association with the Kevin Rudd government's 2009 Defence White Paper, Babbage is rumoured to be a central advisory figure in the new Defence White Paper that the Abbott government has pledged to deliver by 2015 (Nicholson 2013a).

Reportedly a close friend of Abbott since their university days, veteran Australian journalist Greg Sheridan is also a strong supporter of the US pivot strategy and a leading critic of the dovish school of thinking on the US rebalance – particularly the work of White (see, for example, Sheridan 2013). Abbott's international security adviser Andrew Shearer (who served as foreign policy adviser to Prime Minister John Howard), is also a prominent member of the hawkish camp, arguing that Australia should throw its lot in with the United States in confronting China's rise. In a widely cited paper published when he was director of studies at the Lowy Institute for International Policy, for example, Shearer observed that:

> [T]he challenge for Australian diplomacy in the next decade is to explain that if anything Australia is moving *closer* to the United States ... This will require skill and subtlety, particularly as strategic competition between China and the United States intensifies. But it is achievable.
>
> (Shearer 2011: 8, emphasis in original)

Owls

Commentators who can be categorized as belonging to the owls camp locate themselves between those hawks who advocate that Australia provide the strongest possible backing for the US pivot strategy – even including encouragement of that strategy's expansion – and those of the more dovish persuasion who argue that Canberra should instead encourage Washington to moderate the strategy with a view to accommodating China's rise and thereby ameliorating the prospects for strategic competition between China and the United States.

A prominent member of the owls camp is the former senior Australian Department of Defence official Paul Dibb. Dibb has argued consistently that dovish commentators have tended to underestimate the durability and extent of American power, whilst also overlooking the proven capacity of the United States to regenerate at other key historical junctures – such as at the end of the Vietnam War and the end of the Cold War – when many commentators had similarly written the country off (see, for example, Kennedy 1987).

Regarding the pivot strategy, Dibb accuses critics of Obama's US Marine rotation initiative of overreaction, given the relatively small scale of the military forces concerned and Australia's geographic distance from China – a factor rendering its vulnerability to attack from that country next to impossible. Dibb also argues that the risks to Australia due to its alliance relationship with the United States have been much greater at other points in history, particularly during the Cold War years when Australia hosted some of America's most important intelligence facilities. Yet unlike the hawks, Dibb also suggests that efforts to encourage China towards greater levels of cooperative behaviour and military transparency should continue, meaning that it is in Australia's interests to support the 'modest' use of its facilities by the United States (Dibb 2012).

Along similar lines, the respected Australian journalist Paul Kelly is also a prominent member of the owls camp. Interestingly, in Australia's earlier 'China debate', Kelly's views were somewhat closer to those advanced by the hawks, particularly his suggestions that Australia's political leaders had already decided to side with the United States and that any 'China choice' was a false one. Perhaps anticipating the outcomes of the November 2011 Obama visit, Kelly reported one year earlier that the Gillard government had 'sensibly decided to support a bigger American presence' (Kelly 2010). As the US pivot has evolved, however, so too has Kelly's position on it. Writing in mid-2013, for instance, Kelly remained critical of those Australian commentators advocating the accommodation of a rising China, while at the same time urging a greater level of American sensitivity toward 'the strategic dilemma that Australia faces, and of the new debate it has spawned'. In keeping with the owls camp, however, Kelly observes that Australian policymakers have historically exhibited 'a remarkable capacity to integrate their US alliance and their Asian engagements' and he thus remains optimistic regarding their continued capacity to do so, '[a]s long as Sino-American relations do not deteriorate into a raw, zero-sum contest' (Kelly 2013: 67).

As with the doves and the hawks, the owls in Australia's public debate on the US pivot also enjoy support amongst prominent political figures. Most notably, former Prime Minister Howard – whom some regard as a role model of sorts for Abbott, particularly in the area of foreign policy – has struck out at the doves by describing as 'infantile' the notion that Australia faces a choice between its leading economic partner and its long-standing strategic ally. Equally, however, he also provides implicit criticism of more hawkish commentators by observing that 'one of the things that Australia must do is avoid those people who say we have to make choices' (Elliott and Mathieson 2013). Indeed, in a fashion similar to the foreign policy that he followed when prime minister between 1996 and 2007, Howard continues to maintain that 'Australia can expand its trade and investment ties with China while at the same time respecting its longstanding security alliance with the US' (*Australian Financial Review* 2012).

American anxieties

The Obama Administration has been attentive to the public debate regarding Australia's response to the US pivot and there are indications that this debate has generated some sensitivities in Washington. Perhaps the clearest evidence is the statement in August 2012 by Kurt Campbell, then assistant secretary of state for East Asian and Pacific affairs. Campbell publicly intervened in the Australian debate when he criticized White's thesis and the remarks that Keating had made in launching White's book. In particular, Campbell was critical of the 'false assessments' by White and others that the United States is experiencing a period of decline, making a point to 'reject [these] out of hand', and asserting that '[t]he US is going to be a dynamic and powerful player in Asia for many decades to come'. In response to criticisms that the United States needed to go to greater lengths to accommodate China's rise by creating more strategic space for this rising power, Campbell countered that 'no country has taken more trouble to engage with China' than America (cited in Hartcher 2012a).

There have also been indications that American disenchantment with Australia's response to the pivot has extended beyond the public debate and has manifested itself in tensions at the government-to-government level, some of which have again been expressed publicly. Much of this disenchantment has revolved around the decline of the portion of the Australian federal budget allocated to defence expenditure, which according to some commentators has fallen to its lowest levels since 1938 (see, for example, Sheridan 2012). Washington's displeasure on this issue became particularly apparent in the lead-up to the November 2012 AUSMIN meeting when both Campbell and US Pacific Commander Admiral Samuel Locklear expressed concerns regarding the current levels of Australian defence spending (Hartcher 2012b). More recently, former Deputy Secretary of State Richard Armitage delivered the same message even more forcefully, by asserting that Australia's 'free ride' on America must come to an end (Joye 2013).

What explains American anxieties over Australia's defence expenditure at this juncture? As Mark Thomson has observed, '[l]ooking further back, it's clear that we've been free riding at each and every stage of our sixty plus years of formal alliance with the United States, including through the disproportionately small contributions we made to conflicts in Korea, Vietnam, Iraq and Afghanistan' (Thomson 2012: 2). The most likely explanation is that recent declines in the Australian defence budget have been anathema to a central premise of the pivot strategy – and one routinely forgotten amidst all the hype of US force rotations and redeployments to the Asia-Pacific theatre – that Washington expects its strategic partners also to assume a greater share of the responsibility for maintaining stability in this part of the world (for further reading, see Le Mière 2013). Given the perceived level of strategic intimacy between Australia and America, Canberra's response (or meaningful lack thereof) to the pivot thus has the potential to send a dangerous signal to other Asian allies and partners of the United States as to what they can and cannot get away with in terms of meeting Washington's expectations. As the American columnist Anne Applebaum (2013) has observed, 'Australia is a test case, not so much of American willpower but of the US ability to think strategically, plan ahead, and keep allies on board'.

Trouble ahead?

Notwithstanding the issues identified in this chapter, the US-Australian alliance currently remains in remarkably good shape. Australian public support for the alliance is strong. According to recent polling conducted by the Lowy Institute for International Policy, for instance, 82 percent of Australians support the alliance while 61 percent are in favour of allowing America to base forces in their country (Oliver 2013: 7–8). Some commentators even suggest that the US alliance is so much a part of Australia's Western cultural identity that it is a fruitless exercise to contemplate alternatives to this long-standing strategic relationship (see, for example, Dobell 2010). Indeed, it may be that because issues of identity are involved, the views put forward by doves in Australia's public debate regarding the US pivot have provoked such a visceral reaction.

Yet the findings of this chapter also warn against undue complacency. They demonstrate the existence of a marked disjuncture between official Australian pronouncements on the US pivot and the sometimes quite heated public debate that has emerged in the wake of the rebalance, and which has engaged key current and former policy elites. The chapter has also highlighted some of the anxieties that this debate has occasioned amongst US policymakers – as reflected by their public responses – as well as the concerns that Canberra's commitment (or lack thereof) to maintaining defence expenditure have created in Washington. These tensions will require careful monitoring in the years ahead, notwithstanding the growing level of strategic intimacy between America and Australia since the introduction of the pivot strategy. As Stephen Walt has famously cautioned, no alliance relationship should ever be taken for granted. Otherwise, 'the alliance may be dead long before anyone notices, and the discovery of the corpse may come at a very inconvenient moment' (Walt 1997: 167).

References

Age (2012) 'China Drops Hint About a Pacific Cold War', 16 May.

Applebaum, Anne (2013) 'Don't Forget Down Under: Is the United States in Danger of Forgetting the Ally it has in Australia?' *Slate*, 3 May.

Australian Financial Review (2012) 'No Need to Choose Between China and US', 20 November.

Australian Government (2011) Australia in the Asian Century: White Paper, Canberra: Commonwealth of Australia.

Babbage, Ross (2008) 'Learning to Walk Among Giants: The New Defence White Paper', Security Challenges, 4(1): 13–20.

Bell, Coral (1993) Dependent Ally: A Study in Australian Foreign Policy, St Leonards, NSW: Allen & Unwin in association with the Department of International Relations, Australian National University.

Department of Defence, Australia (2013) Defence White Paper 2013, Canberra: Commonwealth of Australia.

Department of the Prime Minister and Cabinet, Australia (2013) Strong and Secure: A Strategy for Australia's National Security, Canberra: Commonwealth of Australia.

Dibb, Paul (2012) 'Modest US Military Presence is in Our Interest', *The Australian*, 4 May.

Dobell, Graeme (2010) 'Torn, Frayed or Rumpled by China?' *The Interpreter*, 9 September.

Earl, Greg (2012) 'US Wrong on China: Keating', *Australian Financial Review*, 7 August.

Elliott, Geoff and Mathieson, Clive (2013) 'US vs China Debate "Infantile", Says John Howard', *The Australian*, 16 May.

Franklin, Matthew (2011) 'Ovations and Flattery in Julia Gillard's Speech to US Congress', *The Australian*, 10 March.

Fraser, Malcolm (2012) 'Overbalancing: The Folly of Trying to Contain China', *Global Asia*, 7(4): 28–33.

Garnaut, John (2012) 'Smith Talks Up "Two Boats" Policy to Wary Chinese', *Sydney Morning Herald*, 7 June.

Hartcher, Peter (2012a) 'No Need To Choose Between America and China: Top US Official', *Sydney Morning Herald*, 23 August.

——(2012b) 'US to Take Up Defence "Freeloading" with Cabinet', *Sydney Morning Herald*, 10 November.

Jakobson, Linda (2013) 'Australia–China Strategic Partnership: Two Years of Fits and Starts', *The Interpreter*, 10 April.

Joye, Christopher (2013) 'Richard Armitage: Why the Free Ride on US Must Stop', *Australian Financial Review*, 19 August.

Kelly, Paul (2010) 'Deeper US Alliance in Response to Strident China', *The Australian*, 10 November.

——(2013) 'Australia's Wandering Eye', *The American Interest*, 8(5): 62–67.

Kennedy, Paul (1987) The Rise and Fall of the Great Powers: Economic Change and Military Conflict From 1500 to 2000, New York: Random House.

Kerin, John (2012) 'Buying US Submarines May Anger China', *Australian Financial Review*, 10 November.

Le Mière, Christian (2013) 'Rebalancing the Burden in East Asia', *Survival*, 55(2): 31–41.

Medcalf, Rory (2012) 'Pivoting the Map: Australia's Indo-Pacific System', Centre of Gravity Paper #1, Canberra: Strategic and Defence Studies Centre, Australian National University, November.

Nicholson, Brendan (2013a) 'Abbott Government Plans a Review of Defence Deals', *The Australian*, 2 December.

——(2013b) 'Defence White Paper Pivots Over China Threat', *The Australian*, 4 May.

Nusa Dua (2011) 'New US Base in RI's Backyard', *Jakarta Post*, 17 November.

Oliver, Alex (2013) 'Australia and the World: Public Opinion and Foreign Policy', Lowy Institute Poll, Sydney: Lowy Institute for International Policy, June.

Robson, Seth (2013) 'Budget Woes Threaten Pacific "Pivot"', *Stars and Stripes*, 21 February.

Shearer, Andrew (2011) 'Uncharted Waters: The US Alliance and Australia's New Era of Strategic Uncertainty', Sydney: Lowy Institute for International Policy, August.

Sheridan, Greg (2011) 'New Australia–US Push Deals India in to Pacific', *The Australian*, 17 September.

——(2012) 'Our Forces Reduced to Impotence', *The Australian*, 12 May.

——(2013) 'Abbott's Job to Re-Pivot Obama', *The Australian*, 19 September.

Slavin, Erik (2013) 'Australian Frigate Embeds with US Navy at Yokosuka, Japan', *Stars and Stripes*, 6 May.

Thomson, Mark (2012) 'How Much is Too Little? Learning to Live with a Smaller Force', ASPI Policy Analysis, 103(15 August).

Turnbull, Malcolm (2012) 'Power Shift: Hugh White's "The China Choice"', *The Monthly*, 81 (August): 53–55.

Walt, Stephen M. (1997) 'Why Alliances Endure or Collapse', *Survival*, 39(1): 156–79.

White, Hugh (2011a) 'Dear Mr President, We Beg to Differ Over the Future of Asia', *Sydney Morning Herald*, 16 November.

——(2011b) 'The Obama Doctrine: The US Plan to Take on China Recalls Harry Truman's Containment of the Soviet Union', *Wall Street Journal Asia*, 25 November.

——(2013) 'Australia's Choice: Will the Land Down Under Pick the United States or China?' *Foreign Affairs*, 4 September.

12 New Zealand's response

Robert Ayson

Since its unveiling in late 2011, the 'pivot' has become firmly entrenched as the Barack Obama Administration's signature tune for US policy towards Asia.[1] Whatever one might say about the sustainability or suitability of the approach it reflects, there is little point in suggesting that the pivot is a complete phantasm. Correspondingly, New Zealand and other regional countries have not been chasing shadows in their perceptions and responses. However, the variety of ways in which we can understand the pivot, and the complexity and uncertainty this variety brings, makes it hard to ascertain exactly what it is that countries in the Asia-Pacific region are reacting to in their own various ways.

It is unlikely, therefore, that New Zealand or any country in the region has a single response to, or a single perception of, the pivot. We are more likely to be talking about a series of smaller responses than one large 'for or against the US pivot' choice, although as will be suggested at the end of this chapter, the former may combine to produce the latter involuntarily. Before coming to that point of view, the analysis that follows tries to understand the pivot from a range of vantage points, including what it says about US priorities, the extent to which it represents something genuinely new in Washington's approach to the region, and the mix of component parts that give the pivot substance. Each of these vantage points will be used to shed light on New Zealand's response to the pivot, including the extent to which the pivot as US strategic policy converges with New Zealand's perception of its own regional interests and priorities.

The priority of the pivot

At one level the pivot is a very simple proposition: it is a US commitment to emphasize the strategic importance of Asia in both intention and action. However, as soon as we break down this proposition by asking some basic but important questions, the complexity of the pivot as a piece of policy emerges fairly quickly. For example, an opening question relates to the main purpose of the pivot. To what extent is the purpose a negative one: a determination that the United States wants to free itself *from* long and complex nation-building efforts beyond East Asia (in such places as Iraq and Afghanistan)? How much is it the positive half of that equation: the desire to shift America's attention *towards* the Asian theatre where China, a peer competitor, has been growing in influence?

For New Zealand, an Asia-Pacific country that had forces deployed in Afghanistan for more than a decade from 2001, the negative purpose is quite important. Successive governments in Wellington have found that their continuing Afghanistan commitment has been very good for building a much more positive security relationship with the United States which had been largely suspended since the mid-1980s ANZUS (Australia New Zealand United States) treaty dispute over nuclear ship visits (for the story of the 1980s crisis in US-New Zealand relations, see McKinnon 1993: 278–301). However, after many long years, New Zealand has welcomed the opportunity that the pivot argument provides for the return of most of its forces from Afghanistan (which took place nearly a year ahead of the corresponding Australian and US drawdown of combat troops).

Moreover, the positive viewpoint – the US pivot towards Asia – is also significant for New Zealand, for which so many commercial and political interests are concentrated in Asia. If we assume for a moment that a greater focus by Washington on Asia helps sustain the environment in which New Zealand can pursue those interests, and indeed invites the possibility of closer US-New Zealand cooperation on regional issues, then Washington's pivot *towards* Asia also works for New Zealand. (If we conclude, on the other hand, that the pivot's long-term effect is to engender a climate of deeper great power tensions, then our answer may be different.)

There are questions here about the extent to which the pivot will be buffeted by other factors. These include the 'pull' factors that will keep the United States attached to the Middle East and surrounding areas in particular, and the domestic factors (constraints) in American decision making which can sometimes pose a challenge to external commitments. Assuming that the pivot can survive these pressures, however, over time the idea of a pivot *from* the Iraq/Afghanistan era in US policy will become an increasingly distant memory. The notion of the pivot *towards* Asia will dominate.

This leads to another question: what sort of American prioritization of Asia does the pivot suggest? To what extent, for example, does it signify a genuine shift of resources from one or more regions to another, so that in a military sense, for example, fewer of them are available to the Atlantic Command, and more for the Pacific Command? Perhaps the best-known aspect of this question are the plans for 60 percent of US naval forces to be deployed in the Western Pacific by 2020 (see Panetta 2012). This number is often repeated as a sign of Washington's medium-term determination to put real meat on the rhetorical bones of the pivot, but as time goes on, and if resource constraints bite, it is not inconceivable that the increased proportion of US forces in Asia will represent a larger slice of a smaller pie. In the end, will Asia get more defence resources in relative but not in absolute terms, or will it be eminently possible to achieve both?

This distinction makes more difference to regional countries for which security depends very directly on America's capacity to exert military power into East Asia (even if we accept that the United States is a 'resident power' in the Western Pacific, it still needs to deploy forces forward if they are to be present in Asia). An increase in America's absolute resources in Asia counts a great deal to Japan, for example, which is concerned (and occasionally unnerved) about any small incremental increase in China's power. It may also matter a good deal to some of the Southeast Asian allies and partners of the United States which sometimes have similar concerns, including one or more of those with claims in the South China Sea which increasingly lives under the shadow of Beijing's intentions. However, it matters less to New Zealand, whose military contacts with the United States were largely suspended for over two decades without too many observable implications for New Zealand's immediate security environment. Even a United States whose absolute power in Asia is declining (but at a slower rate than the decline elsewhere) would continue to look very substantial from Wellington's vantage point. There would likely still be more possibilities for defence cooperation with the United States than New Zealand's small forces (under 10,000 regular personnel) could cope with in an era when the bilateral security relationship has improved substantially.

Another version of America's regional prioritization is the extent to which the pivot means a shift of the distribution of Washington's attention and resources *within* (rather than *to*) Asia. For example, the pivot appears to embody a greater American emphasis on the strategic importance of maritime Southeast Asia. This certainly matters considerably to New Zealand's closest partner, Australia, whose *Defence White Paper 2013* described as 'Indo-Pacific' a strategy that may, in reality, have been little more than a call for a stronger relationship with Indonesia (Department of Defence, Australia 2013). The increased profile of Australia in American thinking (as evidenced by President Obama's announcement of the guts of the pivot while visiting Australia; see Obama 2011) makes a good deal of difference in Wellington. New Zealand has been designing its defence force around possible operations in the South Pacific and less on deployment into Southeast Asia (it completely lacks a relationship with Indonesia which Australia increasingly regards as an asset). It might be wondered in Wellington, therefore, whether the pivot within Asia actually makes it harder for New Zealand to build its most important security relationship across the Tasman Sea.

However, New Zealand is also receiving more than its fair share of attention from Washington (a pattern that the pivot has accelerated but did not begin). This raises the question of whether Wellington will find itself pulled in some challenging directions: will a closer relationship with the United States, partly courtesy of the pivot, take New Zealand increasingly out of its South Pacific comfort zone and offer connections to more challenging neighbourhoods and geopolitics? This does not indicate that New Zealand has been absent from the wider region: its long-standing participation in the Five

Power Defence Arrangements with Australia, Malaysia, Singapore and the United Kingdom is a sign of a wider remit. However, the US connection could increase the spread of New Zealand's military activities in a wider Asia-Pacific context, a development that Wellington should be watching very carefully.

In June 2013, for example, New Zealand personnel participated in Dawn Blitz, a large amphibious exercise off the Californian coast. With substantial Japanese participation, and in the context of sensitivities over the Diaoyu/Senkaku Islands dispute, the exercise drew the ire of China (see Schreer and Ayson 2013). This may be just one sign that as the United States looks further south into the region, New Zealand may end up looking further north. From New Zealand's perspective, a US focus on the bilateral relationship that emphasizes cooperation in the South Pacific, the stuff of the 2010 Wellington Declaration, makes for easier international politics than a broader Asia-Pacific dimension, which was reflected in the 2012 Washington Declaration (both of which are mentioned below). New Zealand cannot rule out the possibility of being involved in issues and areas in ways that might have seemed almost unthinkable a few years ago.

The newness of the pivot

These points raise a further question. The repositioning of US forces *within* Asia was signalled and taking place well before the pivot became part of our vocabulary. These earlier trends included the reduced emphasis on US land forces on the Korean peninsula, the greater use of Guam, and the long-term project to adjust the US posture in Japan. Spreading America's strategic risk further into maritime Asia was already taking place (including the 'places rather than bases' logic) well before the 'p' word become popular. Hence the obvious question: had the pivot simply not come about, which elements of the evolution in America's regional role would we *not* have seen?

New Zealand represents a somewhat unique case here. The once-strained US-New Zealand security relationship was getting back on track well before the middle years of Obama's first term when the pivot was announced. Indeed, positive developments in that direction were occurring in the second George W. Bush term, as Washington was noticing New Zealand's commitment to a common cause in Afghanistan (hence the recent award of a New Zealand Order of Merit to Christopher Hill, the chief Asia policy official in the State Department from that period).

This creates something of a disentanglement problem for our analysis: the pivot may have accelerated America's efforts to develop a closer security partnership with New Zealand which Wellington has welcomed, but the improvement in the relationship predates this additional regional attention. US Secretary of State Hillary Clinton signed the Wellington Declaration, which focuses on the two countries' greater security cooperation in the South Pacific, including disaster response management and renewable energy assistance to regional countries, a year before her well-known *Foreign Policy* article appeared, representing the pivot's early appearance as a piece of diplomacy (New Zealand Ministry of Foreign Affairs and Trade 2010; Clinton 2011). Two years later came the Washington Declaration, signed by defence ministers Leon Panetta and Jonathan Coleman (United States Department of Defense and New Zealand Ministry of Defence 2012). Was this second agreement, which involves the two countries in deeper defence collaboration in the wider Asia-Pacific (especially in maritime affairs; see Ayson 2012: 345–46), a summation of what the *pivot* means for US-New Zealand relations? Or is it a natural evolution of the closer relationship that was going to occur in any case as part of the restoration of deeper US-New Zealand security links?

We might ask the same questions about concrete aspects of that cooperation including New Zealand's return, for the first time in decades, as a participant in Rim of the Pacific exercises, and the participation of the Royal New Zealand Navy frigate *Te Mana* in exercises with the United States near Guam in May 2013. These new opportunities, which New Zealand has happily taken up, are signs of a fresh era in bilateral defence cooperation. To what extent, though, is this New Zealand's endorsement of the pivot per se, or is this about developing a stronger bilateral military relationship which for many years was strained for quite separate and unrelated reasons?[2]

New Zealand's involvement in these and other exercises (including US and New Zealand army personnel exercising in one another's countries) brings to mind another question: what concrete signs of the pivot are in evidence in the region? A great deal seems to have been made, for example, of the rotation of US Marines into Darwin and of US littoral ships into Singapore, but neither of these developments involves more than a very small fraction of the overall US commitment in the region, either before the pivot or after. Neither do such relatively small moves change the distribution of military power in Asia; the core of that American presence, the United States Seventh Fleet, has never left the region. Can we, or should we, count as part of the pivot the *continuation* of this long-standing presence (noting that the pivot will at best augment this existing commitment, and will not come close to doubling it even if the 60 percent deployment target is achieved)? In other words, does the pivot consist of major *new* elements in America's approach, or is it a way of saying that Washington now attaches increasing importance to its long-standing presence? Is the pivot, therefore, more about *attitude* than *presence*? Should we count the welcome that many regional countries have been giving to that long-standing presence (particularly as some are concerned about China's rise) as a sign of their enthusiasm for the pivot? If so, what precisely has changed in the way they have welcomed the American military presence in Asia?

These are important questions in relation to New Zealand's case. Soon after it won office in 1999, the Labour-led government of Helen Clark issued a short 'Defence Policy Framework' document which managed to indicate priorities without once mentioning the United States (New Zealand Government 2000). However, within a few years, Winston Peters, foreign minister of the third Clark coalition administration (who was, admittedly, a leading politician from another party) was on record indicating New Zealand's support for the US role. In one 2006 speech, he argued that 'New Zealand's position on North Korea, our contributions to the campaign against international terrorism, and our commitment to addressing security issues in the Pacific region all serve to support the attainment of US objectives' (Peters 2006). A few years later still, background documents to the *Defence White Paper 2010* published by the National Party-led coalition government of John Key, indicated New Zealand's interest in encouraging a strong US regional presence as a top defence policy priority for New Zealand (for an analysis of these documents, see Ayson 2011: 24–27). It is interesting to note that all of this happened *before* the pivot was part of American policy (at least in terms of the major announcements in late 2011).

The substance of the pivot

This line of questioning encourages us to determine of what we think the pivot consists. How do we know the pivot when we see or hear it? A number of points need to be made here. We should not be surprised if there are gaps between Washington's declaratory policy (its statements of intent) and its operational policy (what it does on the ground – and in the air, sea, space and cyberspace) in Asia.[3] This gap, if it exists, is not just a result of economic limitations during a time of budgetary restraint, or of domestic politics 'inside the beltway'. Neither is it just a question of our assessments of the longevity and sustainability of the pivot which, in New Zealand's case, has focused on how much extra effort the United States will be able to sustain in the South Pacific. It is not just because similar to almost every country in the world, including Australia and New Zealand, America's ambitions often exceed its means. It is also down to the very nature of the pivot itself.

An organizing concept

In my view, the pivot is rather like other *organizing concepts* – such as the 'war on terror' or the 'arc of instability',[4] or even the Cold War strategy of containment – the very declaration of which is an important part of the effect that is being sought. By this I do not mean to invoke the dubious arguments about 'speech acts' that one finds in securitization theory. Instead, I treat the pivot as a conscious, deliberate and serious attempt at political communication and persuasion by the Obama Administration. As an organizing concept, the pivot (especially towards Asia as a whole) reduces the bewildering complexity that arises when one considers Washington's interests, interactions and roles in Asia, and when one tries to keep up with what is happening with Washington's bilateral relationships in the region.[5]

As an organizing concept, the pivot can also help to justify the commitment of extensive resources, even if that commitment simply consists of a continuation of what has come before in a period when resources are being constrained. In Asia, it is a form of communication with Washington's allies and partners in the region on the one hand, and its potential adversaries on the other. It is a form of policy communication or policy guidance from the 'commander in chief', and because Washington's official opinion on issues is an important influence in the world, the very declaration of the pivot is a significant act of policy.

In turn, regional governments are able to welcome this declaratory dimension of the pivot with their own statements. Some of those from Beijing, through official channels and also via sanctioned statements by commentators in the press, have been less than welcoming, evoking suspicions about Washington's true intentions (for an analysis of the variety of responses from Chinese observers, see Swaine 2012). However, the beauty of the declaratory register is that opposition can take place through statements without requiring a material response, an approach which has a long track record in parts of the Asia-Pacific region. Indeed, support for the pivot (amongst allies and partners) can also be found in declaratory endorsements that are not necessarily accompanied by the commitment of extra physical resources. Free-riding is a perfectly acceptable, rational and respectable response to the pivot, especially if the latter is strong on rhetoric.

The declaratory route has been one way in which the New Zealand government has, without too much theatre, welcomed the pivot. The lack of drama is possibly because New Zealand ministers also have their eye on other relationships in the Asia-Pacific region. Accordingly, they have insisted that New Zealand is showing that it is possible to maintain good relationships with a pivoting America and a rising China at the same time.[6] Again, this is something that can simply be declared, although the fact that New Zealand has developed a closer security partnership with Washington without in any obvious way (yet) harming its commercial links with China may be practical evidence for the proposition. However, the ride may not be as free and as easy as they suggest.

The diplomatic angle

On a related front, part of the substance of the pivot is its role as a piece of regional *diplomacy*. Diplomacy is much more than a series of statements. It involves the fostering and exploitation of foreign relationships, and the representation of one's interests overseas. It also involves formal and informal diplomatic processes through which interests are represented, the holding of meetings, the negotiation of agreements, the occasional issuing of demarches, and the establishment of what we call regional security architecture. In this last space, Washington has been very busy. The Obama Administration's decision to sign the Treaty of Amity and Cooperation as a requirement for entry to the East Asia Summit (EAS) deserves to be seen as part of America's action policy and not just its declaratory policy in respect of the pivot. Although the EAS participation decision was yet another thing that happened before the pivot was an explicit part of Washington's policy, a case can be made for the proposition that this is really where the US pivot began.

The EAS commitment and an increasingly high-level American involvement in other regional forums is one sign that the pivot was also part of the rough and tumble of American partisan politics. The Bush/Condoleezza Rice approach was portrayed as short-changing America's influence in Asia, and the Obama team was determined to change that. However, it was also about objective calculations of US national interests that were occurring in Washington and in US missions in the region. No recent act has done more to boost America's reputation in Asia, and in Southeast Asia in particular, than this pre-pivot diplomatic move.

US participation in the EAS was strongly encouraged and warmly welcomed by New Zealand (see McCully 2013). There is a range of interlocking reasons for this. New Zealand takes multilateral diplomacy in Asia seriously for two reasons: first because it has a tradition, born of interest and philosophy, in strong international diplomatic cooperation and the peaceful resolution of disputes; and second because being inside Asia's main multilateral forums (especially the Association of Southeast Asian Nations (ASEAN)+8 grouping reflected in the EAS) is seen as a crucial element in sustaining New Zealand's ability to benefit from the region's dynamism and inject some of its own preferences into what comes next. The prospect of being left out of such discussions and processes is such a nightmare for New Zealand that it is likely why the country was quicker off the mark than Australia to sign the Treaty of Amity and Cooperation. Moreover, in the absence of a defence force and overseas aid budget close to that of Australia, multilateral diplomacy in Asia is, for New Zealand, a relatively more important instrument of external engagement (see Capie 2013). Consequently, to the extent that New Zealand welcomes a more attentive US approach in Asia, the ending of Washington's separation from the EAS (an important piece of the emerging regional architecture) would be a natural priority for Wellington. If New Zealand wishes to have deeper bilateral relations with the United States, Washington's involvement in these multilateral forums provides a suitable opportunity to develop some of these expanding ties.

Similarly, the first Obama Administration's active interest in the Pacific Islands Forum, which included the direct participation of US Secretary of State Clinton and Assistant Secretary of State for East Asian and Pacific Affairs Kurt Campbell, was also positive for New Zealand. For most watchers of the pivot, especially as it affects security in North Asia, the South Pacific is not regarded as a priority area. Indeed, it might not feature at all in some analyses. The pivot as a piece of *strategic* policy hardly seems to connect with this sub-region: there are few compelling reasons for the deployment of American forces in the South Pacific, for example, and this part of the region is unlikely ever to be a major theatre of great-power competition.

However, the great powers' interest in the South Pacific has been growing. For China, the small states in the South Pacific represent quite a grouping of votes in international organizations such as the United Nations (for an analysis of China's growing interest in the South Pacific, see Lanteigne 2012). France is still a significant actor in the region, the United States retains Pacific territories, the European Union and Japan are major providers of development assistance, and in the coming years, one can expect more interest from India and Indonesia (the largest neighbour of Papua New Guinea) in the affairs of the Pacific Island countries.

In these circumstances, and cognizant that neither New Zealand nor Australia has the resources or the inclination to treat the Pacific as their own exclusive sphere of interest, Wellington has generally not sought to deter the interest of the larger players.[7] However, greater US involvement holds the prospect of working with a great power that shares principles more closely with New Zealand about the region's political trajectory (including support for democratic politics). It is also a chance to build the bilateral US-New Zealand relationship in a context far removed from some of the regional hotspots further north (a fact that makes the carefully drafted Wellington Declaration a less risky endeavour for New Zealand than the more speedily arranged Washington Declaration that followed it). However, for similar reasons, the South Pacific dimension of the pivot may become challenging for Washington in terms of sustaining effort and attention, something which cannot be said for obvious strategic reasons in East Asia. Sustaining the South Pacific dimension of the pivot may well rely more on personalities in Washington than on questions of urgent national interest.

The economic dimension

Alongside its South Pacific focus, another abiding element of New Zealand's foreign policy, one arguably most dominant, provides Wellington with a special interest in another aspect of the Obama Administration's regional policy. This is the pivot's economic dimension, especially in terms of Washington's trade policy. There are two elements here, one general and one specific. Generally, among the rationales for the pivot lies the view that in challenging economic times, Asia offers more opportunities for the United States than any other region in the world. This has been one of the strongest arguments for the pivot that was used in the American domestic political context (not least because the pivot was being marketed in the lead-up to the 2012 US elections), but one which is sometimes lost amidst the attention devoted to its military dimension. Specifically, it is interesting to see the way in which Washington's involvement in negotiations for the Trans-Pacific Partnership (TPP) found their way into the Obama Administration's depiction of the pivot as a coordinated inter-agency affair.

The Obama Administration's emphasis on the TPP is good economic news for Wellington, one of the main drivers of the negotiations aimed at enlarging the 'P4' (Brunei, Chile, New Zealand and Singapore) free trade grouping. In the absence of a bilateral free trade agreement with the United States (which is one of New Zealand's leading trading partners), the TPP offers a chance for New Zealand to achieve that relationship by another means. Moreover, given that New Zealand views its bilateral and plurilateral free trade agreements as the most significant signs of its wider engagement in Asia,[8] Washington's greater involvement in Asia's economic integration signifies more than direct economic gains.

However there is a catch for Wellington. It would have been preferable had the Obama Administration simply treated the TPP as a trade agreement, but in selling it as part of the pivot, and in presenting itself as the leader of the TPP exercise (especially since President Obama's push at the Hawaii Asia-Pacific Economic Cooperation meeting in 2011; see BBC News Asia 2011), Washington's line has drawn considerable attention to the TPP's strategic implications. This has not always gone down well in China, with which New Zealand has a very valuable free trade agreement (New Zealand is the first Organisation for Economic Co-operation and Development member to have such an accord). When China has been in a mood to regard the pivot as an instrument of containment (an assertion that Washington has vigorously, and too concertedly, denied), the TPP becomes subject to the same campaign of pressure because the United States has argued that the two are connected. This has led New Zealand ministers to argue that they would never sign a TPP that was designed to exclude China (for example, see the comments of New Zealand Trade Minister Tim Groser in Black 2012). In that context, any signs that Beijing might be interested in participating in TPP discussions, such as those that became evident in mid-2013 (*Bangkok Post* 2013), will be welcomed in Wellington, for which the division of the region into rival trading arrangements would be disastrous.

The military element: the pivot's core?

Beijing's public responses to elements of American policy (such as the TPP) reflect more than an objective calculation of China's interests towards the particular policy in question. More often than not, they are an indication of how China wishes to talk about the overall relationship with the United States. At times, therefore, America's arms sales to Taiwan, while never popular, evoke a much stronger response than in other less tense moments. Perhaps something similar has been happening with the TPP. Beijing's tentative warming towards these negotiations may well be attached to the 'new era' in great power relations that was announced before, during and after the Obama–Xi Jinping summit in June 2013 (for a measured assessment of the relationship, see Zoellick 2013). That meeting, early in Xi's term of office, signalled a more productive relationship between the two players, although it is not the equivalent of the breakthrough that came in the early 1970s between Richard Nixon and Mao Zedong.

Neither will this new era suddenly usher in a situation of deep military trust between the two great powers. This will remain a point of some contention between the United States, the established maritime power that projects itself into East Asia, and China, the traditional giant of the region, a continental power which is also developing the ability to blunt America's long-standing ability to conduct itself freely in North Asia's maritime spaces. While it would be unwise to depict the pivot simply as a sign that America felt its military advantage in Asia vis-à-vis China was slipping, it cannot be denied that this was a central driver for Washington. For that reason, the military dimension of the pivot remains a big part of the overall policy. For that reason too, it is sometimes hard for American diplomats and trade policy officials to compete with the attention that the Pentagon receives as the pivot's most visible parent.

It is also quite clear that while most East Asian countries welcomed America's diplomatic efforts to boost engagement with the region (as in the case of the EAS, as discussed above), their eyes are firmly on Washington's strategic intentions. They will not always say this publicly, but the distribution of military power in Asia (in terms of both capability *and* intention) is often the key factor in their calculations. For those concerned about China (as the main reason for their enthusiastic response to the pivot), they know Beijing watches the military correlation of power even more closely than they do.

However, it is unwise to assume that the amount of military power that the United States is able to project into East Asia is the one and only factor. This becomes an instant problem if we think that there will be real limits to how much extra resources the United States can find to support the pivot. It is quite clear that some US policymakers are aware of these limits (for an example of the public advice that policymakers have been receiving, see Congressional Budget Office 2013). For that reason, the military side of the pivot is as much about the *relationships* that the United States can build with allies and partners in the region as it is about the *power* that the United States can provide and project. The pivot may do more to change the distribution of regional power because of the new regional *alignments* it encourages than because of the additional *resources* the Pentagon can offer. This also means that the attitude that allies and partners take to relatively small military moves by Washington matter. These moves are less important in and of themselves in terms of what they do to the order of battle. Instead, they are more potent in symbolizing the foreign policy ambitions that the pivot brings. Responses to these seemingly small and innocuous moves count more than America's allies and friends might think.

New Zealand is one of a number of regional countries that have been responding to these moves, which may matter less to the distribution of military power in an immediate sense and more to the distribution of political intent to which the use and potential use of force is connected. As an 'emerging partner' (Clinton 2011: 59), despite having once been a close and active ally, New Zealand's alignment (or more specifically its realignment) matters to the United States. However, at the same time New Zealand is a long way from many of the places that matter militarily to the United States and to other regional powers, including China. The distance between Auckland and Tokyo, for example, is about the same as that between Tokyo and Istanbul. Even Southeast Asia is a long way from the New Zealand landmass: the distance between Auckland and Jakarta, for example, is nearly three times that between Darwin and Jakarta. New Zealand will not be the first country to feel the effects of any change in America's military profile in Asia, inasmuch as that this is what the pivot is bringing.

To the extent that America's deepening engagement supports regional security and stability, New Zealand benefits indirectly in a very significant way. These conditions are necessary for sustaining economic growth in many of New Zealand's leading economic partners. Likewise, suitable conditions for the safe passage of seaborne trade, upon which New Zealand depends heavily, are also encouraged by the US presence. To the extent that the pivot ensures that the United States will be more actively engaged militarily in Asia, and to the extent that this greater activity is positive in net terms for wider regional confidence and does not engender dangerous strategic competition, New Zealand's interests are also furthered. Indeed, it is the American contribution to regional confidence in general, rather than more specific military objectives that the US presence might allow, that connects with New Zealand's daily interests in Asia.

This also means that New Zealand does not need the United States to be engaged in Asia in quite the same way as do some of America's leading allies in East Asia. Even in comparison to Australia, New Zealand's direct need for the US regional presence, and for any extra military activity that comes courtesy of the pivot, is amongst the lowest of any small or medium-sized power in the Asia-Pacific region. Yet, as has already been indicated, New Zealand appears to be taking nearly every opportunity for its defence force to work more closely with US forces. While Wellington was silent on its participation in the Dawn Blitz exercise, for example, this involvement suggests something that would have been almost unthinkable only a few years ago: the possibility that in a combat situation in Asia, New Zealand forces might contribute to an action led by the United States.

This was effectively ruled out by the Clark government's policy over a decade ago. It has now become somewhat more likely in an era of more significant great power competition in the region, underscored by the commitment in the Washington Declaration to cooperation between New Zealand and the United States on 'deployable capabilities, in support of peace and security in the Asia-Pacific' (see United States Department of Defense and New Zealand Ministry of Defence 2012: 3). It is disconcerting to find that the present New Zealand government has not stepped forward to explain the implications of these potentially significant words. The debate that New Zealand should be having when additional commitments are being made is not occurring.

This does not mean that major decisions about the future of New Zealand's defence force structure are likely to be shaped by its relationship with the

United States. Those decisions are likely to be shaped by the desire to replace multi-purpose capabilities when they age, by the needs of operating mainly in New Zealand's South Pacific environment (see New Zealand Government 2010: 35), and by the limited expenditure that is available for the New Zealand Defence Force's (NZDF) capital requirements. However, at the very least a US military effort in Asia which has been re-energized by the pivot at a time when the US-New Zealand relationship has been restored, will certainly affect the pattern of exercises and training opportunities for the NZDF. Increased information sharing (including through the 'five-eyes' network) and cooperation over doctrine are also to be expected. New Zealand may not have the maritime military capabilities that make Australia a more attractive partner for the United States in a range of future military scenarios in Asia, but this gap is not a complete barrier to New Zealand's participation in future military action in the region in a coalition led by the United States. New Zealand still boasts some small but well-trained force elements that could conceivably fit into such a mission, and attitude will matter a great deal.

The decision to participate in such a coalition, especially if the United States were going to the assistance of an East Asian ally, and if the mission were opposed by China, would be a politically momentous one for New Zealand. However, the assumption that New Zealand had plenty of room to move out of the way because its defence relationship with the United States was in a state of suspension no longer applies. The fact that New Zealand and the United States are not back in active ANZUS alliance mode is itself no automatic protection; neither is the 1987 nuclear-free legislation, which has become an increasingly lonely sign of New Zealand's determination to retain an independent foreign policy.

Conclusion

New Zealand's stronger alignment with Washington has crept up incrementally, starting with the improvement in US-New Zealand strategic relations which have since been accelerated, but which were not initiated, by the US pivot. Like many other countries in the region, including Australia, New Zealand's position in terms of the US-Chinese factor in Asian affairs is unlikely to come down to a single, all-or-nothing choice at some future moment of crisis. It is more likely to be shaped by a series of small, almost indiscernible, mini-choices. If New Zealand finds that it has moved a bit too close for comfort to the United States, this will not be because of one single move. Rather, it closely aligns with the situation known by some scholars as the tyranny of small decisions, a term originally developed by Alfred E. Kahn (1966) to explain a particular variety of market failure (the loss of a valuable train service in the state of New York). The same idea was later applied to problems of environmental degradation by William Odum (1982: 728), who observed that '[m]uch of the current confusion and distress surrounding environmental issues can be traced to decisions that were never consciously made, but simply resulted from a series of smaller decisions'. Similarly, each small decision made in Wellington about the US relationship may have seemed an entirely sensible and rational choice for the decision makers concerned, but their collective consequences could prove costly for New Zealand in the future.

It is in this light that the pivot, and its implications for regional friends, partners and allies of the United States, might best be understood. The pivot is the collective name for a whole series of actions, some involving US forces and others the US Department of State and other agencies. Even the military aspect of the pivot is hardly a consequence of a single overall move that one might see, for example, when a decision is taken to use force against an adversary in a specific crisis. It is instead composed of a series of smaller developments, some of them more symbolic than materially significant. However, the way in which regional countries respond to each of these signals is important for the positioning they need to undertake to promote their own interests. It is quite likely that the particular individuals responsible for these apparently minor decisions by New Zealand have supported each of these small opportunities, and have regarded them as promising for the country's interests. However, it is not clear who in Wellington is keeping an eye on the overall picture; nor is there any sign that the government wants to encourage (or even acknowledge) the debate that this would involve. The US pivot has quite possibly generated a New Zealand pivot. The former is intentional, but how many New Zealanders even recognize that the latter has been happening?

Notes

1 This chapter deliberately uses the Obama Administration's original language of the 'pivot' rather than the less convincing terminology of 'rebalancing'.
2 The answer is a bit of both, but working out how much *extra* cooperation the pivot has directed is difficult, at least for US-New Zealand links.
3 The relationship between declaratory and operational policy is considered, in a rather different context, in Desmond Ball's work on US nuclear strategy. See, for example, Ball (1983: 516).
4 For the author's analysis of the arc of instability as an organizing concept in Australian thinking and policy, see Ayson (2007).
5 In the latter sense, it is not unlike the relationship between the idea of a San Francisco Treaty System and the numerous individual alliances that the United States has in Asia.
6 For an example, see the remarks of New Zealand's Foreign Minister Murray McCully during a visit with his American counterpart, John Kerry, cited in Backhouse (2013).
7 This includes China, with which New Zealand and the Cook Islands signed a tri-lateral agreement for water projects on the main island of Rarotonga. For coverage from China of this development project, see *China Daily* (2012).
8 This is evident in the inter-agency 'NZ Inc' country strategies that the Key government has rolled out in recent years. At the time of writing these had been produced for New Zealand's relationships with Australia, China and India. See New Zealand Ministry of Foreign Affairs and Trade (2013).

References

Ayson, Robert (2007) 'The "Arc of Instability" and Australia's Strategic Policy', *Australian Journal of International Affairs*, 61(2): 215–31.

——(2011) 'Force and Statecraft: Strategic Objectives and Relationships in New Zealand's 2010 Defence White Paper', *Security Challenges*, 7(1): 11–29.

——(2012) 'Choosing Ahead of Time? Australia, New Zealand and the US–China Contest in Asia', *Contemporary Southeast Asia*, 34(3): 338–64.

Backhouse, Matthew (2013) 'US Coastguard Visit Up To Superpower: McCully', *New Zealand Herald*, 26 May.

Ball, Desmond (1983) 'Counterforce Targeting: How New, How Viable?' in Robert J. Art and Kenneth N. Waltz (eds) *The Use of Force: International Politics and Foreign Policy*, 2nd edn, Lanham, MD: University Press of America, pp. 516–27.

Bangkok Post (2013) 'China to Study Joining TPP', 30 May.

BBC News Asia (2011) 'Obama Outlines Pan-Pacific Trade Plan at Apec Summit', 13 November, www.bbc.co.uk/news/world-asia-15704358 (accessed 27 August 2013).

Black, Joanne (2012) 'Will the Trans-Pacific Partnership Upset China?' *New Zealand Listener*, 3570(24 March).

Capie, David (2013) *Mind the Gap: New Zealand and Regional Institutions in Southeast Asia*, Wellington: Asia New Zealand Foundation, www.asianz.org.nz/sites/asianz.org.nz/files/Mind_the_gap_report_David_Capie.pdf (accessed 27 August 2013).

China Daily (2012) 'China, NZ to Improve Water Mains in Cook Islands', 31 August, www.chinadaily.com.cn/business/2012–08/31/content_15725269.htm (accessed 27 August 2013).

Clinton, Hillary (2011) 'America's Pacific Century', *Foreign Policy*, 189(November): 56–63.

Congressional Budget Office (2013) *Approaches for Scaling Back the Defense Department's Budget Plans*, Washington: CBO, March, www.cbo.gov/sites/default/files/cbofiles/attachments/43997_Defense_Budget.pdf (accessed 27 August 2013).

Department of Defence, Australia (2013) *Defence White Paper 2013*, Canberra: Commonwealth of Australia.

Kahn, Alfred E. (1966) 'The Tyranny of Small Decisions: Market Failures, Imperfections, and the Limits of Economics', *Kyklos*, 19(1): 23–47.

Lanteigne, Marc (2012) 'Water Dragon? China, Power Shifts and Soft Balancing in the South Pacific', *Political Science*, 64(1): 21–38.

McCully, Murray (2013) 'Speech to the US/NZ Partnership Forum', Washington, DC, 21 May, www.usnzcouncil.org/minister-of-foreign-affairs-murray-mccully/ (accessed 27 August 2013).

McKinnon, Malcolm (1993) *Independence and Foreign Policy: New Zealand in the World Since 1935*, Auckland: Auckland University Press.

New Zealand Government (2000) 'The Government's Defence Policy Framework', Wellington: New Zealand Government, June, www.defence.govt.nz/pdfs/archive-publications/def-pol-framework-June2000.pdf (accessed 27 August 2013).

——(2010) *Defence White Paper 2010*, Wellington: Ministry of Defence.

New Zealand Ministry of Foreign Affairs and Trade (2010) 'Wellington Declaration on a New Strategic Partnership Between New Zealand and the United States of America', 4 November, www.mfat.govt.nz/Media-and-publications/Features/665-Wellington-declaration-on-new-NZ-US-partnership.php (accessed 27 August 2013).

——(2013) 'New Zealand Opening Doors Offshore: NZ Inc Strategies', www.mfat. govt.nz/NZ-Inc/ (accessed 27 August 2013).

Obama, Barack (2011) 'Remarks by President Obama to the Australian Parliament', Parliament House, Canberra, 17 November, www.whitehouse.gov/the-press-office/ 2011/11/17/remarks-president-obama-australian-parliament (accessed 27 August 2013).

Odum, William E. (1982) 'Environmental Degradation and the Tyranny of Small Decisions', *BioScience*, 32(9): 728–29.

Panetta, Leon (2012) 'Shangri-La Security Dialogue: As Delivered by Secretary of Defense Leon E. Panetta', Singapore, 2 June, www.defense.gov/speeches/speech. aspx?speechid=1681 (accessed 27 August 2013).

Peters, Winston (2006) 'Foreign Policy: The Next Five Years', Speech, 21 February, www.beehive.govt.nz/speech/foreign-policy-next-five-years (accessed 27 August 2013).

Schreer, Benjamin and Ayson, Robert (2013) 'Amphibious ANZACs?' *The Strategist*, Australian Strategic Policy Institute Blog, 14 June, www.aspistrategist.org.au/author/ robert-ayson/ (accessed 27 August 2013).

Swaine, Michael D. (2012) 'Chinese Leadership and Elite Responses to the US Pacific Pivot', *China Leadership Monitor*, 38(Summer): 1–26.

United States Department of Defense and New Zealand Ministry of Defence (2012) 'Washington Declaration on Defense Cooperation Between the Department of Defense of the United States of America and the Ministry of Defence of New Zealand and the New Zealand Defence Force', 19 June, beehive.govt.nz/sites/all/ files/WashingtonDeclaration.pdf (accessed 27 August 2013).

Zoellick, Robert B. (2013) 'US, China and Thucydides', *The National Interest*, 126(July/August): 22–30.

13 India and the US 'pivot' to Asia

Convergence without change

Mahesh Shankar

Introduction

As the wars in Iraq and Afghanistan began winding down in autumn 2011, top officials in Washington began articulating the Barack Obama Administration's intention to prioritize the Asia-Pacific as a strategy to sustain American global leadership. In an article for *Foreign Policy*, US Secretary of State Hillary Clinton (2011a) offered a first detailed explication of the US decision to implement a multipronged (diplomatic, economic and strategic) 'pivot' or 'rebalancing strategy' towards the Asia-Pacific.[1] During a visit to Australia in November 2011, President Obama reiterated that the United States intended to 'play a larger and long-term role in shaping this region and its future'. As a highly symbolic gesture, he also announced that up to 2,500 US Marines would be rotated through Australia by 2017 (Obama 2011).[2]

This new policy acquired even greater formality in a strategic planning document, 'Sustaining US Global Leadership: Priorities for 21st Century Defense', released by the US government in January 2012 (United States Department of Defense 2012). While the semantics surrounding this strategy have changed over the ensuing months and years, especially with the appointment of John Kerry as secretary of state, American officials have gone to great lengths to reiterate that the substance of the original policy announced by Obama during his Australian visit will remain the guiding light for US global strategy in the years to come (for Kerry's clarification of the issue, see Kerry 2013; also see Donilon 2011).

The core emphasis of this US 'rebalancing' policy has been to increase American economic, diplomatic and military engagement in the Asia-Pacific, particularly in Southeast Asia – a region that had been largely ignored in American global strategy over the last several decades (for recent trends on American engagement in the region, see Tow 2012). However, one extra-regional actor that has attracted a great deal of individual attention from Washington as a likely partner for this rebalancing effort is India. As one analyst has noted when referring to 'Sustaining US Global Leadership', 'India is the only country to merit specific mention as a strategic partner' (Gupta 2012). In fact, as early as 2010, well before the 'pivot' was given expression, President Obama had begun calling on India not just to 'look East', but also 'engage East', a sentiment which Secretary of State Clinton repeated in July 2011 in asking India to 'engage East and act East as well' (Muni 2012: 6).

In her *Foreign Policy* article, Clinton explicitly acknowledged that the United States was making a 'strategic bet on India's future', and indeed characterized the complex of emerging partnerships in the region as an 'Indo-Pacific' one (Clinton 2011a: 60, 62). Secretary of Defense Leon Panetta went even further in remarks made during a visit to New Delhi in June 2012, by declaring that 'defense cooperation with India is a linchpin in this [rebalancing] strategy', and that to this end, the United States is committed to equipping India with the 'best defense technology' (Panetta 2012).[3] These American entreaties coincide with voices emerging recently from within Southeast Asia calling for greater Indian activism in the region.

How then is India likely to respond to these expectations? There are no doubt major convergences in American and Indian strategic challenges and visions which suggest that the prospects for an already maturing US-Indian strategic/security partnership in the region are unprecedented. Indeed, the potential synergies are conveyed by the fact that the American 'rebalance' to the region has been initiated just as New Delhi has begun to redouble its efforts at pushing its until now lacklustre 'look East' policy. Nevertheless, there are several mitigating strategic and domestic considerations likely to render New Delhi largely cautious and circumspect in the enthusiasm with which it embraces the US 'pivot'. As a result, Indian engagement with the United States is likely to see little in terms of a qualitative leap in the realms of traditional security provision and defence co-ordination. New Delhi's efforts are likely to be more focused, keeping to its strategic and domestic prerogatives and limitations, in the domains of economic and infrastructural connectivity, as well as in multilateral efforts at shaping the regional institutional and normative architecture under the Association of Southeast Asian Nations (ASEAN) leadership.

'Rebalancing' and 'looking East': dovetailing policy imperatives

By and large, as in the case of the rest of Asia, the American 'rebalancing' is viewed in India as a positive development. This is unsurprising, given the increased dovetailing of Indian and American strategic imperatives in the region. These include, perhaps most importantly, a common concern with managing the rise of Chinese power in the Asia-Pacific, ensuring maritime security in East and Southeast Asia in the face of Beijing's growing assertiveness in its territorial claims, and a desire to sustain and capitalize on strong regional economic growth to fuel and restore economic dynamism in India and the United States.

Accordingly, in a February 2013 lecture at Brown University, India's ambassador to the United States, Nirupama Rao, conveyed that New Delhi would 'welcome the US engagement in the ... Indo-Pacific ... It is a space that impacts our destinies, whose security and prosperity is vital to both of us, and where we have an increasing convergence of interests' (Rao 2013: 6).

Indeed, just as Washington has decided to ratchet up its engagement in the Asia-Pacific (particularly in Southeast Asia) – notably, by institutionalizing a US-ASEAN summit, and becoming an official participant at the East Asia Summit (EAS) in 2011, following years of neglect – India too has reinvigorated its own 'look East' policy. After a decade of languid progress following its launch in the early 1990s, New Delhi has increasingly prioritized its engagement with Southeast Asia in recent years. At the institutional level, after being accepted as a sectoral dialogue partner by ASEAN in 1992, and then as a full dialogue partner in 1995 (with which came membership in the ASEAN Regional Forum), a summit-level dialogue between India and ASEAN was established in 2002. By 2003, India had acceded to the ASEAN Treaty of Amity and Cooperation; in 2005 it became a founding member of the EAS; and in 2010 it was included in the ASEAN Defence Ministers' Meeting Plus (ADMM+) initiative. At the December 2012 ASEAN-India commemorative summit in New Delhi, with the aim of giving their ties greater substance, both sides agreed to upgrade relations to the level of 'strategic partnership' (Shankar 2013).

On the economic front, while Indian-ASEAN ties have grown significantly in the last two decades, there is recognition on both sides that more needs to be achieved if trade and investment are to approach Sino-ASEAN levels (ASEAN's trade with China amounts to over US$360 billion, compared to US$79 billion with India; see Keck 2012). In the past, ambitious Indian infrastructural connectivity plans, in particular, have suffered from poor implementation, which has impeded India's increased activism in the region (Rao 2013). These concerns mirror those of Washington, where economic connectivity with Southeast Asia has received growing attention, both through existing institutional arrangements – primarily the Asia-Pacific Economic Cooperation grouping – and new initiatives like the Trans-Pacific Partnership, which is aimed at developing regional economic and trade architecture. Indeed, American officials have acknowledged such convergences in their explicit encouragement of what they have termed an Indo-Pacific economic corridor, linking the Indian, Bangladeshi and Southeast Asian economies (Hormats 2013).

India's increasing institutional and economic activism in East and Southeast Asia has been accompanied, as discussed later, by extensive growth in diplomatic and strategic-defence engagements with prominent actors in the region, particularly the United States, China, Japan and the Southeast Asian countries. Such engagement has been operationalized through bilateral and multilateral military exchanges and exercises – most prominently the Malabar series of naval exercises, increased joint patrolling of vital sea lanes, and growing Indian military aid and assistance (particularly training for troops from Southeast Asia) – as well as accelerated strategic-diplomatic engagement, of which the rapid expansion in the India–Japan Strategic and Global Partnership is the most recent and most stark manifestation (for detailed discussions of these developments, see Muni 2011; Naidu 2004, 2011; Panda 2014). What then are the sources of these policy convergences between India and the United States, especially as New Delhi sees them?

The China factor

Strategic convergences that have driven the simultaneous escalation of Indian and American attention to the Indo-Pacific are apparent. Central to these developments, yet seldom explicitly stated, are concerns on both sides about the growing assertiveness of a rising China, and what this portends for regional security. The American decision explicitly to articulate a rebalancing policy emerged from Washington's recognition that earlier attempts at fostering cooperation with Beijing had been read by some Chinese policymakers and analysts as signalling an overall US strategic decline, prompting China's greater assertiveness in the South China Sea (Nye 2011).

For India, similar concerns have become increasingly apparent. Security along the long-disputed land border with China remains a core issue for the Indian leadership, especially given Indian allegations of greater Chinese assertiveness, most recently in an unprecedented Chinese 'incursion' in the Ladakh region (Harris and Wong 2013). India's quest to rival China for status and influence in 'Asia-at-large' suffered grievously with the heavy loss to China in the 1962 Sino–Indian war and a defeat and sense of Chinese perfidy that remains an abiding legacy of the past (see Garver 2001: chapter 3). Yet for India, the strategic stakes vis-à-vis China are now about much more than territorial or historical issues alone. This is especially true given that India's regional and international profile has expanded significantly and has necessitated an increasingly complex Indian engagement with East Asia.

As China's and India's economies have rapidly grown in a globalized world economy, the strategic competition between the two countries has transformed from a continental to a maritime one. With nearly 90 percent of all goods and commodities being traded globally still traversing through international sea lanes of communication, China and India have become increasingly concerned about maritime security (Mohan 2010: 4–5; see also Mohan 2012 for a definitive discussion of the geopolitics of the Indian Ocean region). An increasing proportion (31 percent) of India's trade is now being conducted with East Asian countries, with nearly 55 percent of that trade transported through the South China Sea (Clinton 2011b).

More crucially, as their economies expand, both countries have become massive consumers of energy resources, most of which must be secured overseas. On the one hand, this has led to the two countries' growing dependence on hydrocarbon resources from the Middle East, Central Asia, Africa and Latin America, underscoring their common interest in cooperating to ensure sea lanes stability (Garver 2001: chapter 10; Beri 2005). On the other hand, in addition to the other trade that transits the seas, this strategic reliance on energy has made the securing of sea lanes and freedom of navigation vitally important for national growth and power. As Sumit Ganguly (2005: 50) observes, 'India is in a fundamentally competitive, if not conflictual, relationship with China' to sustain resource access and develop commercial lifelines.

It is in this context that China's growing naval power projection capabilities, accompanied by its increasing activism and assertiveness in the Indo-Pacific, have created consternation in New Delhi and greater apprehension in Washington. Beijing's growing assertiveness in its claims to offshore islands in the East China and South China Seas, most recently witnessed in its declaration of an air defence identification zone over the East China Sea, have stoked fears in India and Washington of Chinese expansionism throughout East Asia (Gladstone and Wald 2013; on Indian concerns over Chinese intentions see, for instance, Kapur 2006: 219–23). At a more operational level, the People's Liberation Army Navy's reported development of anti-access and area-denial strategies in keeping with China's extensive maritime claims, challenges Indian and American perceptions regarding the freedom of maritime navigation at a time when such freedom is increasingly crucial to sustaining India's growing economy and to American plans for economic recovery. Indeed, Chinese leaders have declared the waters from the Indian to the Pacific Oceans as constituting a 'core national interest' of their country (Mohan 2010: 10).

More troublingly from an Indian perspective, such policies on the part of China have translated into greater Chinese activism beyond the East China and South China Seas into the Indian Ocean region, and into India's 'backyard'. In what is characterized by many in India as a 'string of pearls' strategy, Beijing has acquired strategic access to, or is in the process of helping to build, naval ports and facilities along the Indian Ocean periphery, from Gwadar (Pakistan) in the west, to Sri Lanka's Hambantota port project in the south, and several facilities in Myanmar to the east. From China's perspective, these initiatives may just be intended to secure their supplies of energy and other goods and commodities traversing the Indian Ocean. In New Delhi's estimation, however, such Chinese actions have been perceived as at a minimum creating the capabilities for Beijing to project power more effectively in the Indian Ocean, while at the same time surrounding and strangulating India's strategic reach (see Garver 2001: chapters 4, 10; Ladwig 2009: 88–90; Scott 2008).

China's strategic challenges to India have thus increased in recent years and decades. Disconcertingly for New Delhi, this threat intensification has been accompanied by a growing gap between India and China in terms of strategic capabilities, to the former's detriment, a trend that will likely continue in the foreseeable future. Even if one exercises the greatest optimism regarding growing economic interdependence underwriting Sino–Indian relations, the terms of trade have increasingly been in China's favour. Indeed, despite both sides repeatedly stating their intention in recent years to address the issue, India's trade deficit vis-à-vis China in 2012–13 increased to US$39 billion, up from US$37 billion in the previous year (Mehdudia 2013). Chinese capabilities and intentions therefore loom increasingly large in India's strategic calculus in the Indo-Pacific.

India's response to a stronger China: strategically engaging East Asia

New Delhi's response to these developments has, as discussed above, involved a reinvigoration of its activity and engagement in the 'Indo-Pacific'. This has been premised on the belief, as Indian Defence Minister Pranab Mukherjee (2006) stated, that 'India's role is crucial for ensuring and maintaining long-term peace, stable balance of power, economic growth and security in Asia'. Whilst there is a continuing economic and institutional impetus in this effort, keeping up with new strategic imperatives has become more important in unilateral, bilateral and multilateral forms.

On its own, New Delhi emphasizes the modernization of its naval power projection capabilities in the Indian Ocean and beyond. For some time, Indian leaders have articulated a vision of India's maritime sphere of activity and interest as extending from the east coast of the African continent to the South China Sea. As one scholar has argued, even though the Indian Navy's 2004 maritime doctrine suggested a narrower domain of activity from the Persian Gulf to the Strait of Malacca, 'the actions of the Indian Navy ... suggest that the true scope of Delhi's ambition' is in fact larger (Ladwig 2009: 90). The Indian Navy's modernization programme illustrates this trend – its share of India's total defence budget has expanded from 10 percent in the early 1990s to nearly 20 percent in recent years (Ladwig 2009: 90–93). That this build-up is aimed at extending the Indian Navy's strategic reach was made clear in a maritime doctrine document published by the Indian Navy in 2007 (Ministry of Defence (Navy) 2007), and was amply reiterated by naval chief Admiral D.K. Joshi in December 2012. Joshi confidently asserted that his forces were willing and able to deploy to the South China Sea if his country's growing energy interests in the region (including offshore exploitation of oil deposits in conjunction with Vietnam) were to be threatened by Chinese activities (Reuters 2012).

Moreover, support for such operational capabilities has not only involved a build-up of India's naval forces, but also a commensurate supporting infrastructure. In addition to building a naval port near Vizag to bolster its basing network on the country's eastern coast, India has established a Far Eastern Naval Command at Port Blair in the Andaman and Nicobar Islands under a 'tri-service' command structure. This move is expected to bolster India's amphibious warfare capabilities significantly, and enhance its reach into the South China Sea, and especially into the Malacca Strait (Ladwig 2009: 95–96). Interestingly, in contrast to the 1980s when such moves by India at expanding its naval reach provoked consternation in Southeast Asia, shared concerns over Chinese actions have now led ASEAN members to look upon recent Indian activism as a more benign, even a positive development (Sharma 2012).

The gaze of India's Navy has therefore turned firmly eastwards, with the inherent recognition that managing China cannot be a solitary enterprise. Increasing bilateral strategic engagement with major players in the region has occurred. By 1991, India had begun joint naval exercises, as well as exploring other forms of defence cooperation (training, servicing and spare parts supply for military equipment) with Indonesia, Malaysia and Singapore. This process has expanded to include other actors and activities at the bilateral level over the years, setting the stage for strategic partnerships with actors such as Australia, Indonesia, Singapore, the United States, Vietnam and others. In recent years, bilateral exercises with Indonesia, Singapore and Vietnam have been conducted in the South China Sea, reinforcing the expanded domain of Indian naval interest and activity. Since the early 2000s, the Indian Navy has also engaged in periodic joint bilateral exercises with Japan and South Korea (Ladwig 2009: 95–103).[4] Although strategic partnerships in the region have not been a complete panacea for India, they have facilitated a more systematic pursuit of relationships for that country to participate meaningfully and regularly in regional order-building efforts.

In this context, defence cooperation with Singapore has arguably been the most dynamic, and is embedded within the 2003 India–Singapore Defence Cooperation Agreement. As part of this mechanism, both countries have engaged in regular naval exercises (SIMBEX), including anti-submarine warfare drills involving India's Far Eastern Naval Command. New Delhi has also provided Singaporean troops with access to Indian military training facilities (particularly at the Southern Naval Command in Kochi), as well as to the Chandipur missile testing range (Naidu 2004: 338–41).

US-Indian defence bilateral engagement has likewise blossomed in recent years. As part of Washington's efforts to help India to become a major power, the United States and India are actively conducting joint military exercises, and negotiating the sale of weapons and technology to bolster Indian military capabilities. In 2002, the Indian Navy escorted American logistics ships traversing the Malacca Strait to Afghanistan. This set a precedent for increased joint military exercises, regular bilateral strategic dialogue and landmark bilateral defence agreements. In 2005, the two countries signed a ten-year defence framework agreement; in 2008 the US-India Civil Nuclear Agreement was concluded, confirming Washington's de facto acceptance of India as a legitimate nuclear weapon state; and in October 2013, the India-US Joint Declaration on Defence Cooperation was issued, which paved the way for substantial growth in defence technology collaboration (see United States Department of Defense 2011; n.a. 2007).

At the multilateral level also, India has become increasingly active in the defence realm. As noted above, it has become more integrated into East Asian institutional structures. As has been the case at the bilateral level, naval exercises feature prominently, beginning with the Indian Navy's biennial Milan exercise in 1995 that featured regional navies at Port Blair, and which has mushroomed from an initial participation of four countries, to 17 by 2014.[5] According to one Indian naval officer, Milan aims to 'foster bonds of "friendship across the seas", boost interoperability and share views on common maritime issues' (*Times of India* 2012).

The aforementioned Malabar exercise, which began in the early 1990s as a US-Indian affair, now involves a number of participants, including Australia, Japan and Singapore. In addition to increasing the interoperability and coordination of like-minded forces, such exercises help to address more non-traditional security challenges, such as piracy and humanitarian intervention/disaster relief, as exemplified in the aftermath of the 2004 tsunami in Southeast Asia: Australia, India, Japan and the United States formed the core group that coordinated relief and rebuilding efforts following that calamity.

The above developments have been supplemented by Indian participation in more institutional mechanisms. These have included the ADMM+8 process, the Regional Cooperation Agreement on Combating Piracy and Armed Robbery, and the Indian Ocean Rim Association for Regional Cooperation (IOR-ARC). The IOR-ARC, in particular, has become increasingly crucial in Indian perceptions, as Beijing has expanded the scope of its bilateral commercial influence in the IOR countries in line with policy advice from Chinese think tanks specifically advocating greater commercial engagement with the Indian Ocean littoral states (Jha 2013). With growing evidence of Chinese assertiveness in India's 'extended neighbourhood', the strong convergence in interests between India and the US regional alliance system suggests that opportunities for increasing defence coordination between India and that system will accelerate significantly in the future. As India and the United States increasingly project their military power and extend their institutional engagement in the region, they can expand the range and depth of their defence cooperation towards jointly contributing to stable regional security architecture in the Indo-Pacific.

India and US rebalancing: elements of caution

Given the complementarities in strategic imperatives and interests with the United States and its strategic partners in the region, it seems there are undeniable incentives for India to throw in its lot with the American rebalancing initiative. Washington and various Southeast Asian countries have employed such logic in urging New Delhi to increase its commitments to help shape the regional security architecture along the lines they envision as most beneficial. Yet, there are sufficient strategic and domestic reasons to suggest that New Delhi is likely to be more circumspect in seeking to tie itself closely to American regional agendas. No wonder, then, as one analyst has noted, 'Delhi has neither endorsed the US pivot to Asia nor criticized it' (Mohan 2013a).

Mitigating strategic imperatives

India's foreign and security policymaking has a tradition, or culture, premised on the idea of 'strategic autonomy', an idea expressed in India's 'non-alignment' posture developed during the Cold War. It is a leitmotif that has, to various extents, underlined India's approach to world politics since independence. In keeping with this mantra, Indian leaderships have jealously guarded the country's freedom of action by steering clear of close alignment with powers bigger than itself (see Bajpai 2002: 243–86; Bhanu Mehta 2009). For all the ideological underpinnings of 'non-alignment', its doubtful record in the Cold War era, and apparent lack of relevance in the post-Cold War era, the idea of 'strategic autonomy' still commands favour in Indian strategic thinking. It is, moreover, crucial to explaining New Delhi's seeming preference for building 'strategic partnerships' over alliances, a formulation that, as one observer has put it, allows India to practise 'a form of beneficial ambiguity', to exercise caution, and take its time in assessing the desirability of deeper engagement (Panda 2013). Indeed, a prominent set of Indian scholars have emphasized exactly this theme, although with a surprising lack of discussion about relations with the United States (see Khilnani *et al.* 2012; for an American critique, see Tellis 2012).

This traditional emphasis on 'autonomy' that seemingly permeates the Indian body politic – from the elites to public opinion – can moreover manifest itself in an intense sensitivity to any perceived slights to India's 'prestige' or 'status' (for more on the historical roots of such sensitivity, see for instance Miller 2013b). The ferocity of the Indian leadership and domestic population's reaction, for instance, over the spat between the United States and India over the arrest of Indian diplomat Devyani Khobragade, can only be understood – regardless of the merits of the case – with this aspect in mind. The treatment meted out to the diplomat arguably symbolized for New Delhi an affront to its 'honour' and an infringement of its 'strategic autonomy', provoking a reaction that might seem incredible to American commentators (Aziz 2013).

Further encouraging this preference for not aligning too closely with the United States is New Delhi's uncertainty about US intentions and capabilities. On the one hand, there is scepticism about the sustainability of American attention to, and resources earmarked toward, the region. Given Washington's current fiscal straitjacket, there is a justifiable sense in New Delhi that American policies are likely to be in flux for some time. If so, there is little incentive for Indian policymakers to over-commit to the rebalancing initiative under current circumstances. There is particular concern amongst Indian policymakers and independent observers alike that, given the United States' deep economic ties with China, coupled with the American body politic's domestic fatigue and fiscal constraints, little will or capability exists in Washington to sustain regional security commitments in Asia at previous levels.

This concern is further magnified by New Delhi's desire to avoid prematurely provoking a China that already views the American rebalancing initiative as part of a nascent containment strategy directed against itself (see Ross 2012; Nathan and Scobell 2012). While there is no doubt that India's concerns and activities in the region are 'China driven', Indian leaders are nevertheless equally worried about risking derailment of Sino–Indian relations, which have remained largely stable, at least in an economic context, over the past two decades, and at a time when the widening strategic gap between India and China is undeniable (Hathaway 2012; Mohan 2013b).[6]

In many ways, then, Indian officials seek to pursue an approach based on the maxim of 'waiting and watching', or 'biding time' vis-à-vis China while building their own country's strength. This strategy entails sustaining India's economic development and resolving domestic political instabilities.[7] While welcoming greater American engagement in Asia, India refuses to tie itself too tightly to the American agenda in the region. Accordingly, Indian officials have emphasized that ongoing Indian-US engagement is not aimed at China. As Rao has observed, New Delhi does not 'believe that such a construct is valid or sustainable, given the significant overlapping interests that bind us in the region and globally' (Rao 2013: 8). In July 2012, the Indian defence minister similarly cautioned Panetta with regard to the South China Sea disputes, that 'it is desirable that the parties concerned themselves should settle contentious matters in accordance with the international law', further emphasizing that the American 'pivot' 'move at a pace comfortable to all countries concerned' (Press Information Bureau, Government of India 2012).

Mitigating domestic circumstances

Issues in Indian domestic politics are only likely to reinforce New Delhi's strategic ambiguity in response to American rebalancing. Arguably, ambiguity and being 'reactive' (as opposed to 'proactive') is not necessarily a matter of choice for India, but rather a forced constant. India simply lacks the wherewithal to generate that comprehensive type of strategic thinking that underpins successful grand strategy. With a diplomatic service barely larger than that of Singapore or New Zealand and an under-resourced and crumbling university and research infrastructure, the 'software' necessary for sustained strategic thought, and devising means and mechanisms for its implementation, are sorely lacking in India (see Markey 2009; Tharoor 2012). As one scholar has discovered, in addition to the highly individualistic nature of decision making in New Delhi, and fears that 'the notion of the country's rise is a Western construct', these drawbacks have led Indian foreign policy elites to become uncomfortable with talk of the country as a rising power, something that she argues 'should lower Washington's ambitions for its partnership with New Delhi' (Miller 2013a: 14).

Even without this impediment, the contemporary state of India's domestic politics delivers few incentives for leaders to push ambitious international agendas. Since the 1990s, coalition politics has been a fact of life at the centre of Indian politics. This has weakened India's central political leadership and has made it more susceptible to diverse interest groups and political pressures on all policy issues (see Chakrabarty 2006; Mattoo and Jacob 2010). The controversies that surrounded the signing and implementation of the Indo-US nuclear deal illustrates the nature of these new dynamics with regard to Indian foreign and security policymaking (see Rajagopalan and Purushothaman 2012; Mukherjee 2011). Adding to these structural features is the looming threat of a marked deterioration in India's economic fortunes. Economic growth has plummeted from expectations of double-digit growth just a few years ago, to hovering around a disappointing 5 percent in 2012–13 (*Economic Times* 2013). In the political realm, moreover, an array of high-profile corruption scandals, instability in the governing coalition, incidents highlighting the lack of public safety (especially of women), and the apparently emboldened Naxal insurgency, all focus attention on those weaknesses that undermine the Indian state's 'capacity' to govern effectively (on the 'weak state' predicament, see Paul 2010).

All this indicates that the Indian political leadership has relatively less incentive to focus its attention outside India. Dealing with economic downturns and political instability at home was clearly the overwhelming priority in New Delhi when national elections were held in May 2014 and Narendra Modi was elected India's new prime minister. Such domestic imperatives mean that political leaders gravitate towards more cautious strategic options, tending to take a more reactive rather than a leadership role in the international realm.

Implications for Indian responses to US rebalancing

While strategic considerations are strong enough to make India wary of reacting very enthusiastically to American rebalancing, domestic imperatives ensure a further lack of capacity or willingness for the Indian leadership to assume anything more than the ambiguous stance it has adopted. This does not mean that India does not welcome greater American activism in the region – as we have seen, there are ample similarities in the strategic concerns of both countries which have already resulted in a level of defence cooperation and coordination unimaginable scarcely more than a decade ago, following India's nuclear tests in 1998. Indian officials also recognize that they have much to benefit from cooperation with the United States – not least in the acquisition of American military equipment and technology given that India's attempts to balance Chinese power in the region simply cannot be accomplished through 'internal' means.

What is being argued here, however, is that policy constraints remain sufficiently powerful that India is likely to be unwilling to change the nature of its qualified activism in East Asia. This is especially true regarding the qualitative aspects of its bilateral partnership with the United States in the region. While continuing with military exercises, and defence technology-related cooperation with the United States, India will remain sufficiently cautious so as not to be seen as completely in step with, or a mere 'camp follower' of, the United States. Moreover, it is likely to avoid ratcheting up its presence and profile in the region to the degree desired by the United States and those Southeast Asian countries that have been imploring India to do so via their calls for New Delhi to 'act East'.

Rather, India is likely to continue to focus on its internal development, and on pursuing a gradual development of military and diplomatic influence projection capabilities in its growing geographic sphere of interest. It is likely to emphasize 'softer' areas for greater engagement and activism in the region. In particular, there is still a great deal to be achieved in terms of economic connectivity between India and Southeast Asia, and this arena is likely to be the focus of India's current political leaders – both because it is less likely to antagonize Beijing, and because it meets New Delhi's immediate priority to restore the country's economic vibrancy. In terms of defence coordination, while bilateral ties with partner countries in the region will develop, India can be expected increasingly to emphasize multilateral and institutional mechanisms for addressing regional security concerns. In doing so, it is likely to push for ASEAN's centrality to the politics of regional security architecture, and for the engagement and enmeshment of China into that architecture. To what extent this complies with how the United States' rebalancing strategy has evolved to date is questionable.

A reactive Indian foreign and security policy will, of course, respond to the actions of other key regional players, and especially to those projected by China and the United States. Were Chinese assertiveness to become more pronounced, imperilling Indian interests in the process, the shroud of Indian caution towards the American rebalancing might transform into a more explicitly supportive stance. Similarly, were American commitments to the region to begin to appear more credible to New Delhi, or were Washington's policy actions to become viewed as more benign in terms of their potential to spark a Sino-US conflict, Indian leaders might again see more merit in openly supporting rebalancing. On the other hand, to the extent that doubts persist about American commitments, and/or fears remain over how provocative American actions will be to the Chinese leadership, New Delhi will remain reticent in terms of aligning with Washington's rebalancing, and cautious with regard to India's defence activism in the region.

Conclusion

Indian perceptions of the American 'pivot' are still in flux. This is only natural given the lack of clarity and credibility that surrounds Washington's current policies. Given these uncertainties, there is a strategic rationale for Indian ambiguity and caution in terms of its role in the region. Domestic imperatives only strengthen the penchant in New Delhi for a more reactive, softer (less military), and multilateral/institutional role in Southeast Asia.

While this reticence might disappoint the United States and its allies over the short term, this should not be problematic as long as those parties favour diplomatic and institutional ways of managing China in the Indo-Pacific. Were Chinese intentions truly to develop along 'worse-case lines', strategic compatibilities between India and the United States are already strong enough that India is unlikely to be found wanting. The key factor here is what the catalyst would be for transforming India's historically cautious and largely non-aligned posture into one more reflective of a genuine strategic partnership with the San Francisco System. Ultimately, the answer to this question lies in the evolution of China's future strategic behaviour.

Notes

1 Clinton characterized the contemporary period as a 'pivot point' for the United States. An early, comprehensive overview of the various facets of the American 'rebalancing' can be found in Manyin *et al.* (2012).
2 The stopover in Australia was en route to Southeast Asia, where the US government made its maiden appearance at the East Asia Summit (EAS), in addition to visiting Thailand and, surprisingly, Myanmar.
3 'Sustaining US Global Leadership' spoke of the United States 'investing in a long-term strategic partnership with India to support its ability to serve as a regional economic anchor and provider of security in the broader Indian Ocean region'. See United States Department of Defense (2012: 2).
4 Japan and India signed a 'Joint Declaration on Security Cooperation' in 2008, establishing strategic dialogues at several levels between the two governments. See Ministry of Foreign Affairs, Japan (2008).
5 In 2014, the participants included Australia, Bangladesh, Cambodia, India, Indonesia, Kenya, Malaysia, Maldives, Mauritius, Myanmar, New Zealand, Philippines, Seychelles, Singapore, Sri Lanka, Tanzania and Thailand.
6 Such concerns are not exclusive to India. For Southeast Asian concerns, see Emmerson (2013).
7 Several Indian officials expressed this sentiment in a February 2013 track 1.5 conference organized by the Indian Council for Research on International Economic Relations and the Center for Strategic and International Studies, which featured American and Indian officials and scholars, and was held in New Delhi.

References

Aziz, Omer (2013) 'The Case Against India's Diplomat', *The Diplomat*, 27 December, thediplomat.com/2013/12/the-case-against-indias-diplomat/ (accessed 29 January 2014).

Bajpai, Kanti (2002) 'Indian Strategic Culture', in Michael R. Chambers (ed.) *South Asia in 2020: Future Strategic Balances and Alliances*, Carlisle, PA: Strategic Studies Institute, November, pp. 245–303.

Beri, Ruchita (2005) 'Africa's Energy Potential: Prospects for India', *Strategic Analysis*, 29(3): 370–94.

Bhanu Mehta, Pratap (2009) 'Still Under Nehru's Shadow? The Absence of Foreign Policy Frameworks in India', *India Review*, 8(3): 209–33.

Chakrabarty, Bidyut (2006) *Forging Power: Coalition Politics in India*, Oxford: Oxford University Press.

Clinton, Hillary (2011a) 'America's Pacific Century', *Foreign Policy*, 189(November): 56–63.

——(2011b) 'India and the United States: A Vision for the 21st Century', Anna Centenary Library, Chennai, 20 July, chennai.usconsulate.gov/secclinton speechacl_110721.html (accessed 28 January 2014).

Donilon, Tom (2011) 'America is Back in the Pacific and Will Uphold the Rules', *Financial Times*, 27 November.

Economic Times (2013) 'OECD Lowers India Growth Forecast to 5.3% for 2013', 29 May, articles.economictimes.indiatimes.com/2013-05-29/news/39601959_1_paris-based-think-tank-oecd-today-growth-estimate-growth-forecast (accessed 29 January 2014).

Emmerson, Donald K. (2013) 'Challenging ASEAN: The US Pivot in Southeast Asia', *East Asia Forum*, 13 January, www.eastasiaforum.org/2013/01/13/challenging-asean-the-american-pivot-in-southeast-asia/ (accessed 29 January 2014).

Ganguly, Sumit (2005) Prepared Statement to the Committee on Foreign Relations, United States Senate, 'Energy Trends in China and India: Implications for the United States', Washington, DC: US Government Printing Office, 26 July, www.gpo.gov/fdsys/pkg/CHRG-109shrg26670/html/CHRG-109shrg26670.htm (accessed 29 January 2014).

Garver, John W. (2001) *Protracted Contest: Sino-Indian Rivalry in the Twentieth Century*, Seattle, WA: University of Washington Press.

Gladstone, Rick and Wald, Matthew L. (2013) 'China's Move Puts Airspace in Spotlight', *New York Times*, 27 November.

Gupta, Sourabh (2012) 'The US Pivot and India's Look East', *East Asia Forum*, 20 June, www.eastasiaforum.org/2012/06/20/the-us-pivot-and-india-s-look-east/ (accessed 29 January 2014).

Harris, Gardiner and Wong, Edward (2013) 'Where China meets India in a High-Altitude Desert, Push Comes to Shove', *New York Times*, 2 May.

Hathaway, Robert M. (2012) 'India and the US Pivot to Asia', YaleGlobal Online, 24 February, yaleglobal.yale.edu/content/india-and-us-pivot-asia (accessed 29 January 2014).

Hormats, Robert D. (2013) 'US Economic Engagement with the Asia Pacific', Remarks, Asia Society Global Forum, Washington, DC, 12 June, www.state.gov/e/rls/rmk/210563.htm (accessed 28 January 2014).

Jha, Saurav (2013) 'India Seeks Multilateral Partnerships to Counter China in Indian Ocean Rim', *World Politics Review*, 26 July, www.worldpoliticsreview.com/articles/13119/india-seeks-multilateral-partnerships-to-counter-china-in-indian-ocean-rim (accessed 29 January 2014).

Kapur, Ashok (2006) *India: From Regional to World Power*, New York: Routledge.

Keck, Zachary (2012) 'India, ASEAN Celebrate 20th Anniversary with Two FTAs', *The Diplomat*, 21 December, thediplomat.com/2012/12/india-asean-celebrate-20th-anniversary-with-two-ftas/ (accessed 6 February 2014).

Kerry, John (2013) 'Remarks with Australian Foreign Minister Bob Carr After their Meeting', transcript, 18 March, www.state.gov/secretary/remarks/2013/03/206370.htm (accessed 28 January 2014).

Khilnani, Sunil, Kumar, Rajiv, Mehta, Pratap Bhanu, Menon, Prakash, Nilekani, Nandan, Raghavan, Srinath, Saran, Shyam and Varadarajan, Siddharth (2012) *Nonalignment 2.0: A Foreign and Strategic Policy for India in the Twenty First Century*, New Delhi: Centre for Policy Research.

Ladwig, III, Walter C. (2009) 'Delhi's Pacific Ambition: Naval Power, "Look East"', and India's Emerging Influence in the Asia-Pacific', *Asian Security*, 5(2): 87–113.

Manyin, Mark E., Daggett, Stephen, Dolven, Ben, Lawrence, Susan V., Martin, Michael F., O'Rourke, Ronald and Vaughn, Bruce (2012) 'Pivot to the Pacific? The Obama Administration's "Rebalancing" Toward Asia', CRS Report for Congress, Congressional Research Service, 28 March, www.fas.org/sgp/crs/natsec/R42448.pdf (accessed 29 January 2014).

Markey, Daniel (2009) 'Developing India's Foreign Policy "Software"', *Asia Policy*, 8(July): 73–96.

Mattoo, Amitabh and Jacob, Happymon (eds) (2010) *Shaping India's Foreign Policy: People, Politics, and Places*, New Delhi: Har-Anand Publications.

Mehdudia, Sujay (2013) 'Widening Trade Deficit with China Not Sustainable', *The Hindu*, 23 September.

Miller, Manjari Chatterjee (2013a) 'India's Feeble Foreign Policy: A Would-be Great Power Resists its Own Rise', *Foreign Affairs*, 92(3): 14–19.

——(2013b) *Wronged by Empire: Post-Imperial Ideology and Foreign Policy in India and China*, Stanford, CA: Stanford University Press.

Ministry of Defence (Navy) (2007) *Freedom to Use the Seas: India's Maritime Military Strategy*, New Delhi: Integrated Headquarters, Ministry of Defence (Navy).

Ministry of Foreign Affairs, Japan (2008) 'Joint Declaration on Security Cooperation between Japan and India', 22 October, www.mofa.go.jp/region/asia-paci/india/pmv0810/joint_d.html (accessed 4 February 2014).

Mohan, C. Raja (2010) 'India and the Changing Geopolitics of the Indian Ocean', *Maritime Affairs*, 6(2): 1–12.

——(2012) *Samudra Manthan: Sino-Indian Rivalry in the Indo-Pacific*, Washington, DC: Carnegie Endowment for International Peace.

——(2013a) 'China's Rise, America's Pivot, and India's Asian Ambiguity', *India Seminar*, 641(January), www.india-seminar.com/2013/641/641_c_raja_mohan.htm (accessed 28 January 2014).

——(2013b) 'India: Between "Strategic Autonomy" and "Geopolitical Opportunity"', *Asia Policy*, 15(January): 21–25.

Mukherjee, Ktittivas (2011) 'Warming India–US Ties Hit Speed Bump Over Nuclear Trade', Reuters, 20 July, www.reuters.com/article/2011/07/20/india-us-nuclear-idUS L3E7IK1LI20110720 (accessed 29 January 2014).

Mukherjee, Raksha Mantri Shri Pranab (2006) 'Text of Raksha Mantri Shri Pranab Mukherjee's Address at Shangri-La Dialogue in Singapore', 3 June, Press Information Bureau, Government of India, pib.nic.in/newsite/erelease.aspx?relid=18213 (accessed 28 January 2014).

Muni, S.D. (2011) 'India's "Look East" Policy: The Strategic Dimension', ISAS Working Paper No. 121, Singapore: Institute of South Asian Studies, National University of Singapore, 1 February.

——(2012) 'Obama Administration's Pivot to Asia-Pacific and India's Role', ISAS Working Paper No. 159, Singapore: Institute of South Asian Studies, National University of Singapore, 29 August.

n.a. (2007) 'Agreement for Cooperation Between the Government of the United States of America and Government of India Concerning Peaceful Uses of Nuclear Energy (123 Agreement)', www.cfr.org/india/agreement-cooperation-between-government-united-states-america-government-india-concerning-peaceful-u ses-nuclear-energy-123-agreement/p15459 (accessed 28 January 2014).

Naidu, G.V.C. (2004) 'Whither the Look East Policy: India and Southeast Asia', *Strategic Analysis*, 28(2): 331–46.

——(2011) 'From "Looking" to Engaging – India and East Asia', Asie. Visions 46, Paris: Institut français des relations internationals Center for Asian Studies, December.

Nathan, Andrew J. and Scobell, Andrew (2012) 'How China Sees America', *Foreign Affairs*, 91(5): 32–47.

Nye, Joseph S. (2011) 'Obama's Pacific Pivot', *Project Syndicate*, 6 December, www. project-syndicate.org/commentary/obama-s-pacific-pivot (accessed 29 January 2014).

Obama, Barack (2011) 'Remarks by President Obama to the Australian Parliament', 17 November, www.whitehouse.gov/the-press-office/2011/11/17/remarks-president-obama-australian-parliament (accessed 29 January 2014).

Panda, Ankit (2013) 'Why Does India have So Many "Strategic Partners" and No Allies?' *The Diplomat*, 23 November, thediplomat.com/2013/11/why-does-india-have-so-many-strategic-partners-and-no-allies (accessed 29 January 2014).

——(2014) 'India–Japan Defense Ministers Agree to Expand Strategic Cooperation', *The Diplomat*, 8 January, thediplomat.com/2014/01/india-japan-defense-ministers-agree-to-expand-strategic-cooperation (accessed 29 January 2014).

Panetta, Leon (2012) 'Remarks by Secretary Panetta at the Institute for Defence Studies and Analyses in New Delhi, India', 6 June, www.defense.gov/transcripts/transcript.aspx?transcriptid=5054 (accessed 28 January 2014).

Paul, T.V. (ed.) (2010) *South Asia's Weak States: Understanding the Regional Insecurity Predicament*, Stanford, CA: Stanford University Press.

Press Information Bureau, Government of India (2012) 'India and US Hold Defence Talks Asia-Pacific Countries Should Settle Bilateral Disputes as Per International Law: Antony', 6 June, pib.nic.in/newsite/erelease.aspx?relid=84715 (accessed 28 January 2014).

Rajagopalan, Rajeswari Pillai and Purushothaman, Uma (2012) 'Role of the Indian Political System in Shaping India's Nuclear Policy', *International Journal of Nuclear Law*, 3(4): 246–58.

Rao, Nirupama (2013) 'America's "Asian Pivot": The View from India', Lecture, Brown University, 5 February, brown.edu/initiatives/india/news/2013-02/nirupama-rao-americas-asian-pivot-view-india-full-text (accessed 29 January 2014).

Reuters (2012) 'Indian Navy Prepared to Deploy to South China Sea to Protect Oil Interests', 3 December, www.reuters.com/article/2012/12/03/us-china-sea-india-idUS BRE8B20KY20121203 (accessed 29 January 2014).

Ross, Robert S. (2012) 'The Problem with the Pivot', *Foreign Affairs*, 91(6): 70–82.

Scott, David (2008) 'Sino-Indian Security Predicaments for the Twenty-First Century', *Asian Security*, 4(3): 244–70.

Shankar, Mahesh (2013) 'India and Southeast Asia: Building LEP Momentum', RSIS Commentaries, Singapore: S. Rajaratnam School of International Studies, Nanyang Technological University, 26 April.

Sharma, Rajeev (2012) 'The Garuda, ASEAN Need Not Fear the Indian Navy's Strategic Eagle', *Jakarta Globe*, 17 September.

Tellis, Ashley J. (2012) 'Nonalignment Redux: The Perils of Old Wine in New Skins', Washington, DC: Carnegie Endowment for International Peace.

Tharoor, Shashi (2012) 'In the Ministry of External Affairs', *The Caravan*, 1 July, caravanmagazine.in/reporting-and-essays/ministry-eternal-affairs (accessed 29 January 2014).

Times of India (2012) 'Navy to Host 14-Nation "Milan" Exercise from Feb 1', 31 January.

Tow, William (2012) 'The Eagle Returns: Resurgent US Strategy in Southeast Asia and its Policy Implications', *Policy Analysis*, Canberra: Australian Strategic Policy Institute, 13 February.

United States Department of Defense (2011) 'Report to Congress on US–India Security Cooperation', November, www.defense.gov/pubs/pdfs/20111101_NDAA_Report_on_US_India_Security_Cooperation.pdf (accessed 28 January 2014).

——(2012) 'Sustaining US Global Leadership: Priorities for 21st Century Defense', Washington, DC: United States Department of Defense, January.

14 Balancing the risks of US rebalancing

Tongfi Kim

What explains the commonality and variations of Asia-Pacific (hereafter 'Asian') states' responses to the US rebalancing strategy now under way? Each Asian state has its own tradition of foreign policy and historical relationship with the global superpower on the other side of the Pacific. Acknowledging the risk of oversimplification, this chapter offers an explanation of Asian states' adaptations to the US 'rebalancing to Asia' strategy by focusing on key factors that drew particular attention in the previous chapters. Although their expressions and emphases vary, the contributors to this volume have discussed how their countries balanced the risk of being abandoned by the United States with the risk of being entrapped in a conflict with China, while also balancing the risk of emboldening China with the risk of provoking the country. In other words, Asian states have adapted their response to the US rebalancing to cope with what Glenn Snyder (1984, 1997) called the 'composite security dilemma'. The concept originally concerned alliance politics, but it is also useful for analysing more loosely aligned partners.

The composite security dilemma concerns two closely interconnected relationships: between cooperation partners and between adversaries.[1] In this volume's context, an Asian state can support US rebalancing to reduce the risk of abandonment by the United States and to deter China, but such a move provokes China and increases the risk of entrapment into a political, economic and military conflict with China.[2] An Asian state can alternatively withhold support for US rebalancing to reduce tension and the risk of entrapment, but the move encourages China to demand more and alienates the United States. There is a trade-off to be made, and the actual policies of Asian states have been neither a total embrace nor a complete rejection of the US strategy.

A good relationship with the United States has been valuable to many states regardless of China, but the rapid expansion of China's military and economic power has intensified the Asian states' fear of abandonment and entrapment by the United States. China's increasing military power has aroused particular concern in the region and made the possibility of abandonment more consequential. The military 'rise of China' is exemplified by the country's defence spending. For example, China's official defence budget in 2013, which is considered to be significantly lower than its true spending level, was larger than those of Japan, South Korea, Taiwan and Vietnam combined (IISS 2014). While the United States still maintains an edge in military power and technologies (Beckley 2011), many perceive a shift in the relative capabilities of the United States and China.

Meanwhile, the increased importance of the Chinese economy – now the second largest in the world – has made friction with China very costly. In comparison, in 1995 and 1996, at the time of the third Taiwan Strait crisis, China's gross domestic product was only eighth and seventh in the world, respectively (World Bank 2014). Strong economic interdependence, which one observer calls 'mutual assured production' (Katz 2013), has developed between China and many states, although China's dependence on smaller economies may be minor. A military conflict involving China will significantly disrupt the global economy. Moreover, given China's suspicion of American motives, mere support for US (military) rebalancing means antagonizing China, thereby causing economic problems.

The dragon/panda in the room

The trade-off involved in policy toward US rebalancing is complicated by China's position not simply as a dragon that presents a threat, but also as a panda that entices Asian states with the lure of economic opportunities. As Fu-Kuo Liu (Chapter 7) argues, 'Taiwan has to maintain a balanced policy between China (for market reasons) and the United States (for security)'. Given that even Taiwan needs to balance desires for prosperity and security concerns, it is no wonder that other countries are ambivalent about their choices. The United States itself is torn by questions of prosperity versus security, and Asian states cannot expect the United States to side with them automatically and sacrifice its own economic relations with China.

Abandonment and entrapment in alliance theory are predominantly discussed in military terms, but they have political and economic dimensions as well (see, for example, Snyder 1997: 357; Press-Barnathan 2006: 280–81). For instance, the increased importance of the Chinese economy to all states of Asia-Pacific and beyond has made Asian states recognize economic entrapment as a serious threat. Robert Ayson (Chapter 12) explains that the military dimension of the US rebalancing is not so important to New Zealand because of the country's location, but he suggests that the US rebalancing strategy entails a risk of economic entrapment of New Zealand by the United States and that the Trans-Pacific Partnership designed to exclude China is not welcomed in Wellington.

Concomitant with China's rapid economic development, no Asian state – even countries such as the Philippines and Japan, which now both prefer a more hard-line US policy – wants the US rebalancing to be just a sword to slay the Chinese dragon. Slaying the dragon means killing the panda as well. Indeed, the economic interdependence with China gives an important commonality of cautiousness to Asia's adaptation to US rebalancing and is also an important consideration for both the United States and China. The US rebalancing for 'America's Pacific Century' (Clinton 2011), for instance, involves a genuine desire for economic cooperation with China – so much so that Indian policymakers and observers are sceptical about Washington's will to sustain regional security commitments at levels now in place (see Mahesh Shankar, Chapter 13).

At the same time, Asian states do not want the US rebalancing to be too weak since the economically seductive Chinese panda has as much potential to exercise its increasingly powerful muscles as a threatening dragon. All chapters of this volume argue that a US strategic presence in Asia through the rebalance strategy has a positive impact for the region at large as long as it does not provoke China; the generally positive view towards the role of the United States in regional security is another commonality of Asian attitudes towards US rebalancing. When Ralf Emmers (Chapter 10) argues that Singapore favours a modest US rebalancing because it fears great power competition, he carefully qualifies this by adding 'for now at least'. As Changsu Kim (Chapter 6) points out in observing South Korea's adaptation, states in the region encourage the US rebalancing to be 'more than mere political rhetoric' and to move 'beyond existing policies'. In sum, Asian states want the 'US ability to ensure order so that … the region can have constructive and mutual benefits from relations with China' (Limaye 2013: 50).

Geography and the varying responses

If the dual nature of China's rise – as economic virtue and potential security threat – is the background to the commonality of Asian states' adaptation to US rebalancing, what explains the variations in their responses?[3] Geography and proximity to China are likely to play a role. In explaining Thailand's perception of a Chinese threat, Kitti Prasirtsuk and William Tow (Chapter 9) emphasize that Thailand neither shares a contiguous border with China nor has territorial claims involving Chinese counter-claims. Geography affects other states' attitude toward US strategy as well. For instance, offshore balancing by the United States (Layne 1997) will mean strategic abandonment to many in Japan (see Ken Jimbo, Chapter 5), but will worry New Zealanders much less (Ayson, Chapter 12).

Geographic proximity increases perception of threat and the chance of having overlapping territorial claims, but this does not necessarily mean that states closer to China will be more supportive of the US rebalancing to Asia. States geographically closer to China (which more strongly perceive China as a threat) do desire US support, but some immediate neighbours in particular recognize that the cost and risk of antagonizing China is also very high – sometimes too high. This might explain why in Southeast Asia there is a 'loose, geopolitical division within the region between continental and maritime states … with the "offshore" insular countries better disposed towards an invigorated US presence' (Graham 2013: 325). Japan and the Philippines have larger benefits in countering China with American help because of their territorial disputes with China, but they may also believe that they face a lower risk in doing so because the barrier of the ocean protects them. From the US perspective, too, it is easier to balance the rise of China with offshore partners than with states in continental Asia (Ross 1999, 2013).

Close neighbours of China have a strong need for US support, but that support needs to be long-lasting and non-provocative. China will not cease to be their neighbour, and they do not want to face a vindictive neighbour after Americans withdraw their support. Neither do they want to be burnt in a fire in the neighbourhood. In other words, the fear of eventual abandonment and the fear of entrapment mitigate their desire to tighten partnership with the United States simply to reduce the risk of abandonment now. The land contiguity and the memory of war with China make Vietnam cautious in expanding its relationship with the United States, despite strong interests by some on both the US and Vietnamese sides (Graham 2013: 315–16). Similarly, India (Shankar, Chapter 13) and South Korea (Kim, Chapter 6) are wary of prematurely making commitments to the US rebalancing.

On a related note, geography may also affect the likelihood of a 'Georgia scenario' (Goldstein 2011), 'where a state in the region takes too seriously Washington's assurances and takes on a bigger fight than it can handle itself, only to find out that Washington had no intention of going to war in its defense over that particular issue' (Logan 2013: 14). From the US perspective, the fear is of emboldening its allies and having to abandon them later. Jeffrey McCausland (Chapter 4) therefore suggests that Washington should frequently communicate with its allies and partners to clarify expectations – and restrain them. The Georgia scenario, however, is more worrisome to junior partners that may be eventually abandoned than to the United States, so the junior partners have their own incentives to be cautious. In particular, the immediate neighbours of China should be less likely to fall victim to the Georgia scenario because they know that they cannot get away from China even if they make short-term gains by taking a hard line.

The future of US rebalancing

Assertiveness by China makes the US rebalancing an attractive idea for Asian states (Keatley 2013; Charmaine Misalucha, Chapter 8), but rebalancing as a signal faces difficult problems, especially if its recipients are risk averse. From the Chinese perspective, the United States lacks credibility when it insists that the rebalancing strategy is not intended to contain the rise of China, because the United States is likely to claim innocence even if it has a plan of containment. As Douglas Stuart (Chapter 2) points out, for its own interest, 'Washington cannot ask, or be perceived to be asking, Asia-Pacific governments to support a strategy of anti-Chinese military containment'. Accordingly, despite all the efforts by the Barack Obama Administration to allay the Chinese fear of containment, the Chinese government is highly suspicious of the US strategy (see, for example, Liao 2013; Ling 2013).

From the perspective of US allies and partners, the United States also lacks credibility to remain engaged in the region. The rhetoric of rebalancing is itself not a sufficiently costly signal to many regional states, and the US intention might anyway change over time. Unless the US commitment is reinforced by measures that have a recognizable cost to the United States (for example, increased forward presence or support for allies' policy), allies and regional partners will remain doubtful to US commitment to the rebalancing strategy. Moreover, even then demonstrations of a strong US commitment will raise Asian states' concerns about over-militarization and entrapment (see William Tow, Chapter 3).

On the other hand, both China and other Asian states have reasons to be assured about the nature of the US rebalancing strategy. The United States does indeed benefit economically from its cooperative relationship with China, and Washington also has a strong incentive to retain its influence in the Asia-Pacific regardless of who is in the White House. As American policymakers emphasize, rebalancing is not just about military balance. Even if China and the United States are in 'a contest for supremacy' and 'the struggle for mastery in Asia' (Friedberg 2011), the struggle is about the future order and not just immediate military balance. A 'constructive' relationship is often a euphemism, but the United States, China and the regional states all have a mutual interest in realizing a peaceful order.

Notes

1 It is not accurate to depict China as an adversary of Asian states, but for this analysis China will be portrayed as an adversary and the United States as a partner, because the United States has broader and more meaningful security cooperation with other states in the region than does China.
2 'Abandonment is defection by an ally, and it may take a variety of specific forms: the ally may realign with the opponent; he may merely de-align, abrogating the alliance contract; he may fail to make good on his explicit commitments; or he may fail to provide support in contingencies where support is expected ... Entrapment means being dragged into a conflict over an ally's interests that one does not share, or shares only partially' (Snyder 1984: 466–67). For a more technical discussion of entrapment, see Kim (2011).
3 As Brendan Taylor (Chapter 11) demonstrates, attitudes toward the US strategy have important variations within a country as well.

References

Beckley, Michael (2011) 'China's Century? Why America's Edge will Endure', *International Security*, 36(3): 41–78.

Clinton, Hillary (2011) 'America's Pacific Century', *Foreign Policy*, 189(November): 56–63.

Friedberg, Aaron (2011) *A Contest for Supremacy: China, America, and the Struggle for Mastery in Asia*, New York: W.W. Norton.

Goldstein, Lyle (2011) 'The South China Sea's Georgia Scenario', *Foreign Policy*, 11 July.

Graham, Euan (2013) 'Southeast Asia in the US Rebalance: Perceptions from a Divided Region', *Contemporary Southeast Asia*, 35(3): 305–32.

IISS (International Institute for Strategic Studies) (2014) *The Military Balance 2014*, London: International Institute for Strategic Studies.

Katz, Richard (2013) 'Mutual Assured Production: Why Trade will Limit Conflict between China and Japan', *Foreign Affairs*, 92(4): 18–24.

Keatley, Robert (2013) 'How China Helps the Pivot', *The National Interest*, 21 March.

Kim, Tongfi (2011) 'Why Alliances Entangle but Seldom Entrap States', *Security Studies*, 20(3): 350–77.

Layne, Christopher (1997) 'From Preponderance to Offshore Balancing: America's Future Grand Strategy', *International Security*, 22(1): 86–124.

Liao, Kai (2013) 'The Pentagon and the Pivot', *Survival*, 55(3): 95–114.

Limaye, Satu P. (2013) 'Southeast Asia in America's Rebalance to the Asia-Pacific', in Daljit Singh (ed.) *Southeast Asian Affairs 2013*, Singapore: Institute of Southeast Asian Studies, pp. 40–50.

Ling, Wei (2013) 'Rebalancing or De-Balancing: US Pivot and East Asian Order', *American Foreign Policy Interests*, 35(3): 148–54.

Logan, Justin (2013) 'China, America, and the Pivot to Asia', *Policy Analysis*, 717(8 January), Washington, DC: Cato Institute.

Press-Barnathan, Galia (2006) 'Managing the Hegemon: NATO under Unipolarity', *Security Studies*, 15(2): 271–309.

Ross, Robert (1999) 'The Geography of the Peace: East Asia in the Twenty-First Century', *International Security*, 23(4): 81–118.

——(2013) 'US Grand Strategy, the Rise of China, and US National Security Strategy for East Asia', *Strategic Studies Quarterly*, 7(2): 20–40.

Snyder, Glenn (1984) 'The Security Dilemma in Alliance Politics', *World Politics*, 36(4): 461–95.

——(1997) *Alliance Politics*, Ithaca, NY: Cornell University Press.

World Bank (2014) 'GDP (Current US$)', data.worldbank.org/indicator/NY.GDP. MKTP.CD/countries (accessed 4 March 2014).

Index

www.ingramcontent.com/pod-product-compliance
Ingram Content Group UK Ltd.
Pitfield, Milton Keynes, MK11 3LW, UK
UKHW020354010325
455677UK00021B/455